GROWING UP IN THE UK
ENSURING A HEALTHY FUTURE FOR OUR CHILDREN

May 2013

Editorial board

A publication from the BMA Science and Education department and the Board of Science

British Library Cataloguing-in-Publication Data.
A catalogue record for this book is available from the British Library.

ISBN: 978-0-9575831-0-8
Cover photograph: iStockphoto
Printed by the BMA publications unit

Board of Science

This report was prepared under the auspices of the Board of Science of the British Medical Association, whose membership for 2012/2013 was as follows:

Approval for publication as a BMA policy report was recommended by the BMA Board of Professional Activities on 28 February 2013 and by UK BMA Council on 20 March 2013.

The Board of Science, a standing committee of the BMA, provides an interface between the medical profession, the Government and the public. The Board produces numerous reports containing policies for national action by Government and other organisations, with specific recommendations and areas for action affecting the medical and allied professions.

Acknowledgements

The Association is grateful for the help provided by the BMA committees and outside experts and organisations. We would particularly like to thank:

- Professor Sir Al Aynsley-Green Kt (Professor Emeritus of Child Health, University College London; Founder and Director Aynsley-Green Consulting)
- Dr John Harvey (Co-Chair, Faculty of Public Health, Child Public Health Special Interest Group).

Declaration of interest
Declarations of interest for outside experts can be found in **Appendix 1**.
For further information about the editorial secretariat or Board members please contact the BMA Science and Education Department, which holds a record of all declarations of interest: info.science@bma.org.uk

Abbreviations

This list only contains abbreviations used more than once in this report

ADHD	attention deficit hyperactivity disorder
ARM	Annual Representative Meeting
ASD	autistic spectrum disorders
BFI	baby friendly initiative
BMI	body mass index
CAF	Common Assessment Framework
CAMHS	child and adolescent mental health services
CASH	contraceptive and sexual health
CB	commissioning board
CCG	clinical commissioning group
CEMACH	Confidential Enquiry into Maternal and Child Health
CHD	coronary heart disease
COMA	Committee on Medical Aspects of Food and Nutrition Policy
CQC	Care Quality Commission
DALY	disability-adjusted life year
DCD	developmental coordination disorders
DDA	Disability Discrimination Act
DCSF	Department for Children, Schools and Families
DfE	Department for Education
DWP	Department for Work and Pensions
DH	Department of Health
DHSSP	Department of Health, Social Services and Public Safety
EAR	estimated average requirement
ECM	Every Child Matters
EDCM	Every Disabled Child Matters
EHC	education, health and care
FASD	fetal alcohol spectrum disorders
FEV1	mean forced expiratory volume in one second
FNP	Family Nurse Partnership
FRS	Family Resources Survey
GMC	General Medical Council
GP	general practitioner
HBAI	Households Below Average Income
HCP	Healthy Child Programme
HENRY	Healthy Exercise and Nutrition in the Really Young
HPSR	health policy and systems research

IFS	Infant Feeding Survey
IGF	insulin-like growth factor
IQ	intelligence quotient
MAOA	monoamine oxidase A
MCS	Millennium Cohort Study
MIHL	minimum income for healthy living
MIS	minimum income standard
NCMP	National Child Measurement Programme
NDNS	National Diet and Nutrition Surveys
NFP	Nurse Family Partnership
NHS	National Health Service
NICE	National Institute for Health and Clinical Excellence
NIDDM	non-insulin dependent diabetes mellitus
NSF	National Service Framework
NSP	non-starch polysaccharide
NSPCC	National Society for the Prevention of Cruelty to Children
NS-SEC	National Statistics Socio-economic Classification
OECD	Organisation for Economic Co-operation and Development
Ofsted	Office for Standards in Education, Children's Services and Skills
PbR	payment by results
PCT	primary care trust
PSA	public service agreement
SACN	Scientific Advisory Committee on Nutrition
SEN	special educational needs
SGA	small for gestational age
SRE	sex and relationship education
SSLP	Sure Start Local Programme
UIC	urinary iodine concentration
UN	United Nations
UNCRC	United Nations Convention on the Rights of the Child
UNICEF	United Nations Children's Fund
USA	United States of America
WFS	welfare food scheme
WHO	World Health Organization

Glossary

Attention deficit hyperactivity disorder: a condition associated with inattentiveness, overactivity, impulsivity, or a combination. For these problems to be diagnosed, they must be out of the normal range for a child's age and development.

Child and adolescent mental health services: these are healthcare service-provided services for children. They provide a range of assessments and therapeutic interventions to promote the emotional and psychological wellbeing of children, young people and their families.

Child protection: child protection work aims to prevent, respond and resolve the abuse, neglect, exploitation and violence experienced by children in all settings. Child protection services are statutory services coordinated by local authority children's services.

Child protection plan: a plan that contains details of how children's services will check on the child's welfare, what changes are needed to reduce the risk to the child and what support will be offered to the family. It is drawn up by the core group of professionals and the family. It is part of statutory services offered to children who have been judged to be suffering significant harm from abuse or neglect.

Common Assessment Framework: a standardised approach to conducting an assessment of a child's additional needs. It takes account of the role of parents, carers and environmental factors on their development, in deciding how those needs should be met, and was designed to be used across agencies.

Family Nurse Partnership (UK): a preventive programme for young first-time mothers. It offers intensive and structured home visiting, delivered by specially trained nurses (family nurses), from early pregnancy until the child is two.

Improving Access to Psychological Therapies: a UK initiative to improve access to psychological therapies. The aim of the project is to increase the provision of evidence-based treatments for anxiety and depression by primary care organisations. This includes workforce planning to adequately train the mental health professionals required.

Monoamine oxidase A: one of a family of enzymes that catalyse the oxidation of monoamines. They are found bound to the outer membrane of mitochondria in most cell types in the body.

National Institute for Health and Clinical Excellence: the organisation responsible for providing national guidance on the promotion of good health and the prevention and treatment of ill health in England and Wales.

Nurse Family Partnership (USA): a nurse-led, evidence-based public health programme that helps transform the lives of vulnerable mothers and their children.

Post-traumatic stress disorder: an anxiety disorder that some people get after seeing or living through a dangerous event.

Safeguarding: safeguarding work covers child protection and also the broader remit of preventing impairment of a child's health and development, and ensuring they have safe and effective care to reach adulthood.

Sure Start Local Programme: a programme which aimed to enhance the life chances of young children and their families by improving services in areas of high deprivation. The programmes were set up between 1999 and 2003 and were experimental in the sense of trying out different ways of working with deprived communities where provision had been poor for years.

Foreword by Professor Sir Al Aynsley-Green Kt

Professor Emeritus of Child Health, University College London; Founder and Director Aynsley-Green Consulting

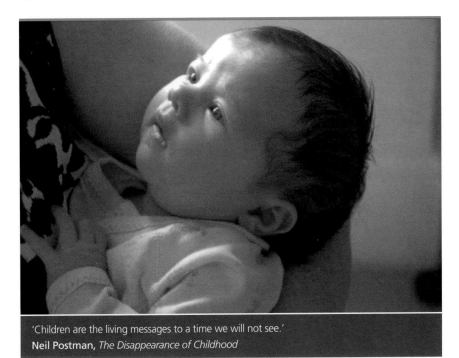

'Children are the living messages to a time we will not see.'
Neil Postman, *The Disappearance of Childhood*

This book is about children and their health today. The image above reminds us of the species we are talking about. She is a beautiful newly born infant girl, a citizen in her own right, showing her hard-wired ability to manipulate her caring adults by her rapturous gaze at the adult face. This eye-to-eye contact is a fundamental trigger in attachment – the process whereby the brains of adults, especially mothers, experience a surge of love hormones including prolactin and oxytocin that trigger our nurturing instincts. The gaze also stimulates the infant's own brain in its journey of emotional competence. Our love and commitment for our babies and children in our families triggered by these precious early moments of adult-child dialogue has ensured the survival of the human species.

Like all other newly born babies, she is defenceless, exquisitely vulnerable, and depends critically for her survival and for her long term potential on the care given to her by adults. The nurture of babies and children is not just the responsibility of parents and families, as vital as that is, but it should be everybody's business – communities, faiths, schools and professional staff as well as politicians.

Understanding, support and effective advocacy for the needs of children by politicians is especially relevant to the content of this book, since governments determine political priorities, define policy through legislation and allocate funding from taxation.

It could be argued that nations should be judged on their enlightenment not only by the commitment they give to children in policies but through the reality of their health, education and social outcomes as they progress into adulthood. These outcomes are a direct reflection of the quality of services and the nurture in society they have received.

Children are our nation's most precious resource. Political theorists from Karl Marx, through Winston Churchill and Tony Blair and Gordon Brown, have recognised this fundamental truth. I first visited Eastern Europe in 1979 and saw the high priority given to children, as the workers of the future, in those communist societies. Similar priority has been given to children's health in Cuba. Sadly, and without supporting a totalitarian approach to society, I have witnessed the progressive diminution of that priority as former Eastern European communist countries have moved to capitalist economies. Winston Churchill also reminded us that: 'There is no finer investment for any community than putting milk into babies' ('Four Year Plan for England' broadcast on 21 March 1943). More recently European Union theoreticians have argued the cause of investing in children to create the 'child-centred social investment strategy', and this became manifest in England through the *Every Child Matters* policy of the New Labour government.

Political rhetoric is important in setting a context and flying a signal, but it is ephemeral, subject to change in party political focus, and driven by external circumstance. What should matter most is sustained cross-party political will to recognise the importance of children and translate fine words into practical policy that supports the lives of children and their families.

So, how well are we doing for children and young people in the UK? Are the services fit for the purpose of supporting their needs?

Children, generally, are healthy and few die compared to 50 years ago. The culture of services has been transformed, for example, by accepting that parents should have unlimited access to their sick children in hospital, and be involved in making decisions in their care.

The increasing importance of the voice of children and young people is being realised based on Article 12 of the United Nations Convention on the Rights of the Child that states: 'Children have the right to say what they think should happen when adults are making decisions that affect them, and to have their opinions taken into account'.

No one today would inflict a procedure or a treatment without fully involving the child, depending on its level of understanding. But even young children receive patient-controlled analgesia after surgery, in which within very tight limits, they can adjust the rate of morphine infusion to meet their needs for pain relief.

Resources and facilities have improved such as attractive new children's hospitals that include wards purpose-designed for adolescents.

Major scientific advances in molecular medicine and genetics have transformed the understanding of the pathogenesis of diseases, their diagnosis and treatment, and immunisation has diminished the toll of polio, pertussis, rubella and meningococcal meningitis.

Take two-day old baby Peter (not his real name), for example, suffering from severe congenital neonatal hypoglycaemia due to excessive release of insulin. Until recently, this baby would have spent weeks in hospital with the ever-present risk of severe neurological damage caused by persistent hypoglycaemia during months of volatile medical treatment, eventually requiring total pancreatectomy to control the relentless hypoglycaemia. Now, advances in molecular genetics linked to new methods of imaging of the pancreas allow laparoscopic resection of a focal area of excess insulin release in the pancreas. Peter can expect to go home cured of the disorder without brain damage within a few days of diagnosis. There are countless other stunning examples of progress in every sub-specialty in paediatric medicine.

Despite these important and welcome developments, the result of the hard work of dedicated scientists and medical staff, the content of this book exposes the inconvenient paradox that all is not well for children and their health in the UK, with so many outcomes for our children falling way below the benchmarks of other developed nations. Why is this the case?

In 2000, Sir Ian Kennedy published his critical Inquiry into the scandal of children's cardiac surgery in Bristol, which amongst other conclusions found that 'more children died than might have been expected in a typical PCS [paediatric cardiac surgery] unit'. He exposed that nationwide, care for children was subordinated to the demands of adults; lack of understanding of what is different about children's services in people who matter; the view that children are healthy and services are satisfactory, and the ability to admit a sick child being a major success.

But he also exposed that children were not mainstreamed in government policy – they were an 'add-on', with key adult-centric priorities in the NHS that were not relevant. Children and young people being unable to vote have little political traction, and this coupled with a failure of leadership and of political advocacy by professional organisations led to their needs being under-recognised.

Ten years later, Kennedy re-visited children's health services and showed that whilst there were patches of excellence, cultural barriers in government, and in services, perpetuated the isolation of policy, lack of responsibility for policy, no identified funding, poor use of data, the NHS not working with others, and a lack of financial investment.

The Kennedy Inquiry triggered the then Government to launch 'a new crusade to improve the nation's children's health', including a new role to be responsible for defining standards of care in a National Service Framework with the promise of ring-fenced money, imperatives, and hard targets to meet. The rhetoric created a massive expectation in the children's health sector that at last there would be a transformation in the low standing of those services.

After four years of work, expense and involving over 300 experts – coupled with rigorous evidence as to what works and extensive consultation not least with children and young people themselves – the National Service Framework was ready for publication. It received international acclaim as an outstanding process for defining standards for children's health care.

But then, unexpectedly, children were betrayed by politicians with the defined 'must do's' turning to nothing more than 'aspiration' over a ten year period. The lack of political will to provide imperatives and resources created fury in the sector with a shadow of distrust lasting until now. A unique opportunity at a time of financial abundance to give children the priority they deserve was lost evermore.

Why did this happen? The inconvenient truths are:
- the 'churn' of ministerial appointments (six Ministers and three Secretaries of State in five years)
- failure to get continued focus for children's health from the Government through successive Secretaries of State in the Department of Health
- overtaken by political fashion – 'shifting the balance of power' becoming the mantra in the Department of Health
- political indifference for children
- failure of Parliament to hold the Department of Health to account
- lack of media pressure
- silent voice of the sector and lack of concerted, effective and sustained advocacy.

In 2007, the New Labour Government launched *The Children's Plan* incorporating five outcomes – 'be healthy, stay safe, enjoy and achieve, make a positive contribution and achieve economic well being'.

As with the National Service Framework, this policy received international acclaim for the comprehensive way in which children and their services were regarded, with all Departments of State being held to account for their work that related to children and young people.

In 2010, within minutes of the new Coalition Government being announced, every image of the *Every Child Matters* policy was removed in what had been the Department for Children, Schools and Families, now re-named the Department for Education, the former Plan being systematically dismantled.

The Department of Health published in 2010 its policy statement, *Achieving Equity and Excellence*, timed to coincide with and, arguably, to neutralise Sir Ian Kennedy's highly critical report on the lack of progress in improving children's services. It has now published its report of the Children and Young People's Outcomes Forum, the product, as for the National Service Framework, of hard work by outstanding contributors. It defines principles with the potential to change the focus of children's health care to accountability through defined outcomes: putting children, young people and families at the heart of what happens; acting early and intervening at the right time; integration and partnership; safe and sustainable services; workforce, education, and training; knowledge and evidence; leadership, accountability and incentives.

The sceptic experiences déjà vu, seeing philosophies and words identical to those of the National Service Framework, and believes that without any political commitment to the outcomes, let alone the funding streams for implementation, the publication is destined to gather dust on the library shelves alongside the many other unimplemented policy declarations in recent years.

On the 19 February 2013, the Government announced a national pledge to reduce the number of excess deaths in children (some 1,600 per annum when compared to other developed countries), and starting a data revolution so the NHS and local authorities get better information they can use to improve the health of young people. The announcement also includes making sure children and young people are at the heart of the new health and care system, and that their voices are heard; and new roles and bodies have been created, including input by the Chief Medical Officer to make sure the issue stays top of the agenda by bringing health leaders together to improve children's health.

These comments and pronouncements are welcome, but the history of children's health policy is such that there is limited confidence that anything meaningful or substantial will change especially against the backdrop of national financial austerity.

The chapters of this book provide a compendium of hard evidence on the circumstance of children's health in the UK today. What the incontrovertible overall data cannot do, however, is to expose the real human cost of this circumstance on the day-to-day lives of individual children and their families. The voices of children and families are not evident. Who is listening to them?

Take, for example, Rachel and Simon (not their real names), the parents of five-year old Emily (not her real name), a child with complex congenital malformations and learning difficulties. 'Wading through treacle', they say. 'Who is in overall charge of my child? Why do I need 10 different appointments at different times to see the specialists involved in her care? What is going to happen to her as she grows up and becomes an adult? Who is responsible for integrating her education, health and social care needs? Why do we have to fight every inch of the way for her entitlements? Who cares?'

Or take Becky (not her real name), a 16 year-old with severe anorexia nervosa requiring admission to a specialist in-patient unit 150 miles away from her home because of the lack of specialist provision where she lives. Her parents express their frustration and exhaustion in having had to fight endlessly for their concerns to be taken seriously, coupled with the financial and social cost in travelling a round trip of some 300 miles to visit their sick daughter.

These are but two illustrations of the lived experiences that lie hidden behind the hard facts of the inadequacies of current services and the failure of political will that this book exposes. Who can deny the fear, the anguish, and despair, in seeing a much-loved child who has a disability or becomes sick? No one chooses to be the parent of such a child, and the children themselves certainly do not, yet where is there compassion in our society? Any one of us could be confronted with these realities in our families.

As Ingrid Wolfe, quoting Charles Dickens says in her chapter, 'It was the best of times, it was the worst of times'. The Victorian times were devastating for the lives of countless children.

Here is Elizabeth Barrett Browning in her poem, *The Cry of the Children*, published in 1843:

'Now tell the poor young children, O my Brothers
  Look up to Him and pray;
So the blessed One who blesseth all the others,
  Will bless them another day.
They answer, "Who is God that He should hear us
  While the rushing of iron wheels is stirred?
When we sob aloud, the human creatures near us
  Pass by, hearing not, or answer not a word.
And we hear not (for the wheels in their sounding)
  Strangers speaking at the door;
Is it likely God, with angels singing round Him,
Hears our weeping any more?"'

But in the midst of so much despair, some people did listen and a social conscience began to stir. The social reformers – including Bramwell Booth, Joseph Rowntree, Josephine Butler, W.T. Stead, the Rev Waugh, Dr Barnardo and, above all, Charles Dickens – were leading public figures driven by outrage over how they saw the effects of society at that time on the lives and deaths of children. They founded famous organisations, many of which are still with us today, and courageous politicians including Lord Shaftesbury introduced education and employment legislation that transformed the lives of children.

Of course we cannot compare directly the appalling circumstance of children 150 years ago with today. But, are there not parallels? In 2013 we are currently experiencing the most challenging era for children, young people and their health for the last 30 years, driven by a disastrous financial environment leading to deep cuts to public services, coupled with political turmoil caused by ideological dogma as exemplified by the NHS re-organisation that continues apace.

Should there not be outrage that the lives of so many children and their families are blighted by the facts exposed in this book, despite current difficulties, still one of the richest countries of the world? Who speaks for them? Where is the evidence of concerted and effective political advocacy from the professional organisations that claim to have their best interests at their heart?

I issue a call to action by all who are concerned by the current plight of children and the threats to their services. The incontrovertible facts and a menu of recommendations are here in this outstanding book. So, to every reader, my challenge is if you really care about children, then what are you going to do about it?

As well as striving for national political focus and action through membership of our professional organisations, it is from the local level that change for children should be driven – the power of parents in exposing poor practice; the new responsibilities of staff in the light of the Inquiry into the scandal of care in Stafford to be 'whistle-blowers'; effective leadership through the brigading of medical, nursing and all professional staff involved in the care of children – there is much to do and as Neil Postman said in his book *The Disappearance of Childhood*, 'Children are the living messages to a time we will not see!'.

Their future lies in our hands now, and we cannot afford to continue to fail them.

Professor Sir Al Aynsley-Green Kt
Professor Emeritus of Child Health, University College London

Sir Al Aynsley-Green

Professor Sir Albert Aynsley-Green Kt

Sir Al started his career in medicine in London at Guy's Hospital, then developing his speciality of paediatric endocrinology through training and research in University hospitals in Oxford, England and Zurich, Switzerland.

He was Clinical then University Lecturer in Paediatrics and Fellow of Green College, University of Oxford, Professor of Child Health and Head of the School of Clinical Medical Sciences, University of Newcastle upon Tyne and then Nuffield Professor of Child Health and Executive Director for Clinical research and development at the Institute of Child Health and Great Ormond Street Hospital for Children, London.

He was appointed Chair of the first NHS Children's Taskforce and then the first National Clinical Director for Children in the Department of Health where he was responsible for defining the first national comprehensive standards of health care services for children, young people and expecting mothers. He was appointed the first independent Children's Commissioner for England in 2005, a post created by Parliament to be the independent voice for children and young people, implementing new ways of engaging with them, particularly those most invisible in society. Among his achievements was the exposing to public and political view the injustices faced by children with mental ill health, those in conflict with the law, and those seeking asylum.

He stood down after his five years of tenure as Children's Commissioner in 2010 and is now Professor Emeritus of Child Health at University College London, and Founder and Director of Aynsley-Green Consulting, engaging with governments and organisations worldwide on children, childhood and children's services.

Foreword by Professor Averil Mansfield

Chairman, BMA Board of Science

Doctors have a unique and vested interest in child health that goes beyond their roles as parents and grandparents. Many will be directly involved in the medical care of children and young people, while others dedicate their professional lives to managing long-term conditions that have their origins in childhood, or in planning and delivering preventative health services.

Child health has been a central feature of the BMA's work on areas such as nutrition and physical exercise, mental health, sexual health, smoking, alcohol and drug use. There is also a need to look more broadly at the medical and social care of children in the UK, from the way child health services are commissioned and coordinated, to the factors that affect the conditions in which they live, learn and develop from young children to adolescents.

The BMA first considered this issue in its 1979 report, *Our children's health*, which was followed in 1999 with the publication of *Growing up in Britain: ensuring a healthy future for our children*. While there have been some improvements since our 1999 report, this is not distributed evenly across the socioeconomic spectrum. It is distressing that in the 21st Century, the future health and wellbeing of a child born in the UK remains dependent on their social position. The UK is also lagging behind many other European countries on a range of health outcomes for children and young people without good reason.

This report sets out what is needed to move towards an equitable society where all children are given the best start in life. It highlights the importance of coordinating children's health services, and the processes and structures that enable them, in the interests of children and families. In building on the improvements that have been made in child health policy in recent years, we support a life-course approach where health and wellbeing are integrated on a continuum from pre-conception to adolescence. The key elements for this include:
- measures to tackle poverty and reduce inequalities before birth and continuing throughout the life of the child
- ensuring child health policies are evidence based and informed by robust data, to improve the 'match' between children's healthcare needs and the services provided to meet these needs

- establishing accountability at Ministerial level for children's health and wellbeing that includes a framework of monitoring, reviewing, and remedying processes
- providing children's services that are family centred and focused on the importance of parenting, where the child and family are embraced as a unit
- meeting the needs of children at risk through early intervention and multi-disciplinary working between social services, education authorities, healthcare teams, police services, and others.

As healthcare professionals, we have an opportunity, indeed a duty, to push for change for the benefit of our nation's children. I am therefore very grateful to all those who have contributed to this report, which provides an authoritative resource for advocacy. My hope is that the next report we publish on this subject is a celebration of the successes that have been achieved, and not a further acknowledgement that society in the UK is continuing to fail its children.

Averil O. Mansfield.

Professor Averil Mansfield
Chairman, BMA Board of Science

Professor Averil Mansfield

Professor Averil Mansfield

Averil Mansfield is a graduate of Liverpool University and was formerly a consultant surgeon in Liverpool until her move to St Mary's Hospital in London in 1982. She became Director of the Academic Surgical Unit and Professor of Vascular Surgery at St Mary's/Imperial College in 1993. Her research centered around venous thromboembolism, carotid surgery and extensive aortic aneurysms.

She was Vice President of The Royal College of Surgeons and President of The Association of Surgeons of Great Britain and Ireland, The Vascular Surgical Society, and the Section of Surgery of the Royal Society of Medicine.

She was President of the BMA from 2009 to 2010 and became Chairman of the Board of Science in 2010.

Contents

Chapter 1: Introduction

We cannot overstate the importance of children and young people's health. A healthy start in life is at the heart of a happy childhood and the ability of every young person to achieve their potential and grow up well prepared for the challenges of adolescence and adulthood.
Healthy lives, brighter futures, 2009[1]

The BMA has a longstanding interest in child health inequalities in society and their impact on health. We have developed a number of policies and published many reports on child health, including: nutrition, obesity, body image, mental health, sexual health, smoking, alcohol and drug use (see **Appendix 2** for a full list of BMA policy and a summary of BMA work on children's health).

The care of children at all stages of their development is a key focus. The BMA published its first major report on child health in 1979, *Our children's health*, from which followed a number of reports and web resources, including in 1999 *Growing up in Britain: ensuring a healthy future for our children*, which examined child development from conception to age five, in particular in relation to the impact of social and economic inequality on child health. It considered a number of key areas including childhood nutrition, abuse and non-accidental injury, disability, mental health, behavioural problems, and the origins of adult disease.

At the BMA's 2010 Annual Representative Meeting (ARM), members agreed that the Board of Science should prepare an updated version of the 1999 report and make recommendations that will help ensure a healthier and happier future for our children.

Child health is a critical issue of concern to everyone, including the family, the community, the nation and the international community. Enhancing children's lives and improving child wellbeing should be a central objective of public health policy. This means continuous improvement of services for all children and their carers, as well as doing more for the most vulnerable, to reduce inequalities in health. The Marmot review emphasises the importance of investment in children to reduce health inequalities at all ages.[2] Although the past decade has seen some improvements in children, young people and families' health services, the care provided by UK child health services is inferior in many regards to that in comparable European countries.

A 2007 study for the United Nations Children's Fund (UNICEF), ranked the UK bottom out of 21 industrialised countries for wellbeing enjoyed by children, based on a range of measures.[3] An updated version of this study was published in April 2013 (see **Box 1.1**).[4] While few direct comparisons are possible (because the later study included more countries, and used different measures), the UK was found to have shown a modest improvement, moving from 21st (joint last) to 16th position. It is worth noting that these data cover the period up to 2009/10, so do not reflect any policies implemented post the 2010 election, and will not account for the impact of the Coalition government's austerity policies. This is discussed in further detail in **Chapter 2**.

Other international benchmarks point to outcomes for our children that are already far from satisfactory, being way below those achieved in other high-income countries. These include the concluding observations of the United Nations (UN) Committee on the Rights of the Child, 2008,[5] the Organisation for Economic Co-operation and Development (OECD) Report, 2009,[6] the Good Childhood Inquiry, 2009,[7] and the UNICEF Innocenti Report Card 9, 2010.[8]

The 2012 *Report of the Children and Young People's Health Outcomes Forum*, highlighted the failures in child health in the UK.[9] It noted that too many health outcomes for children and young people are poor and that, despite important improvements, more children and young people are dying in this country than in other countries in northern and western Europe. This makes a compelling case for change.

Box 1.1: The child wellbeing index

The chart below presents the findings of this Report Card in summary form. Countries are listed in order of their average rank for the five dimensions of child wellbeing that have been assessed. A light grey background indicates a place in the top third of the table; mid-grey denotes the middle third and dark grey the bottom third.

		Overall wellbeing	Dimension 1	Dimension 2	Dimension 3	Dimension 4	Dimension 5
		Average rank (all 5 dimensions)	Material wellbeing (rank)	Health and safety (rank)	Education (rank)	Behaviours and risks (rank)	Housing and environment (rank)
1	Netherlands	2.4	1	5	1	1	4
2	Norway	4.6	3	7	6	4	3
3	Iceland	5.0	4	1	10	3	7
4	Finland	5.4	2	3	4	12	6
5	Sweden	6.2	5	2	11	5	8
6	Germany	9.0	11	12	3	6	13
7	Luxembourg	9.2	6	4	22	9	5
8	Switzerland	9.6	9	11	16	11	1
9	Belgium	11.2	13	13	2	14	14
10	Ireland	11.6	17	15	17	7	2
11	Denmark	11.8	12	23	7	2	15
12	Slovenia	12	8	6	5	21	20
13	France	12.8	10	10	15	13	16
14	Czech Republic	15.2	16	8	12	22	18
15	Portugal	15.6	21	14	18	8	17
16	UK	15.8	14	16	24	15	10
17	Canada	16.6	15	27	12	16	11
18	Austria	17	7	26	23	17	12
19	Spain	17.6	24	9	26	20	9
20	Hungary	18.4	18	20	8	24	22
21	Poland	18.8	22	18	9	19	26
22	Italy	19.2	23	17	25	10	21
23	Estonia	20.8	19	22	13	26	24
24	Slovakia	20.8	25	21	21	18	19
25	Greece	23.4	20	19	28	25	25
26	United States	24.8	26	25	27	23	23
27	Lithuania	25.2	27	24	19	29	27
28	Latvia	26.4	28	28	20	28	28
29	Romania	28.6	29	29	29	27	29

Source: United Nations Children's Fund (2013) Child well-being in rich countries: a comparative overview. Innocenti report Card 11. Florence: United Nations Children's Fund Innocenti Research Centre.

1.1   Child health policy since 1999

The health of children across the UK has improved somewhat in recent years, although it is important to note it has not become distributed more fairly. The fact that child health is only rarely dictated by individual policies emphasises the complex causal pathways and changes in health outcomes determining inequalities in health. During the course of the last 10 years, a number of child health policies, implemented on an inadequate scale for insufficient time periods, have focused on overall health improvement instead of addressing the issue of child health inequalities.[10] Real and sustained improvements in child health can result if political will is brought to bear on the issues. The future of the UK depends on it.

The importance of investing in, and concentrating services on, the early years of life cannot be overstated. As highlighted by Marmot, the determinants of health and wellbeing, whether good or bad, start before birth and accumulate over a lifetime, with a particular importance attached to the early years.[2] Giving every child the best start in life is crucial in improving the health and wellbeing of the population as a whole and tackling health inequalities.

The past decade has seen some improvements in health services for children, young people and families. New services and public health campaigns have been put in place to support families in tackling some of the current and future health threats facing the modern world: pandemics, obesity, smoking, mental health, drugs and alcohol. New technologies and innovations have led to improvements to treatments, as well as to new ways of providing information and advice. The care provided by UK child health services remains inferior in many regards to that in comparable European countries.[11] Much more effort and investment are essential in the crucial early period of life, if services are to influence how children grow up and prosper. While there is much more to be achieved, the Government has begun to put down foundations for the future. Professor Sir Ian Kennedy's 2010 review, *Getting it right for children and young people* acknowledged the concerted effort, at least at the level of policy, to raise the profile of services for children and young people, and to give them a higher priority.[12] The following paragraphs detail some of the key cornerstones of child health policy in the UK.

England
Introduced in 1999, Sure Start Children's Centres, a service for 0 to five year olds, have been established to help provide health and education services in the early years of a child's life alongside schools, community health services and general practitioner (GP) practices. There are 3,600 children's centres in England, enabling over 2.7 million children under five and their families to access a range of integrated services. The House of Commons Children, Schools and Families Select Committee 2010 report recognised that the Sure Start programme 'is one of the most innovative and ambitious Government initiatives of the past two decades'.[13] The Committee endorsed Sure Start's approach to

ensuring that children's centres serve all communities, recognising that 'this was the right policy to pursue' and that 'only universal coverage can ensure that all the most disadvantaged children, wherever they live, can benefit from the programme'.[13]

In 2004, the Department of Health (DH) and the Department for Education and Skills (DfES)[a] published a key National Service Framework (NSF): *The National Service Framework for Children, Young People and Maternity Services*.[14] This 10-year programme was intended to stimulate long-term and sustained improvement in child health. It set out the standards that services for children and young people were to meet and aimed to ensure fair, high-quality and integrated health and social care from pregnancy, right through to adulthood.

In 2003, the Government published its Green Paper, *Every child matters* (ECM).[15] It proposed a range of measures to reform and improve child care. In 2004, following consultation the Government published *Every child matters: change for children*.[16] It set child health and wellbeing in the context of the Government's commitment to their welfare. The *Children's Act 2004* was also passed, providing the legislative spine for developing more effective and accessible services focused around the needs of children, young people and families.[17]

In 2007, the DCSF published the *Children's plan*, which set out the Government's strategy for improving the wellbeing, health and opportunities available to children and young people in England.[18] It included a commitment from Government to publish a child health strategy jointly between the DH and the DCSF. In 2009, *Healthy lives, brighter futures: a strategy for children and young people's health* was launched.[1] This joint strategy presented the Government's vision for children and young people's health and wellbeing. It set out how Government would build on progress through: world-class outcomes; high-quality services; excellent experience in using those services; and minimising health inequalities.

Public service agreements (PSAs) were introduced by the Government in 1998 to transform the health and social care system so that it produced faster, fairer services that deliver better health and tackle health inequalities.[19] The *PSA 12*, published in 2007, called for the improvement of the health and wellbeing of children and young people. Another two PSAs addressed the same aim, by itemising the need to keep children safe (*PSA 13*, published in 2009) and to focus on young people's health (*PSA 14*, published in 2007).

---

a   The DfES was the government department responsible for education and children's services in England between 2001 and 2007. In 2007, its responsibilities were split between the Department for Children, Schools and Families (DCSF) and the Department for Innovation, Universities and Skills. The Department for Education (DfE) was formed in 2010, with responsibility for children's education in England.

In 2008, the DH launched the *Healthy Child Programme* (HCP), a public health initiative for children, young people and families, which focused on early intervention and prevention.[20] It offered a programme of screening tests, immunisations, developmental reviews, information and guidance on parenting and healthy choices. Due to its universal reach, the HCP aimed to identify families requiring additional support or that are at risk of poor health outcomes. The programme was made up of three documents; *Healthy Child Programme: pregnancy and the first five years;*[21] *Healthy Child Programme: the two year review*[22] and *Healthy Child Programme: from 5 to 19 years old.*[23]

Lord Laming's 2009 report, *The protection of children in England: a progress report*, confirmed that robust legislative, structural and policy foundations were in place and that ECM 'clearly has the support of professionals, across all of the services, who work with children and young people' and provided 'a sound framework for professionals to protect children and promote their welfare'.[24] He reported that 'a great deal of progress has been made' and highlighted the positive difference that people on the front line are making to children. Lord Laming, was clear, however, that more needs to be done, calling for a 'step change in the arrangements to protect children from harm'. He challenged national Government to 'inject greater energy and drive into the implementation of change and support local improvement' and leaders of local services to 'translate policy, legislation and guidance into day-to-day practice on the frontline of every service'. The Government responded, detailing their plans to deliver the step change that Lord Laming's report called for.[25]

In March 2010, the DfE published its revised guidance on *Working together to safeguard children*. This document set out how organisations and individuals should work together to safeguard and promote the welfare of children and young people in accordance with the *Children Act 1989*[26] and the *Children Act 2004*.[18] The DfE is currently consulting on *Working together to safeguard children*,[27] in the context of the National Health Service (NHS) reform agenda as set out in the *Munro review of child protection*.[28]

In June 2010, the Secretary of State for Education asked Professor Eileen Munro to conduct an independent review of child protection in England. The review, published in February 2011, explained that while previous reforms have been well meaning and well informed, they have not delivered positive long-lasting improvements at the front line. Changes during the past 40 years have been made in reaction to high-profile cases and have focused on parts of the system in isolation, rather than looking at the system as a whole.[28]

Professor Sir Ian Kennedy's 2010 review, *Getting it right for children and young people*, concentrated on understanding the role of culture in the NHS in delivering child services.[29] Kennedy recognised the efforts by Government departments to improve the health and wellbeing of children and young people but highlighted the fact that these developments have not always been matched by results. The review exposed many cultural barriers standing in the way of improving services for children and young people. These were created, and operate, at a number of levels, from Whitehall, through regional and local organisations, to contacts between individual professionals, and with children, young people and those looking after them. Kennedy proposed a new approach, which contemplates the integration of services, working collaboratively within the NHS and across other agencies.

Kennedy's 2010 review corroborates the view that, despite a wealth of Government publications and targets, far too many children and young people's services remain highly unsatisfactory. The DH's 2010 document *Achieving equity and excellence for children*, draws together information from the white paper and the associated consultation documents, to create a vision of how the proposed new arrangements for the NHS could improve services for children and young people.[30]

In July 2012, the Children and Young People's Health Outcomes Forum published its report following a request from the Secretary of State for Health to look at how best the health outcomes of children in the UK could be improved.[9] The report noted that while there have been some improvements in measured outcomes for children and young people in recent years, the UK lags behind comparable countries in northern and western Europe. Some of the most important health outcomes for children and young people in the UK are worse than in many of these countries. The report set out recommendations for the new health system, which would start to address the key obstacles to improving children and young people's health outcomes.

Scotland

In 1999, the white paper *Towards a healthier Scotland* identified child health as a key driver in improving the health of the people of Scotland.[31] *For Scotland's children*, published in 2001, found that agencies did not work together to help children.[32] Children and their families had to negotiate their own way around and between agencies. Agency resources were not aligned according to need or around a child. It recommended greater joining up between agencies at all levels. The audit and review of child protection was published in 2002. The report, *It's everyone's job to make sure I'm alright,* noted that children did not get the help they needed when they needed it.[33]

In April 2004, the Scottish Government published their consultation on the review of the Children's Hearings system – *Getting it right for every child*.[34] The Scottish Government developed a programme of reform across a number of agencies and Scottish Government departments in order to deliver the necessary improvements that had been signalled. *The getting it right for every child* programme is an integrated programme of action and legislation to reform children's services. In June 2005, the Scottish Government published *Getting it right for every child – proposals for action*. This called for views on a wide number of reforms to improve child services.[35]

In 2005, the Scottish Government published *Health for all children*, which offered guidance to support implementation of the recommendations of the Royal College of Paediatrics and Child Health's fourth review of routine child health checks, screening and surveillance activity.[36] The guidance aimed to promote effective and integrated provision of universal and tailored services for children and families, and described the activity needed for implementation at national and local levels.

In 2008, the *Early Years Framework* was launched, signifying a commitment to the earliest years of life being crucial to a child's development.[37] The framework signalled commitment across the public sector to break this cycle of inequality through prevention and early intervention and to give every child in Scotland the best start in life. This is supported by the wider policy document *Equally well*, also published in 2008, which highlighted the need to provide the best possible environment for children's earliest years and to end cycles of poverty and poor health passed down from parent to child.[38] *Early Years Framework: Progress so far*, was published in 2011.[39]

In 2010, the Scottish Government launched the *Maternal and early years* website, to provide accessible information to early years professionals across all sectors.[40] The site aims to improve joint understanding of the role professionals can play in improving outcomes for Scotland's children and families, and support the delivery of consistent messages to parents across all services.

The 2011 report, *Growing up in Scotland* detailed the aspects of day-to-day parenting that are important to child health and whether variations in parenting account for social inequalities in child health outcomes.[41] In June 2012, the Scottish Government updated its *Getting it right for every child guide*.[42] In July 2012, the Scottish Government announced that plans to introduce legislation to ensure investment in early years are not an optional extra. It also planned to explore legislative options to ensure that *Getting it right for every child* is embedded throughout the public sector.

Wales

In 2000, the Welsh Assembly Government published *Children and young people: a framework for partnership*, to ensure a new approach to the planning and delivery of services for children and young people.[43] It proposed a way in which all local partners could work together in an integrated framework designed to meet the needs of children and young people. *Everybody's business*, published in 2001, was a 10-year strategy for improving child and adolescent mental health services (CAMHS) in Wales.[44]

In 2002, the National Assembly for Wales developed *Seven core aims for children and young people* which summarised the United Nations Convention on the Rights of the Child (UNCRC) as a basis for planning, decisions on priorities, and objectives, both nationally and on a local level.[45]

In 2004, the Welsh Assembly Government published *Children and young people: rights to action*, which set out plans to support all children and young people to achieve their potential and committed to assisting children and young people who are disadvantaged, for example through disability, poverty, family and community circumstances, illness, neglect or abuse.[46] The *All Wales youth offending strategy* was published jointly in 2004 and was the result of the Welsh Government, the Youth Justice Board and local agencies working together to develop a strategy that provided a national framework for preventing offending and re-offending among children and young people in Wales.[47]

In response to the *Children's Act 2004*, the Welsh Government issued guidance in July 2006 called *Stronger partnerships for better outcomes*.[48] This guidance showed how local authorities in Wales could produce a 'children and young people's plan'. These plans have been the key mechanisms for delivering sustainable improvement in local service delivery for children and young people.

The NSF, launched in 2005, set out the quality of services that children, young people and their families have a right to expect in Wales.[49] This framework incorporates national standards based on the UNCRC. The *Integrated children's system* was in force by the end of 2006 and was designed to provide information to practitioners working with children and families.[50]

The child poverty strategy and implementation plan, published in 2006, contained proposals, targets and milestones to halve child poverty in Wales by 2010 and eradicate it by 2020.[51] In 2007, the Welsh Assembly Government published *Towards a stable life and a brighter future*.[52] This provided guidance and regulations on measures to strengthen arrangements for the placement, health, education and wellbeing of looked-after children and young people. *Getting it right*, published in 2009, provided a five-year rolling action plan for Wales setting out key priorities and actions to be undertaken by the Welsh Assembly Government in response to the concluding observations of the UNCRC 2008.[53]

In 2011, the Welsh Assembly Government published their Childcare Policy Statement, *Nurturing children, supporting families*, outlining a vision to promote high-quality, affordable and accessible child care across Wales.[54] In 2012, the *Children's rights scheme* was published, setting out the arrangements for having due regard to the UNCRC.[55]

Northern Ireland

In 1988, the Royal College of Paediatrics and Child Health established a joint working party to review existing child services in the UK. The first edition of *Health for all children* was published by this multidisciplinary working party in 1989.[56] The emphasis at the time was on development of partnerships between parents, children and health professionals. The 2003 edition of *Health for all children* promoted the gradual shift from a highly medical model of screening, to one with a greater emphasis on health promotion, primary prevention and active intervention for children at risk.[57] The Child Health Promotion Programme within Northern Ireland, introduced in 2006, is based on *Health for all children: guidance and principles of practice for professional staff*.[58] *Healthy child, healthy future*, published in 2010, is intended to strengthen the existing programme and is recognised as being central to securing improvements in child health.[59]

In 2006, the Office of the First Minister and Deputy First Minister, published *Children and young people: our pledge*.[60] This provided a 10-year strategy on the commitments to prevention and early intervention. In 2008, the early years was identified as one of the six priority areas of the *Ten year strategy for children and young people (2006-2016)*.[61] This led to the publication, in June 2010, of the draft *Early years 0-6 strategy* for consultation.[62] The strategy emphasised that education begins at birth, and that the most critical period in human development is that of the early years. In 2010, the Department of Health, Social Services and Public Safety (DHSSP) published *Health futures 2010-2015*.[63] This focused on health visitors and school nurses within integrated children's services.

In July 2012, the DHSSP published *A maternity strategy for Northern Ireland 2012-2018*.[64] This strategy aims to provide women and their partners, health and social staff, commissioners and policy makers with a clear pathway for maternity care in Northern Ireland from preconceptual care through to postnatal care. This strategy highlights the importance of giving every person the best start in life through promoting and protecting the health and wellbeing of baby, mother, father and family members.

1.2 An overview of the report

This report focuses on the child, from conception to age five, and on the impact of social and economic inequality on child health. Some areas cover childhood more broadly and within the framework of cycles of development. For the purpose of this report, health is defined not simply as the absence of ill health and disease, but more broadly as developing a sense of wellbeing – physically, emotionally, intellectually, psychologically and spiritually.

Chapter 2 gives a brief overview of the key issues in child health today and **Chapter 3** draws on the evidence of inequalities that are present in child health within the UK, including discussing Marmot's work on health inequalities. Marmot noted that although there was around a three-point improvement in the percentage of five year olds achieving a good level of educational development between 2010 and 2011 – from nearly 56 per cent to 59 per cent – this left almost 250,000 children failing to meet the standard set by schools.[65] Assessment of development is measured by tests which include being able to dress and concentrate, and the ability to speak and recognise words. The remaining low level of results for testing is evidence that the UK is failing its young children on a grand scale. There are significant inequalities in child development, with many not achieving basic levels of social and emotional development.

The report cannot deal with all child health issues in depth, but a number of key issues have been identified to illustrate inequity in child health, highlight the efficacy of certain interventions and point to the need for a total rather than service-orientated approach in addressing inequity and poor health and wellbeing during the early years of life.

The report considers issues relating to nutrition (**Chapter 4**), maltreatment (**Chapter 5**), disability (**Chapter 6**) and emotional and behavioural problems (**Chapter 7**).

Chapter 8 considers the origins of adult disease and how this can be programmed in utero and early childhood. **Chapter 9** draws conclusions and **Chapter 10** presents a broad range of recommendations for actions that need to be taken if the UK is to provide an environment in which children are nurtured and their health in the early years of life recognised as key to the future health and wellbeing of the population.

We hope that this BMA report will be a valuable resource for doctors and other healthcare professionals working with children, including health visitors, members of the primary healthcare team and paediatricians. Policy makers and workers involved in health, education, social and voluntary sectors may also find this report a useful reference point for their work.

Why are we publishing this report?
The BMA has three main aims in producing this report:
- to acknowledge and celebrate the significant improvements that have been achieved and the considerable amount of work that has gone into child health policy;
- to highlight the fact that, despite these achievements, international benchmarks continually rank the UK low in the league in terms of child health and wellbeing;
- to encourage health professionals, policy makers and the public to consider what more can and should be done and to provide an authoritative resource for effective advocacy.

Chapter 2: Setting the scene

Dr Ingrid Wolfe

> *It was the best of times, it was the worst of times, it was the age of wisdom, it was the age of foolishness, it was the epoch of belief, it was the epoch of incredulity, it was the season of light, it was the season of darkness, it was the spring of hope, it was the winter of despair, we had everything before us, we had nothing before us, we were all going direct to Heaven, we were all going direct the other way – in short, the period was so far like the present period, that some of its noisiest authorities insisted on its being received, for good or for evil, in the superlative degree of comparison only.*
>
> *A tale of two cities*, Charles Dickens[1]

Charles Dickens vividly documented the poverty and pain of childhood in the UK in the nineteenth century. It is 200 years since Dickens was born, and child health in the UK, in many ways, is better than ever. In 1999 when the BMA published *Growing up in Britain*, the death rate for children aged under 14 years was 58.11 per 100,000. This fell to 45.98 per 100,000 by 2009, meaning that over 1,200 extra children survived in the past decade.[2] But mortality figures are an incomplete measure of child health, and although it is an undoubted success that so many more children survive today, what happens to these children? Are they healthy and happy? Do they thrive and fulfil their potential? Dickens would surely recognise some aspects of children's lives today.

This chapter will set the scene by examining child health outcomes and considering the underlying explanations, and drawing upon these to make recommendations.

2.1   Child health and wellbeing

Children are among the most vulnerable members of society, and children's wellbeing therefore indicates the state of our entire society. The UK is a signatory of the UNCRC, recognising that children are vulnerable and need special care and protection. Yet the UK is lagging behind many of its European counterparts in terms of child wellbeing,[3] and one in every ten British children is unhappy.[4]

Why are some half a million children so unhappy?[5] Is our health system prepared for the new morbidities, the chronic diseases, and mental ill health of children and young people? How well do we, as citizens, look after and nurture our children? What is our role, as health professionals, in the lives of children?

The UK is failing its young children on a grand scale, according to Professor Sir Michael Marmot. Children's wellbeing is inadequate in all of the aspects examined by UNICEF. In a 2013 UNICEF study of 29 of the world's most advanced economies, the UK was ranked overall in the middle third range of countries.[3] This is a modest improvement however, since in 2007, a previous study[6] by the same institution found the UK to rank lowest of the 21 countries examined. Although the more recent study included more countries, and used different measures, some direct comparisons of the two reports are possible. The UK has improved from 21st (joint last) to 16th position. These data cover the period up to 2009/10 however, so it is unlikely that much of the effects of the economic downturn could have been detected, nor can any inferences be drawn about the impact of the Coalition government's austerity policies.

The five UNICEF dimensions of wellbeing noted in the previous paragraph are similar to the five important outcomes of the ECM framework: being healthy, staying safe, enjoying and achieving, making a positive contribution, and economic wellbeing.[7] The ECM philosophy explicitly recognised the importance of health and social care, and the interface between them. Although the ECM framework has been superseded by more recent reports, its influence is reflected in current strategy such as the Children's Outcomes Forum report.[8] Accordingly, the chapters of this book focus on these topics that are of central importance in determining the life chances and wellbeing of children. It is in these areas that we must focus our efforts in improving the lives of children.

This report focuses on the early years of childhood, and takes the optimistic approach of emphasising the conditions that need to be put into place to promote healthy lives and development for children rather than services that are needed once things go wrong. These categories, however, are not and cannot be mutually exclusive. The life-stages of childhood are continuous and interdependent; the youngest children grow into older children, adolescents, and adults and what happens in the earliest stages is reflected later in life. Child health is affected both by upstream determinants such as socioeconomic conditions and social institutions and by downstream determinants such as health services necessary to help children who are ill and suffering with their immediate problems. Finally, since demand for health services continues to rise, and since parents seek help with problems of all types through the health sector, this is where we start our investigation of growing up in the UK.

2.2   Health services

How well is our health service helping children? This is a difficult question to answer; health services research for children is at an early stage of development compared with biomedical research,[9] and one reason is because the research methods for answering questions in this field are different. Whereas the strength of evidence in biomedical research may be loosely judged according to a hierarchy, with randomised controlled trials as the gold standard, health policy and systems research (HPSR) is a transdisciplinary research field which defines new methods, and new standards for evaluating evidence and making recommendations. This sort of research must often be able to produce recommendations on the basis of 'best available knowledge rather than the most desirable evidence'[10] in order to help us understand how well systems work, and what should be done differently to strengthen child health system performance.

Death is a health outcome that no one wishes were necessary to consider. Fortunately fewer children die now than ever before (see **Figure 2.1**) This success is tempered by stark social inequalities in death rates within the UK. The death rate among infants from routine socioeconomic groups is nearly twice that of professional and managerial groups.[11] When we compare the UK's childhood mortality rate with similar European countries, there are further causes for concern; we lag behind comparable countries, and are at or above the EU average rate for child deaths (see **Figure 2.2**).

Figure 2.1: Child mortality in the UK – deaths among children aged 0-14 years, all causes

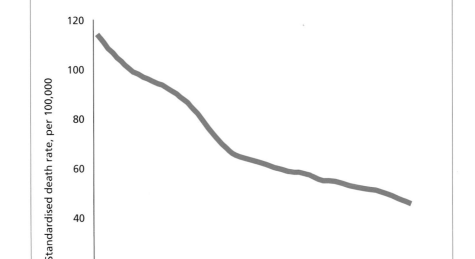

Source: *European health for all database* (World Health Organization). Figure provided by Dr Ingrid Wolfe.

Figure 2.2: Trends in child mortality (0-14 years): UK compared with European countries, 1980-2010

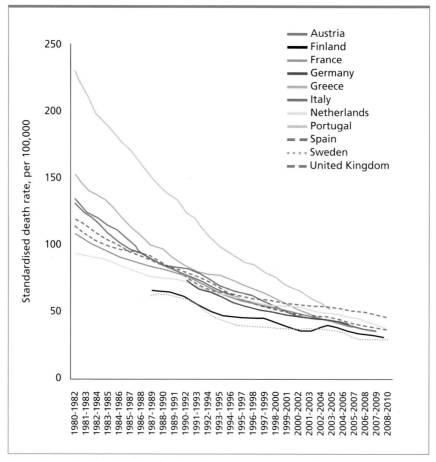

Source: *European health for all database* (World Health Organization). Reproduced from Wolfe I, Thompson M, Gill P et al (2013) Health services for children in Western Europe. *The Lancet.* Published online March 27, 2013 http://dx.doi.org/10.1016/S0140-6736(12)62085-6

What might be causing the higher child death rate in the UK? It is often argued that the UK's higher child poverty rate may be to blame. Poverty and other socioeconomic conditions contribute to differences in disease incidence and prevalence, and to access to health care. But dig a bit deeper, and the poverty explanation is insufficient. Many children in the UK die from causes that should be preventable with adequate health care. These deaths should not be happening.

The concept of avoidable or amenable mortality as a measure of health systems and healthcare effectiveness has gained increasing currency among high income countries health systems.[12] This method, however, has limited use for measuring the quality of children's health services for the felicitous reason that the number of deaths is small enough to render interpretation difficult. Avoidable mortality is an extremely useful concept, and there are two broad ways it can be used for assessing the quality of children's health care. First is through individual case audit. This method has been put to use effectively by the Confidential Enquiry into Maternal and Child Health (CEMACH) which produced the report *Why Children Die*. This work was a meticulous audit of the events leading to the deaths of a representative sample of children. Its findings are alarming: identifiable failures in the child's direct care, in just over a quarter of deaths, and potentially avoidable factors in a further 43 per cent of deaths. A further striking finding is that errors were particularly common among staff with inadequate paediatric training or supervision.[13] Case audit does not confirm causality, but it can point towards areas meriting further inquiry. The second way is examining mortality by avoidable cause, and by combining data for several years. This method allows some comparison between countries (as regions or hospitals would have numbers too small for statistical analysis). Focusing on death rates from illnesses that ought not to kill children in high-income countries with highly developed health systems reveals useful insights: death rates from pneumonia, asthma, and meningococcal disease are higher in the UK than in comparable European countries.[14] If the UK had the same all-cause death rate as Sweden, around 1,900 children's lives could be saved each year.[15] Although a complex interaction of social and economic forces shape children's life chances and risk of death, equitable access to high quality health care is an important determinant, and these are signals of concern: children's health services are not performing as well as they could. We should be doing better than this. A concerted effort is required to understand and correct these failures of health systems and services to match children's needs.

2.3   Physical health

There is no annual report documenting the state of child health in the UK. If there were such a resource, planning health services to meet health needs in an effective and efficient way would become a great deal easier. Describing what children need from health care services is a challenging task. There are no comprehensive childhood disease incidence and prevalence databases, with indicators of wellbeing, development, and risk profiles, all linked to demographic information. Such a resource should, ideally, be available on a geographic basis to allow health service planning and evaluation, and would provide a normative indication of healthcare need. Perceived need for healthcare is an important factor determining its use. Significant progress has been made recently with the Child and Maternal Health Observatory, although this resource can only ever be as good as the data available, which remain insufficient.[16] Similarly Joint Strategic Needs Assessments are ambitiously designed to encompass both health and social care needs, but nevertheless are still reliant on the data that is available. Health service planning usually still relies on past evidence of service use, since there remains a lack of comprehensive data on needs. The result is a rather circular situation in which services are planned on the basis of what is already provided. A more rational system of health service planning is warranted. For the time being, information has to be gleaned piecemeal and indirectly.

So we need to ask some questions, about what kills children, and what ails children, and how these things are changing with time, and how children in different areas, communities, and families may experience health and illness. With this information we can start to build a picture of child health needs, examine in more detail how well those needs are matched by services, and consider what we could do to make things better.

What are the main causes of children's deaths? Congenital abnormalities and external causes of death and injury such as accidents, injuries, and poisoning are the most common causes of death.[2,17] Accidents and injuries in children are strongly linked to socioeconomic conditions, and are highly preventable through public health intervention.[18]

Infectious diseases, respiratory illnesses, gastroenterological problems – the acute illnesses on which our hospital-centric health service configuration is largely based – are relatively small causes, and non-communicable disease are becoming more common (see **Figure 2.3**).

Since the NHS was founded over 60 years ago, there has been a shift in the causes of death in childhood. In recent years, long-term or ongoing conditions and accidents and injuries have become more frequent causes of mortality, accounting for 95 per cent of deaths, while communicable diseases are more commonly prevented or cured (see **Figure 2.3**). There has also been a notable change in the age distribution of deaths in childhood. Mortality rates in younger children have declined more quickly than in older children and adolescents. Fewer young children die of infectious diseases, while violence and injury-related death rates in young people aged 15 to 24 years have increased.[19] Adolescents, and boys in particular, have not benefited as much as younger children have from the improvements in health in recent decades.

Figure 2.3: Shifting causes of childhood deaths (aged one to 14 years) – mortality in the 15 pre-2004 countries of the European Union, 1960-2010

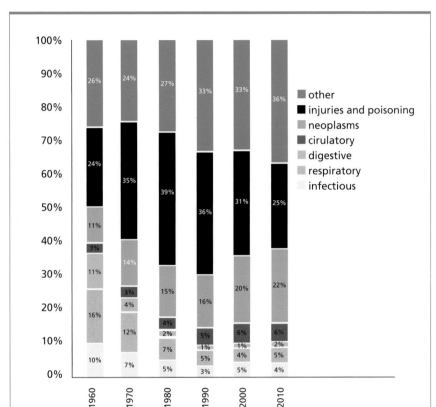

Source: *European health for all database* (World Health Organization). Reproduced from Wolfe I, Thompson M, Gill P et al (2013) Health services for children in Western Europe. *The Lancet*. Published online March 27, 2013 http://dx.doi.org/10.1016/S0140-6736(12)62085-6

Chronic diseases and other long-term conditions are now the most common cause of illness and suffering among children and young people. There is an epidemiological shift away from acute infectious diseases towards ongoing conditions, and the new morbidities associated with environment, family and psychosocial conditions. Just over three-quarters of all childhood diseases are attributable to chronic conditions (see **Figure 2.4**), and around 7 per cent of children in the UK have a disability; the commonest involve difficulties with learning, communication, and mobility.[20]

Figure 2.4: The causes of illness and disability in childhood (aged 0 to 14 years), Western Europe, 2004

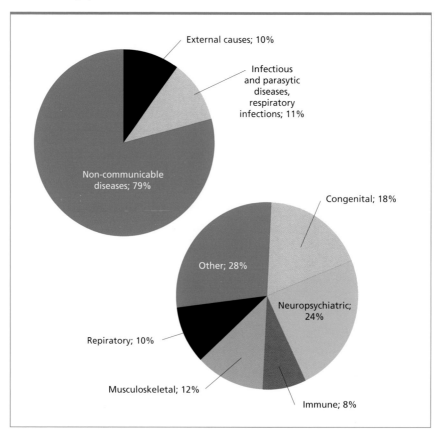

Source: Data from the Global Burden of Disease Study 2010 (Institute of Health Metrics and Evaluation). Reproduced from Wolfe I, Thompson M, Gill P et al (2013) Health services for children in Western Europe. *The Lancet.* Published online March 27, 2013 http://dx.doi.org/20.1016/S0140-6736(12)62085-6

Asthma is one of the commonest chronic diseases in childhood, and is responsible for the largest number of disability-adjusted life years[a] (DALYs) lost of any single childhood chronic illness.[18] There is conflicting evidence on whether the prevalence of asthma in the UK is increasing or decreasing, and what the differences in trends are between young and older children.[21-23] It is indisputable that our health services are not providing universally high-quality care for children with asthma. Only 3 per cent of children with asthma have written plans to prevent and manage exacerbations of symptoms, which contribute to preventable admissions to hospital,[24] and there are preventable deaths from asthma.[13,15]

a   A DALY is a measure of overall disease burden, expressed as the number of years lost due to ill-health, disability or early death.

Diabetes mellitus is becoming increasingly common in children, and presenting earlier in life than ever before. Current trends suggest that the incidence of type I diabetes mellitus will double in children under five years of age, and the prevalence in children aged under 15 years will increase by 70 per cent between 2005 and 2020.[25] Less than 5 per cent of children with diabetes receive care consistent with guidelines, and therefore preventable complications of disease such as diabetic ketoacidosis occur. Children in the UK die from diabetes. These deaths ought to be entirely preventable.[26]

Epilepsy is a common chronic disease of childhood, yet children with epilepsy do not always get the care they should have. A recent national audit revealed significant gaps in services, for example only 65 per cent of children had an appropriate first assessment, and 35 per cent did not have a complete assessment, nearly half of the children did not receive appropriate specialist neurology care when it was necessary, and less than half of services employ a specialist epilepsy nurse.[27]

Although this book focuses on the first five years of life, the consequences of early years health and development are often revealed later in childhood. Self-rated health in adolescents and young people is important as a subjective indicator but also because it reflects events earlier in life, and predicts objective health later in life. There is a link with living conditions since poor or fair self-rated health is significantly associated with family poverty (see **Table 2.1**).

Table 2.1: Children who self-rated health as fair or poor*

	11 year olds		13 year olds		15 year olds	
	Boys	**Girls**	**Boys**	**Girls**	**Boys**	**Girls**
England	11	13	19	21	18	32
Wales	17	23	20	30	20	33
Scotland	13	14	16	25	18	34
Average (WHO European region, USA & Canada)	11	13	12	18	13	23

*No data given for Northern Ireland.

Source: Currie C, Levin K & Todd J (2008) *Health behaviour in school-aged children: World Health Organization collaborative cross-national study (HBSC): findings from the 2006 survey in Scotland*. Edinburgh: Child and Adolescent Health Research Unit, The University of Edinburgh. Reproduced with the permission of the authors.

2.4   Mental health and wellbeing

It is especially noteworthy, partly because it is often overlooked, that the largest category cause of non-communicable illness among children and young people is neuropsychiatric illness.[28] Unipolar depression is the commonest single cause. Emotional and behavioural problems affect one in five children, and mental health conditions affect one in eight.[29] Six per cent of the child and adolescent population have a diagnosed conduct disorder, 4 per cent an emotional disorder, 3 per cent have attention deficit hyperactivity disorder (ADHD), and 1 per cent have other conditions including autism.[30] The Centre for Maternal and Child Enquiries (CMACE), formerly the CEMACH, report identified mental health as an important area to focus efforts in reducing preventable deaths, since the majority of young people who die following suicide or substance misuse had not been in contact with mental health services. The DH has recognised the importance of these problems and recently issued a strategy for preventing mental illness and intervening early in childhood.[31] This is to be welcomed. Implementing such a strategy effectively at a time of tremendous upheaval in the NHS and severe budget cuts will be challenging.

2.5   Social determinants of child health

Virchow's statement that medicine is a social science, is especially relevant to child health, since early development is such a vulnerable and important stage of life.[32] The aetiology of emotional, behavioural, and mental conditions in children and young people is complex. There is, however, no doubt that changes in family structures, and social and economic factors influencing the whole of society play an important role. There are a variety of frameworks setting out plausibly how causal relations between social and economic stressors could affect health.[33,34] Although the exact mechanism is difficult to describe, there is no doubt that the relationship exists. Social risk factors for disease include proximal ones such as smoking, and more distal ones such as poverty.[34] These distinctions are fairly arbitrary since, for example, smoking and harm caused from alcohol consumption are strongly linked to socioeconomic status, and consumption is amenable to price and fiscal policy. The distinctions gain meaning only in how these risk factors are measured and in how policy should be devised to deal with the problems. Political solutions to the structural causes of ill health are required, even if the manifestations are seen and measured in the health sector.

2.6   Family

Parents are vital influences in the early years of children's lives and their social and emotional development. Furthermore there is evidence that the parent-child relationship may be a life-course health determinant. Young children whose parents show resentment or hostility have an increased risk of poor health in later childhood. Indeed higher levels of these negative parenting qualities predict greater likelihood of ill health, and higher use of health services. These results are independent of socioeconomic factors such as poverty.[36] Poor parent-child relationships can affect health much later in life too, even into adulthood.[37] These are important findings; first poor parenting is common (in the

Waylen study 34% of parents showed high levels of hostility towards their young child, up to 70% were moderately resentful, and around a third of parents hit their children frequently); and second because of the potential for universal and targeted public health interventions to improve the parenting relationship and, therefore, also possibly health.

Changes in family structure, together with wider social pressures, affect children's lives and health in fundamental ways. The UK ranks twenty-fourth out of 27 European countries in a composite measure of pressure on families, and the UK has the highest proportion of children living in a household where no one is employed.[38] Such is the strain on families and their consequent malfunction that over 64,000 children in the UK live in the care of local authorities rather than with their parents. Most of them are there because of abuse or neglect.[39] The UK has among the highest rates of out-of-home care in Europe.[40] The numbers of children referred for out-of-home care has been rising steadily and the past year, 2011 to 2012, has seen the highest number ever recorded – 10,199 referrals, an increase of over 10 per cent in the one year.[41] The phrase 'in care' is all too often inadequate, as there are widespread deficits in the quality of care for children in such circumstances. Children 'in care', for example, are often made to change home without notice (23% were informed on the day of their move, and 55% had less than a week's notice), representing major disruptions in the lives of children who crave stability. Nearly three-quarters of siblings are separated from each other while in care. Twenty-nine per cent of care-leavers were not in education, employment or training, and only 12 per cent of those leaving care go to a job or training post, thus perpetuating the social instability and stressors from which they came.[42]

Far more common than children in care, in terms of family disruption, are those whose parents have divorced. Twelve per cent of British children (age 11 to 15 years) live in step-families and 16 per cent in single-parent families. These figures are higher than other Western European countries, though lower than the USA.[43] Looking beyond the structure of families to how they function and what they do together is important. Thirty-three per cent of children, aged 15 years, eat main meals with their parents less than twice a week. Family meal times are important social and nutritional experiences. The changes in family behaviour that this may indicate could be related to the finding that fewer than two-thirds of five year olds had achieved a good level of development in 2011. This means that 250,000 children a year are failing to meet a school standard of good development, which examines such things as ability to concentrate, speak, recognise words, and dress themselves.[44]

2.7   Education

Early years education, at home, as well as formally, is a crucial part of child development.[45-47] The early years are vital in enabling children and future adults to develop empathy and to form healthy relationships.[48] Socially well-adjusted children are more likely to benefit from education.[49] It is an indictment of our culture that, in a country with such a strong literary heritage, one-third of children in Britain aged between 11 and 16 years do not own a book.[50] Children and young people's school experiences are important. According to UNICEF, the UK scores 24th (out of 29 countries) for education,[3] and the OECD ranks it twenty-second of 30 countries.[51] The quality of school life is, however, at least partly better: the OECD scores the UK fourth of 30 countries, and the UK mostly scores above average for 11 year olds. The proportions decrease with age and vary across the nations (see **Table 2.2**).

Table 2.2: Percentage of children who like school a lot*

	11 year olds		13 year olds		15 year olds	
	Boys	**Girls**	**Boys**	**Girls**	**Boys**	**Girls**
England	52	56	22	25	26	24
Wales	30	36	19	21	17	19
Scotland	33	45	31	33	22	16
Average (WHO European region, USA & Canada)	33	43	22	27	18	22

*No data given for Northern Ireland.

Source: Adapted from Currie C, Levin K & Todd J (2008) *Health behaviour in school-aged children: World Health Organization collaborative cross-national study (HBSC): findings from the 2006 survey in Scotland*. Edinburgh: Child and Adolescent Health Research Unit, The University of Edinburgh. Reproduced with the permission of the authors.

It is interesting to note that much larger proportions of children report feeling pressured by school work (family affluence is not a significant factor) in the UK than in Scandinavian countries. Educational outcomes for the UK are, however, generally comparable for both reading and mathematics.[52]

2.8   Friends and peers

Peer relationships are important for social development, but both healthy and harmful influences can occur. A large majority of children aged 11 to 15 years report close friendships with three or more children, which is well above the average.[53] Time spent out with friends in evenings, however, is strongly associated with risk behaviour in adolescence, especially with substance misuse. The UK scores poorly in this area, compared with the average across surveyed countries (see **Table 2.3**).[54]

Table 2.3: Percentages of children who spend four or more evenings per week out with friends*

	11 year olds		13 year olds		15 year olds	
	Boys	**Girls**	**Boys**	**Girls**	**Boys**	**Girls**
England	32	25	40	27	40	31
Wales	42	32	52	45	47	34
Scotland	46	39	54	46	53	40
Average (WHO European region, USA & Canada)	25	19	29	25	34	27

*No data given for Northern Ireland.

Source: Adapted from Currie C, Levin K & Todd J (2008) *Health behaviour in school-aged children: World Health Organization collaborative cross-national study (HBSC): findings from the 2006 survey in Scotland.* Edinburgh: Child and Adolescent Health Research Unit, The University of Edinburgh. Reproduced with the permission of the authors.

2.9   Risk to health and wellbeing

Smoking usually begins in adolescence, and early initiation of smoking predicts likelihood of addiction to tobacco, and also problems with alcohol later in life[55] and later use of illicit drugs.[56] Around one-quarter of British 15 year olds report having first smoked at the age of 13 years or younger; the rate is higher in teenage girls than boys. The likelihood of early smoking in girls, but not boys, is related to family poverty. Just under one-fifth of 15 year olds smoke at least once a week, again more commonly in girls than boys.[53] Smoking remains the leading cause of preventable morbidity and mortality in the UK. The BMA has a long history of supporting comprehensive tobacco control measures since the pioneering work of Professor Sir Richard Doll in 1950 (further information on the BMA's work on tobacco control can be found on the BMA website).

Alcohol over-consumption is a serious problem in the UK, and it begins in early life. Binge drinking is a particular feature of adolescent and young people's drinking behaviour. Around 40 per cent of 15 year olds, and just under 20 per cent of 13 year olds drink alcohol at least once per week. There is no significant association between weekly alcohol consumption by young people and family affluence, but the harm from excess alcohol consumption falls disproportionately on poorer families.[53] The burden of alcohol-related harm represents a significant threat to public health in the UK. The BMA has a long history of supporting comprehensive measures to reduce alcohol-related harm. Since its first publication on alcohol and young people in 1986, the BMA has led the medical profession in calling for tough action to redress the excessively pro-alcohol social norms in the UK. The BMA has produced a number of reports on alcohol including *Reducing the affordability of alcohol* (2012), *Under the influence: the damaging effect of alcohol marketing on young people* (2009), *Alcohol misuse – tackling the UK epidemic* (2008), *Fetal alcohol spectrum disorders – a guide for healthcare professionals* (2007), and *Adolescent health* (2003). Further information on the BMA's work on alcohol control can be found on the BMA website.

Over 20 per cent of children entering school (age 4+ years) are overweight or obese and are therefore at increased risk of ongoing overweight and obesity and of incurring the physical health problems such as diabetes, coronary heart disease (CHD), and early osteoarthritis in later life.[57] Physical activity, which is an important contributor to optimal weight, is also associated with physical and mental health gains in short and long term. Fewer than half of children aged 11 to 15 years engage in at least one hour per day of moderate to vigorous physical activity, and the rate decreases with age.[53] The BMA's 2005 report *Preventing childhood obesity* is a guide on childhood obesity for GPs and other healthcare professionals. The report highlights the impact childhood obesity can have on children's current and future health.

Environment can be both beneficial and harmful to health. The physical home environment is important for health, wellbeing and safety. Housing in deprived areas is more likely to be considered unsafe for children.[58] Poverty, adult alcohol consumption, and maternal depression are associated with injury in children aged under five years.[59] These risk factors are modifiable, and can enable early identification of children at risk of injury and so target prevention. The wider environment can increase or mitigate the risk of injury, which is not only a leading cause of childhood disability and disease, but is also largely preventable.[18]

2.10 Poverty

Poverty and social inequalities are some of the most important stressors on family life and are crucial determinants of children's health and wellbeing. The UNICEF league table on inequalities in childhood wellbeing assesses and ranks countries according to three related dimensions of inequalities: material, education, and health.[60] It tells us interesting and important things about the UK today. It demonstrates our relatively low position in the league tables of inequality, but also has a subtler message. The report focuses on what has become known as 'bottom-end inequality', that is how far below the median children who are at the margins of society live. The UK scores poorly in its overall inequality record for childhood, as well as in measures of bottom-end inequalities. The consequences are stark: social inequalities in health continue to widen, and while average life expectancy increased by 0.3 years from 2007/09 to 2008/10, the gap between the richest and poorest widened.[44]

The Labour Government that took office in 1997 pledged to halve child poverty by 2010, to eradicate it within 20 years, and to reduce health inequalities. Too many of the health policies that followed these pledges focused on modifying individual health behaviours, and taxation policies were not sufficiently progressive to achieve the redistribution of wealth that was promised.[61] The 2010 target was not met and although as the 2013 UNICEF report shows,[3] some progress has been made, the situation faced now by the UK's children is one of deepening poverty. Nearly a third (27%) of children in the UK live in poverty,[62] and there are areas where poverty is particularly concentrated in specific places such that between 50 and 70 per cent of children are growing up in poverty.[63] Current Government austerity policies are predicted to cause child poverty to rise substantially (see **Table 2.4**).[64]

Table 2.4: Current and predicted child poverty rates in the UK

	1998/99*	2009/10*	2010/11**	2015/16**	2020/21**
Children in poverty (before housing costs)	3.4 million	2.6 million	2.5 million	2.9 million	3.3 million
Children in poverty (after housing costs)	4.4 million	3.8 million	3.5 million	3.9 million	4.2 million

* Data taken from Harker L (2006) *Delivering on child poverty: what would it take? A report for the Department for Work and Pensions*. London: Department for Work and Pensions.

** Data taken from Child Poverty Action Group (2012) *End child poverty: child poverty map of the UK*. London: Child Poverty Action Group.

Compiled by Dr Ingrid Wolfe.

The 2013 UNICEF report on child wellbeing makes important points about social protection policy and child wellbeing.[3] Compared with other European countries, data until 2009/10 showed that the UK had done comparatively well in reducing child deprivation, ranking 9th of 20 countries, with 5.5 per cent of children in deprivation. However it had done less well in reducing child poverty (defined for this study as the number of children living in households below 50% of the median income), for which the UK ranked 22nd of 35 countries, with 12.1 per cent of children in poverty.

The scale of the gap between child poverty and deprivation is partly accounted for by policy. Governments can reduce the impact of poverty through social protection policy. Sweden has lower child deprivation rates than other countries of similar wealth, because of differences in policy providing support for single parent families, for example. The UK too has had a fairly good social protection record, providing cash and public services to families in need. Up until 2009, the UK would have had three times the child poverty rate if the Government had not adopted the policies they did on cash transfers, tax credits, and public services for children.[65]

As shown in **Table 2.4**, child poverty is projected to increase, and the full impact of the Government's cuts to social protection policy, and austerity economics, are yet to be determined. The moderate progress for children made in the years since the 2007 UNICEF report[6] is likely to be lost.

2.11   Bringing it all together

The increasing numbers of children and families in poverty and widening social inequalities present enormous challenges for the health system. The rising numbers of children with chronic conditions has direct social and economic implications in terms of reduced school participation, and indirectly through reduced productivity for their parents at work. It also has substantial impacts on the health services since the hospital-centric structure of child health services was designed to suit an episodic illness model when infectious diseases predominated. When the current model was devised, children's medicine and healthcare was considered largely to be a subset of adult practice. Children's health needs are now accepted to be distinct from those of adults, and children's health care has become a sophisticated specialty with a discrete knowledge base. Health services, however, have failed to adapt sufficiently to meet children's needs adequately. Health systems still prioritise acute services modelled around the demands of running hospital wards and emergency departments. Services are used inefficiently as a result, and chronic care takes second place to urgent services.[15,66] Despite the emphasis on acute care, there are still significant numbers of children whose deaths are avoidable.[13]

Children with long-term conditions often require complex packages of care coordinated by different health professionals working in different organisations across health and other sectors such as social and educational. It remains to be seen whether the Health and Social Care Act 2012 facilitates or impairs integration between services. Health policy analysis suggests that the emphasis on competition rather than collaboration may impair efforts to integrate services and reduce equity of access to care.[67-69] A further significant impediment to reform is the size of the paediatric workforce; there is a mismatch between the number of paediatricians being trained, the number of funded consultant posts, and the number required safely and legally to staff existing acute hospital services.[70]

Prevention of chronic disease and improving life chances are priorities for the entire health system, and the greatest gains will accrue from starting at the earliest stage of life. Social and economic conditions are profoundly important determinants of children's health. A direct attack on the determinants of disease and deficits of wellness in children is necessary both comprehensively to deal with the problems children face today, and to improve our chances of ensuring a healthy and happy future for the next generations. Just as there has been a shift in disease burden among children, there has been a shift in the distribution of risks they face. Undernutrition is a less important risk for the UK's child population now than is over-nutrition. Although of note there are pockets of malnutrition, and the rising prevalence of rickets is a significant concern. Tobacco, alcohol, physical inactivity, overweight, lack of fruits and vegetables in the diet, and road traffic safety are important risk factors for child health.[71] Early years development is critical and sustained investment is needed. The life-course health development approach aims to provide rational interventions that deliver sustained improvements in health and wellbeing.[33] Tackling the complex social and economic determinants of chronic ill health and of unfulfilled lives requires a multidimensional policy response across Government departments. It is important to get this right; children's health and development determines the strength of nations.[72] In these straitened economic times, investment in public health must be strengthened and protected as a vital part of our efforts to improve children's health and wellbeing.

Wellbeing in childhood encompasses a diversity of aspects of children's lives, summed up as the quality of children's lives. The OECD and UNICEF attempt to measure children's wellbeing by examining various dimensions of their lives, and then provide a score, and rank countries accordingly.[3,51] Both organisations measure dimensions of wellbeing based on the UNCRC.[73] The 2009 OECD report focuses especially on aspects of wellbeing that are amenable to policy interventions. Of 30 OECD countries, the UK ranks poorly in each domain except for quality of school life.[51] In its 2007 study, UNICEF ranked the UK as the worst performing of the 21 countries it assessed, based on an average ranking for six dimensions of children's wellbeing.[6] As noted in Chapter 1, its update to the 2007 study (published in April 2013),[3] found that the UK had shown a modest improvement, moving from 21st to 16th position. Further direct comparisons are not possible as the two studies used different measures and assessed different countries.

When UNICEF's 2007 report was published, David Cameron, then in opposition stated 'If today, Britain is the least family-friendly country in the developed world, the aim of the next Conservative Government is to make it the most family-friendly'. This pledge was repeated often during the election campaign, and into the early months of the Coalition Government. To date, the current administration's policies are unlikely to be described by health policy analysts as family-friendly. There are cuts to child benefit, Sure Start centres (which provide child care for working mothers, parenting support, behavioural and other early interventions to prevent family problems and later reliance on social services, and improve early years education) have been closed, and regressive tax policies have been implemented that differentially affect women and children (see **Chapter 7** for a more detailed discussion on parenting).

There is a new Welfare Reform Act and a Health and Social Care Act that many health professionals and policy analysts argue will have profoundly deleterious effects on the most vulnerable patients.[67-69] Despite an enormous amount of current policy change, there remains little comprehensive policy analysis to examine the effects of these changes on children's health and lives. This is compounded by the relatively small amount of work in children's health services research and comparative health systems analysis which could inform future policy direction. The updated UNICEF study, published in April 2013,[3] reports data from 2009/10, just before the Coalition government took office. Although some progress in improving child wellbeing was reported, the time lag in data availability means that it does not reflect the Coalition government policies. It is unlikely, given the current economic situation and policy environment, that the trend in improving child wellbeing will continue for the next few years.

The Court Report in 1976, the NSF for Children in 2004, and the Marmot Review and Kennedy report in 2010, are major Government reports that emphasised the importance of health professionals working closely together, in integrated services, serving the best interests of children and young people.[35,74-76] Each made recommendations to improve children's health and health services and each contributed towards improving children's health. There remains, however, a great deal more work to be done in implementing the recommendations of those reports. It is to be hoped that the BMA's *Growing up in the UK* report can help to reinforce these preceding reports, and contribute towards realising the goals that are shared by all those who work to promote the interests, health, and wellbeing of the UK's children.

2.12   Recommendations

The recommendations in this chapter are intended to complement and support those in the children and young people's health outcomes strategy[8] published in 2012.

A life course approach to improving child health

Reducing risk and promoting health are fundamental to our efforts to improve the lives of children. The life-course approach to health defines health as a developmental process, and builds on chronic disease epidemiology, developmental epigenetics, early development research, and neurobiology.[77] A combination of reducing risk and promoting health, therefore, influences the life-course trajectory (see **Figure 2.6**).[33]

A 2012 report by the Royal College of Paediatrics and Child Health states that despite the commitment made by successive governments and progress in research, there remains a historic society-wide reluctance to involve children in research in the UK.[78] Children's research is needed to define the causal biological mechanisms, alter the development of aberrant trajectories, preserve health, and reduce the costs of healthcare in adult life. The report calls for a need to work together to effect a sea change in the recognition of the importance of child health research for the entire population. From a national perspective the economic arguments in favour of children's research activity are compelling. Improving child health accumulates advantages throughout the life-course and investment in the earliest years will reap the biggest rewards.

Figure 2.6: A life-course approach to health

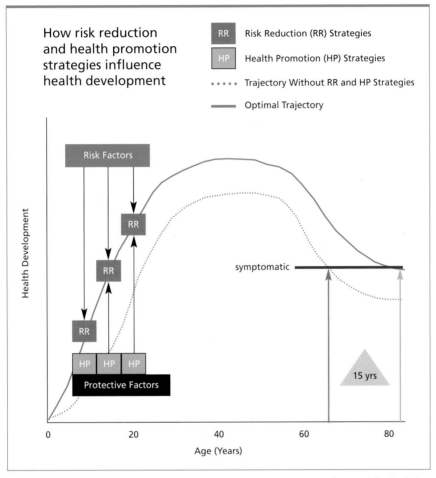

Source: Halfon N & Hochstein M (2002) Life Course Health Development: an integrated framework for developing health, policy, and research. *Milbank Quarterly* **80**: 433-79. Reproduced with permission of the authors.

Adopting a life-course approach to improving child health means that a variety of interventions across different sectors will be required. The aim is to ensure that all children are given the best possible chance to develop along a healthy trajectory (see **Figure 2.7**) and by the time they reach five years old, they should be ready to learn.

Figure 2.7: Strategies to improve early development

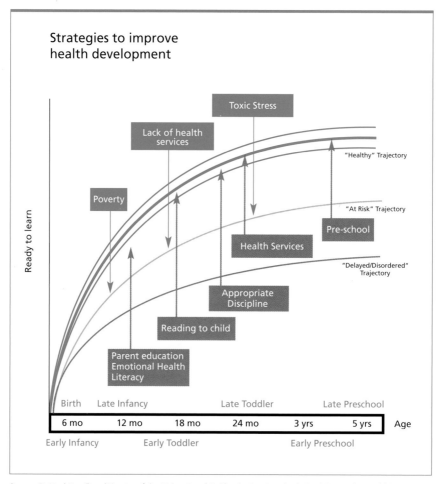

Source: Dr Neal Hamilton (Director of the University of California, Los Angeles (UCLA) Center for Healthier Children, Families & Communities). Reproduced with permission of the author.

Key aims and recommendations
Overarching themes
- Policy should serve to improve the 'match' between healthcare needs and services.
- Children's services, and the processes and structures that enable them, should be coordinated in the interests of children and families. This will require financial and organisational coordination, supportive local and national policy, and adequate resources invested for sufficient time to enable improvement.
- Accountability for children's health and wellbeing is key to ensuring progress is made:
  - responsibility and accountability should be at Ministerial level within the Cabinet
  - a framework of monitoring, reviewing, and remedying processes is needed to enable accountability
  - a national oversight mechanism, with responsibility for child health services, should be set up, and report to the Minister with the power to implement remedying action when problems are detected.
- Every aspect of children's health services and systems should be committed to providing for children. The defining culture should be 'I exist to serve' rather than 'I am a professional, and this is what I do'.

Health services
- To reduce the numbers of healthcare amenable deaths among children.
- To improve the quality and efficiency of first contact care for children:
  - first contact care for children should be improved by ensuring that all staff are appropriately trained and supervised.
- To support and strengthen child and adolescent mental health through services:
  - the DH's strategy for preventing mental illness and intervening early in childhood must be accompanied by sufficient and protected funding.
- Chronic care for children should be improved by developing chronic care health service models, appropriate for children's needs, and effectively managing transitions to adults' services.
- The planning, commissioning and evaluation of children's health services should be informed by child public health professionals.
- To improve the child-friendly qualities of health services, ensuring that the views of children, young people, and their parents form an integral part of health service planning and evaluation.

Prevention, policy, and public health
- Strengthen early years development and readiness for school and promote a culture of playing outside.
- Adapt the social and physical (built) environment to prevent child obesity.
- Policy and regulatory action should be taken to reduce alcohol and tobacco use.
- Improve and support the health knowledge and behaviours of school age children.

- Support parents and families through universal public health and targeted interventions:
  - parents and families, particularly in areas of high need, should be supported through targeted interventions, while preserving and strengthening the universal approach of child services
  - the universal services provided by health visitors working closely with GPs in strong primary care teams should be supported and strengthened.
- Strengthen public health interventions to prevent childhood accidents and injuries:
  - the built environment should be improved to support healthy lives for children and families and to reduce accidents and injuries.
- National and local policy on matters affecting the social and economic determinants of health should be devised and evaluated according to the ECM outcomes, and with reference to the needs and interests of children. Consideration of the five ECM categories of outcomes: health; safety; enjoyment and achievement; meaningful social contribution; and economic security and wellbeing remains the ideal way to ensure that the most important aspects of children's wellbeing are covered in policy.

Infrastructure and enablers
- We recommend that an annual report on the health of children, similar to the Chief Medical Officer's report on the State of the Public Health, should be published, with a view to monitoring health trends in children so that remedial action can be taken where needed and progress monitored.
- Comprehensive, reliable, regularly collected data on child health and health care needs are required to inform health services planning and evaluation. Work should build on current outcomes frameworks to strengthen the data resources available for health services. The Early Development Index could be included to ensure a comprehensive perspective.
- Evidence-based commissioning and evaluation, and strengthened child health services research to improve the 'fit' between health care needs and health services.
- Evaluation of policies that affect children's lives, health, and wellbeing is essential. Children's health services research and HPSR should be strengthened in order to continue to improve the care we deliver to children and families.
- Money for health and welfare of children – including for health (primary, secondary and community), education, social care – should be consolidated in one fund, to enable the joined-up planning and delivery of care that children need and deserve.

Key evidence
- Improve the skills and supervision of all staff providing first contact care for children.[13,14,79]
- Healthcare models that integrate services and bridge the gap between primary and secondary care are likely to be helpful in improving the quality and efficiency of first contact and planned care.[14,15]
- Integration within and between sectors, with professionals working closely together

to cooperate in the best interests of those they serve, is likely to be the best way forward for children; and successful integration requires supportive policy.[76,80-83]

- Children's health and health needs are distinct from those of adults. Planning, commissioning and evaluating child health services are specialist skills that rely on specialist skills and data.[84]
- Accountability can be strengthened through a framework of monitoring, reviewing, and remedying processes.[85]
- The Council of Europe has ratified a strategy to adopt 'child friendly healthcare' based on the UNCRC.[86]
- The Early Years Development Index measures physical health and motor development; social and emotional development; and language, communication and cognitive skills. It is a systematic means of tracking child development and has been evaluated in the USA as a means of measuring development trajectories, health and wellbeing determinants, assessing quality of services, and driving improvement.[87]
- The National Healthy Schools Programme is associated with strengthening health-promoting environments in schools, specifically leading to improved health knowledge, choices and behaviour, as well as achievement.[88]
- Children in Sure Start areas are less likely to be overweight, more likely to experience better physical health, and to have a better learning environment at home. Families in Sure Start areas use less harsh means of discipline and are more likely to have someone in the household become employed by the time the child reaches the age of five years.[89]
- There are effective interventions for preventing child behaviour problems which also have benefits in other aspects of family life.[90] Parenting skills can be improved and strengthened through education and training support[91] and an on-going randomized controlled study should provide further evidence.[92]
- Strengthen the universal services provided by health visitors working closely with GPs in strong primary care teams.[35,93]
- The built environment is an important determinant of health and wellbeing and can be designed to improve children's and families' lives.[94,95]
- Child obesity can be prevented through a combination of healthy eating and physical activity, through changing social norms and physical environments.[96]
- Accidents and injuries in childhood are highly amenable to prevention.[18]
- Minimum pricing per unit of alcohol is an effective means of reducing alcohol consumption.[97]
- Plain packaging of tobacco make cigarettes less appealing to young people. Plain packaging may help in preventing young people from taking up smoking.[98-100]
- Children's health research, health services research and policy analysis are important for improving the care we deliver and ultimately for improving children's health and wellbeing.[9]

2.13   Conclusions

Charles Dickens would have railed against the rising levels of child poverty and the increasing unfairness in life chances among the UK's children. Although the social determinants of child health are diverse and complex, and causal pathways are complicated, there is no shortage of information on their effects on the health and life chances of children. Nor is there a lack of information on how to improve the lives of children. What is missing is sustained economic investment and political will.

Last year marked the bicentenary of Dickens' birth. It is also 10 years since the death of John Rawls. His thinking gives an insight into our current predicament, and perhaps signals a way forward. Rawls was in many ways Dickens' successor, taking forward the same focus on social inequality and injustice.[99] 'Principles of justice' are 'the basic structure of society' he wrote. Every person (child) has the equal right to basic liberties that 'nullifies the accidents of natural endowment'. Rawls made inequality a contemporary political concern, and would doubtless have agreed with the principle 'fair equality of opportunity', which should be the philosophy of all those seeking to promote the welfare and wellbeing of children.

Chapter 3: Inequalities in child health

Dr Elizabeth Rough (PhD), Mr Peter Goldblatt (Marmot Review Team), Professor Sir Michael Marmot & Professor Vivienne Nathanson[a]

> *The foundations for virtually every aspect of human development – physical, intellectual and emotional – are laid in early childhood. What happens during these early years, starting in the womb, has lifelong effects on many aspects of health and wellbeing [...] To have an impact on health inequalities we need to address the social gradient in children's access to positive early experiences.*
> The Marmot Review, *Fair society, healthy lives*, 2010[1]

Overall, the health of children in the UK is improving. Between 1980 and 2009 the mortality rate for children aged one to 14 years fell by 61 per cent from 31 deaths per 100,000 population in 1980 to 12 deaths per 100,000 population in 2009.[2] This was accompanied by a steady decline in neonatal mortality rates (deaths under 28 days) and post-neonatal mortality rates (deaths between 28 days and one year) in England and Wales since 1980. Common infectious diseases of childhood are also coming under control through a combination of successful immunisation programmes, health promotion, disease prevention and treatment. While recent outbreaks of measles in the UK suggest that such improvements are fragile, the overall trends are encouraging.

National data can obscure variations between regions, social classes and ethnic groups. The difference in male life expectancy at birth between the most and least disadvantaged classes increased from 4.9 years in 1982/86 to 6.2 years in 1997/2001:[3] by 2008, males in the least deprived areas could be expected to have 14.6 more disability-free years than their counterparts in the most deprived areas.[4] While mortality and morbidity rates for some conditions like ischaemic heart diseases[5] are declining, such declines have been more rapid in people from higher socioeconomic groups. As a result, the socioeconomic gradient of mortality has become steeper.[6]

These brief examples are illustrative of a broader trend; health inequalities between groups in society appear to be widening. This is vividly captured by the rate of child poverty in the UK. A powerful indicator of the wellbeing of children, child poverty is

---

a   This chapter is based on Chapter 3, 'Inequalities in Child Health', of *Growing up in Britain* (1999), which was authored by A Quick and R Wilkinson.

usually measured as the percentage of children falling below 60 per cent of contemporary median income without deducting housing costs. A 1999 UNICEF report showed that by 1994/5 Britain had the third highest rate of child poverty out of 25 industrialised countries, at 21.3 per cent. Only Russia and the United States scored higher.[7] Following a Government commitment in 1997 to eliminate child poverty, the rate began to decline, only to rise again after 2004/05. While data from 2009/10 shows that child poverty fell by 2 per cent between 2008 and 2010 to 20 per cent, forecasts produced by the Institute of Fiscal Studies indicate that child poverty will remain broadly constant between 2009/10 and 2012/13, before rising slightly in 2013/14.[8] Differences between regions, ethnic groups, and family types are particularly striking. A Department for Work and Pensions (DWP) report found that black Caribbean and Indian children had rates of poverty of 26 and 27 per cent respectively, rising to 35 per cent for black African children, while over half of Pakistani (54%) and Bangladeshi (58%) children were in poverty according to 2006/7 statistics.[9]

Despite these disappointing figures, the UK has arguably led the world in research aimed at identifying and tackling health inequalities.[10] Since the publication of the landmark Black report[11] in 1980 – which found social gradients to be present for many different causes of morbidity and mortality – evidence for the effects of social and economic inequalities on health has grown. In 2010, the critically acclaimed Marmot Review categorically stated that 'social and economic differences in health status reflect, and are caused by, social and economic inequalities in society'.[1] Like the Black report, the Marmot Review team found that 'the relationship between social circumstances and health is […] a graded one'; put simply 'the higher one's social position, the better one's health is likely to be'.[1]

Underpinning the Review is a life-course perspective. This recognises that social and biological influences on development begin before conception, accumulate through pregnancy, and impact upon the child at birth. From then onwards, the child will experience a wide range of shifting social, economic, psychological and environmental factors as they progress through the different stages of life. It is the accumulation of, and interaction between, these influences that the Marmot Review identifies as casting '"a long shadow" over subsequent social development, behaviour, health and wellbeing of the individual'.[1]

3.1   Definitions of disadvantage

While it is now well established that social and economic deprivation is associated with poor health outcomes, difficulties remain with both measuring deprivation and categorising individuals accordingly. Social class is a widely used measure, though it is not necessarily an indicator of 'material' wealth nor is it the only determinant of life chances. In 2001, the National Statistics Socio-economic Classification (NS-SEC) replaced 'Social Class based on Occupation' (formerly Registrar General's Social Class), and 'Socioeconomic Groups', as the measure used for all official statistics and surveys. The NS-SEC is an occupationally-based classification: it differentiates positions within labour markets and production units in terms of their typical 'employment relations'.[1] The NS-SEC categories thus distinguish different positions (not persons) as defined by social relationships in the work place and uses these as the basis from which to allocate socioeconomic status. The eight NS-SEC classes are as follows:

1.1   large employers and higher managerial occupations
1.2   higher professional occupation
2   lower managerial and professional occupations
3   intermediate occupations
4   small employers and own account workers
5   lower supervisory and technical occupations
6   semi-routine occupations
7   routine occupations
8   never worked and long-term unemployed.

'Deprivation indices', such as the Carstairs deprivation index and the Index of Multiple Deprivation, are also employed to gauge disadvantage.[12] These types of measures calculate 'deprivation scores' for people living in a predefined geographical area using either a weighted or unweighted combination of indicators. Carstairs scores, for example, are based on the unweighted combination of four variables (unemployment, overcrowding, car ownership, and low socioeconomic class) taken from the 2001 Census.

For children it is not only material wealth that matters; their wellbeing is directly related to their emotional environment and the social circumstances into which they are born and continue to grow, live, work, and age.[13] A child may come from a materially privileged family, yet problems will arise if they are unwanted or resented, neglected or abused. Wellbeing, in other words, cannot be assessed by focusing on a single factor or variable; it is multidimensional. This is recognised in the 'ecological perspective' on child development which aims to locate a child's wellbeing in the context of the family, friendship networks, school, and the neighbourhood, rather than solely in the context of material wealth.[14] It is also important to remember that such factors may interact to produce complex, and sometimes unexpected, outcomes:[13] socioeconomic factors such as poverty, unemployment or homelessness may exert their effects on the child by the overall reduction in parental capacity to meet their own, and their children's, emotional needs. With regard to children, social disadvantage can be usefully understood, in part, in terms of the quality of child care. Good child care involves a mutually affectionate relationship based on respect and empathy with one or, preferably, more adults; consistent discipline based on positive reward for good behaviour rather than punishment for bad; and intellectual stimulation appropriate to the child's level of development.

3.2   Socioeconomic inequalities and health

- A boy born in Kensington and Chelsea has a life expectancy of over 84 years; for a boy born in Islington, less than five miles away, it is around 75 years.[15]
- Children with a high cognitive score at 22 months but with parents of low socioeconomic status do less well (in terms of subsequent cognitive development) than children with low initial scores but with parents of high socioeconomic status.[1]
- The 2003 Children's Dental Survey found that, among five year olds, 13 per cent from social classes IV and V had never visited the dentist compared with 2 per cent from social classes I, II and III.[16]
- Childhood mortality from injury and poisoning fell between the early 1980s and early 1990s for all social classes; the differential between the classes increased, owing to the smaller decline occurring in social classes IV and V as compared to social classes I and II.[17]
- Low birth weight is the strongest risk factor for infant mortality. In 1994 in England and Wales, the average birthweight in Social Class V was 115 grams lighter than in Social Class I for births inside marriage and 130 grams lighter for births outside marriage registered by both parents.[17]

3.3   Social classes

Infant mortality is a key measure of the health of the nation.[18] Since 1980, the post-neonatal mortality rate in England and Wales has fallen by 68 per cent, from 4.4 deaths per 1,000 live births in 1980 to 1.4 deaths per 1,000 live births in 2009. A similar decline has been observed in the neonatal mortality rate which, between 1980 and 2009, fell by 60 per cent from 7.7 deaths per 1,000 live births to 3.1 deaths per 1,000 live births.[2] Despite these improvements at the aggregate level, a class gradient persists. Drawing on the NS-SEC classification, data from 2005/6 shows that the infant mortality rate stood at 3.0 deaths per 1,000 births when parents were from the 'higher and professional' group. This compares with a rate of 4.8 deaths per 1,000 births for the 'routine occupations'.[19] The difference between socioeconomic groups is even more pronounced when deprivation scores are examined. Babies born to the 'least deprived' parents, as calculated using the Carstairs index, had an infant mortality rate of 2.9 deaths per 1,000 births in 2005/6. Using the same index and years, babies born to the 'most deprived' parents had an infant mortality rate of 5.9 deaths per 1,000 births.[19] A gender difference can also be discerned, with boys remaining at a consistently higher risk than girls: in 2008, the UK infant mortality rates were 5.1 per 1,000 live births for boys compared with 4.1 per 1,000 live births for girls.[20]

While there are a range of established risk factors associated with infant mortality, low birth weight (under 2,500g) and prematurity are the most significant in terms of strength of association and consistency.[19] Both factors are highly associated with socioeconomic status and deprivation: recent research has shown that young mothers (aged under 20 years), who were born outside the UK and were solely responsible for registering the birth of the child had an elevated risk of giving birth prematurely to a low birth weight child.[18,19] Together, these three risks led to a higher infant mortality rate when compared to babies born to other groups.[18] Analysis of data from the Millennium Cohort Study (MCS)[b] on birth weight produced broadly similar findings: the risk of low birth weight was found – after controlling for other factors – to be higher for mothers in poverty, underweight mothers, mothers who smoked during pregnancy, and mothers from minority ethnic groups.[21] The last point is borne out in the 2009 gestation-specific infant mortality statistics for England and Wales. These show that 'small for gestational age' (SGA)[c] babies were most prevalent in Indian (18.3%), Bangladeshi (17.9%) and Pakistani (15.6%) ethnic groups.[22] The Marmot review is not alone in suggesting that, based on the figures outlined in this section, one-quarter of all deaths under the age of one year would potentially be avoided if all births had the same level of risk as for women with the lowest level of deprivation.[1]

The role of unequal societies in the health of children is also revealed by comparing the relative poverty in different countries with infant mortality rates. Using the UNICEF index of child wellbeing, Pickett and Wilkinson examined associations between child wellbeing and material living standards (as measured by average income); the scale of differentiation in social status (income inequality); and social exclusion (children in relative poverty) in 23 high-income countries. They found that the overall index of child wellbeing was closely and negatively correlated with income inequality ($r=0.64$, $p=0.001$) and children in relative poverty ($r=0.67$, $p=0.001$) but not with average income.[23] Table 3.1 taken from Pickett and Wilkinson's paper, lists two of the six components of the UNICEF index of child wellbeing (material wellbeing; health and safety) and 10 of the 39 individual measures.

---

b A longitudinal survey of 18,296 singleton children born in the UK between September 2000 and January 2002.
c SGA: birthweight below tenth percentile for each gestational age.

Table 3.1: Correlations of two of the six components of the UNICEF index of child wellbeing with income inequality, child relative poverty and average income

	Income inequality		Child relative poverty		Average income	
	r	P value	*r*	P value	*r*	P value
Overall UNICEF index	-0.64	0.001	-0.67	0.001	0.15	0.50
Material wellbeing						
Overall	-0.36	0.10	-0.37	0.10	0.40	0.06
Deprivation:						
Low affluence	-0.41	0.08	-0.40	0.11	0.80	<0.001
Few educational possessions	0.00	0.99	-0.26	0.25	0.29	0.19
Few books	-0.37	0.08	-0.34	0.14	-0.08	0.72
Work:						
No employed parent	-0.23	0.29	0.03	0.88	0.04	0.87
Health and safety						
Overall	-0.53	<0.01	-0.71	<0.001	0.16	0.45
Health at birth:						
Infant mortality	-0.76	<0.001	-0.66	<0.001	-0.13	0.55
Low birth weight	-0.42	0.048	-0.62	0.003	0.25	0.26
Immunisations:						
Measles	-0.11	0.60	-0.06	0.80	-0.26	0.22
Diptheria	-0.04	0.86	-0.32	0.16	-0.13	0.56
Polio	-0.05	0.82	-0.49	0.02	-0.06	0.79
Child mortality:						
Accident/injury mortality	-0.27	0.21	-0.40	0.08	0.38	0.08

Source: Pickett K & Wilkinson RG (2007) Child wellbeing and income inequality in rich societies: ecological cross sectional study. *British Medical Journal* 335: 1080. Reproduced with the permission of the British Medical Journal.

Another indicator of child health inequality is accident rates. The Black Report identified accidents as one of the most important causes of death among children aged between one and 14 years, and also one of the causes of childhood mortality with the steepest socioeconomic gradient.[11] Figures from 2001 to 2003 show that the risk of accidental death for all children aged between 28 days and 15 years was 4.5 times higher in the routine class (NS-SEC class seven), and 5.3 times higher in the non-occupied class (never worked, long-term unemployed, full-time students or unclassified) than for a child with at least one parent in a higher managerial or professional occupation.[24] Deaths associated with accidents are declining: in 2008, 'external causes of morbidity and mortality' (which includes accidental injuries and poisonings) were responsible for 11.40 per cent of childhood deaths, falling to 9.55 per cent in 2009. The most common cause of death for children aged between one and 14 years in England and Wales has, since 2008, been 'congenital malformations, deformations and chromosomal abnormalities'.[20]

The factors operating to cause such wide differences in morbidity and mortality between socioeconomic groups obviously need to be identified if action is to be taken to improve the current situation. An explanation for the relationship is still far from clear, though a number of theories have developed. The favoured explanation in recent years has emphasised that risk 'factors [...] combine and accumulate over the life course' and vary by social position.[25] The life-course perspective, and the idea that disadvantage accumulates throughout life, is central to the influential Marmot Review: the review stresses that the close links between early disadvantage and poor outcomes over time can only be broken by taking action to reduce health inequalities before birth, and continuing these throughout the life of the child.[1]

3.4 Housing
There is clear evidence of the importance of a 'healthy' environment in the early years, in order to protect current health and prevent future ill health. In 2003, the BMA reported that poor quality housing – as indicated by the presence of damp or mould, disrepair, overcrowding and the lack of central heating and/or adequate cooking, preparation and storage facilities – is strongly associated with low income levels.[26] Poor quality housing, together with homelessness and living in temporary accommodation, all pose particular risks to health, especially the health of children. Research conducted by the housing charity Shelter in 2006 estimated that, in England alone, over one million children live in bad housing.[27] As well as being associated with debilitating, and even fatal, accidents, children living in overcrowded, inadequate housing are also more likely to contract meningitis, experience respiratory difficulties, and have mental health problems, such as anxiety and depression.[27] Physical and mental health conditions related to poor housing can also have associated impacts on a child's education: the Shelter report found that children in unfit and overcrowded homes miss school more frequently due to illnesses and infections and may experience delayed cognitive development.[27]

Reducing the impact of poor housing on health inequalities was a component of the DH's 2003 report, *Tackling health inequalities*.[28] By 2007, the DH reported that, '[B]etween 1996 and 2006, the proportions of vulnerable private sector households and of social sector tenants living in non-decent housing decreased, with a narrowing of inequalities between these groups and non-vulnerable private sector households in both absolute and relative terms'.[29] Differences between ethnic groups persist: statistics from 2005 show that 31 per cent of non-white minority ethnic households lived in non-decent homes, compared with 26 per cent of white households.[29]

Living in a cold home poses additional risks to health. In 2008, 18 per cent of households in the UK were estimated to be living in fuel poverty, defined as having to spend 10 per cent or more of a household's net income in order to heat their home to an adequate standard of warmth.[30] Living in fuel poverty is a function of three factors: the size and energy efficiency of the house, which will determine how expensive it is to heat; the type and cost of heating fuel required; and the household income, which determines how much a 10 per cent spend on heating would amount to.[30] Using data from the Families and Children Study (FACS), a large-scale, UK Government-sponsored survey of families with dependent children, Barnes, Butt and Tomaszewski found that children growing up with a black mother, in a lone parent family, or with family debts, were between two to three times more likely to experience inadequate heating on a persistent basis than other children.[31] Earlier research has shown that children living in damp, mouldy homes (factors that are more likely to occur in cold, poorly insulated buildings) are between one and a half to three times more prone to coughing and wheezing than children in dry homes.[32] In a 2011 report, commissioned by Friends of the Earth, the Marmot Review team also found that the negative, physical effects of cold housing on children were evident in terms of: 'infants' weight gain, hospital admission rates, and developmental status'.[30]

Not all those who are income poor are fuel poor, yet the risk of fuel poverty rises sharply as average income falls.[30] One factor that cannot be overlooked in providing a 'healthy' environment is an adequate income. Although poverty is not the only factor that may lead to adverse outcomes for individuals, it is a factor that exacerbates, and contributes to, many other risk factors.

3.5 Definitions of poverty

Poverty can be measured in a number of different ways. The *Child Poverty Act 2010*[33] established a set of four indicators.

1. Relative low income – proportion of children living in households where income is less than 60 per cent of median household income for the financial year before housing costs.
2. Absolute low income – proportion of children living in households where income is less than 60 per cent of median household income in 1998/99, adjusted for prices but before housing costs.
3. Persistent poverty – proportion of children living below 60 per cent of median equivalised net household income in three out of the last four years before housing costs.
4. Low income and material deprivation – equivalised net income for the financial year is less than 70 per cent of median equivalised net household income, before housing costs, for the financial year.

The Coalition Government's *New approach to tackling child poverty*, published in 2011, lists a further 11 indicators of child poverty, including the proportion of children living in workless households, low birth weight, school readiness, teenage pregnancy, school attainment and young offending.[15] While the statistical sources for these indicators vary, those that focus on income rely on the Family Resources Survey (FRS). This is a continuous survey of the incomes and circumstances of private households conducted by the Office for National Statistics and the National Centre for Social Research. The annual target sample size is 24,000 private households.

The Households Below Average Income (HBAI) is a series based on the FRS data and is used to discern the number of children living in impoverished households. In 2009/10, 20 per cent of children (2.6 million) were in households in the UK with incomes below 60 per cent of contemporary median net disposable household income before housing costs, and 29 per cent (3.8 million) after housing costs.[34] Compared to 2008/09, this represents a fall of two percentage points (0.2 million) on a before housing costs basis and a fall of one percentage point (0.1 million) on an after housing costs basis.

International, OECD data shows that, in the early 2000s, child poverty rates fell fastest in those countries with historically high levels of poverty, such as Mexico, the United States and the UK.[35] The reduction in the UK was largely attributable to the 'cash-transfer-focused' policies, including tax credit payments, rolled out during this period.[35] The same OCED report highlights that higher average family incomes are not necessarily associated with greater family income inequality: while the UK has shown above-average growth in family income, it has simultaneously achieved a sharp reduction in the level of child poverty.[35] By 2009, the UK's progress had slowed considerably. Figures from a

DWP report show that the UK had higher than the OECD inequality average for material wellbeing, placing the UK in a group of countries in the bottom two-fifths for overall inequality.[15] The same report also found that, in contrast to European counterparts, the UK has a higher proportion of children living in workless households than almost any other EU country.[15]

All of the indicators outlined above have drawbacks. Absolute measures assume that standards of living, and notions of what is essential or necessary, remain static and do not adapt over time. Relative measures have been criticised on the grounds that 60 per cent of median equivalent income is an arbitrary measure that is not rooted in an understanding of the income people need to live. Recognising these problems, and the fact that there is not a socially agreed minimum income standard (MIS), Bradshaw and colleagues sought to answer the question: 'What level of income is needed to allow a minimum acceptable standard of living?' Their work relies on another type of indicator – 'budget standards'.[36]

Budget standards identify the income needed to afford an adequate, acceptable standard of living. They often are costed on the basis of a 'basket of goods and services' – things deemed as essential to living. Since everybody's needs are different, Bradshaw and colleagues are careful to specify that a national MIS does not create an acceptable standard of living for every individual. What this work suggests is a minimum below which it is socially unacceptable for any individual to live. For a couple with two children the MIS per week, excluding child care and rent, is £370.05. This is £240 less than actual average expenditure, £83 higher than similar families on income support, and £33 higher than similar families in social housing. For a lone parent plus toddler, the comparable MIS is £210.31; £5 less than actual average expenditure, £49 higher than a lone parent on income support, and £27 more than lone parents in social housing spend.[36]

3.6   Income and health

Missing from the work on the MIS is an explicit acknowledgement of the connections between income and health: Bradshaw and colleagues consider what is needed for individuals to have 'sufficient resources to participate in society and to maintain human dignity' and to consume 'those goods and services regarded as essential in Britain'.[36] The Marmot Review recognises that the relationship between income and health can operate in multiple ways: 'low income can lead to poor health and ill health can result in a lower earning capacity'.[1] While the mechanisms that link societal income distribution to health still require further elucidation, a number of pathways have been proposed. Kawachi has drawn attention to the 'psychologically mediated effects of relative deprivation'. He argues that the (perceived) widening of deprivation – the gap between wealthy and poor – can lead to frustration among those for whom conditions are not improving, with potential adverse consequences for health.[37] Wilkinson has focused on the ways in which income inequality may affect health through disrupting the social fabric of society. Social cohesion and tight-knit social relationships have been shown to break down as inequality grows.

This can exert a negative impact on public health.[38] The Marmot Review notes that people on low incomes refrain from purchasing goods and services that can improve or maintain health, perhaps because they cannot afford, or do not see the benefit of, them. They may also feel that they have no alternative but to buy cheaper goods and services that can increase health risks.[1]

Researchers from the London School of Hygiene and Tropical Medicine have worked to fill the gap in the minimum income requirements literature and have proposed the concept of 'minimum income for healthy living' (MIHL).[39] The concept is based on assembling the current best evidence in health needs while estimating the minimal costs entailed in meeting them for defined population groups. Components of the MIHL include physical activity, housing, psychosocial relations/social inclusion, personal transport, medical care and hygiene.[39] One of the Marmot Review's key recommendations is 'to develop and implement standards for minimum income for healthy living'.[1] This should reduce the numbers in persistent and reoccurring (child) poverty while reducing 'adverse health outcomes attributable to living on low incomes'.[1]

3.7   Poverty and family composition

Certain groups are over-represented among families experiencing income poverty. Data from the HBAI series from 2009/10 indicate that 31 per cent of children in lone-parent families live in 'low-income and materially deprived households' compared to 11 per cent of children in families with two adults.[34] Overall, the percentage of lone-parent families with children in poverty is declining: of those children living in absolute low-income households (before housing costs), 26 per cent were in lone-parent families in 2009/10 compared with 43 per cent in 1999/2000.[34] Over the same period, of those children living in absolute low-income households (before housing costs), the percentage where two adults are both not in work has risen from 17 per cent in 1999/2000 to 23 per cent in 2009/10.[34] Children from black and minority ethnic families are almost twice as likely to experience material deprivation as children from white families: in 2009/10, 29 per cent of children living in households with an income below 70 per cent of the contemporary median income (before housing costs) were black or black British; 28 per cent were Asian or Asian British; and 15 per cent were white.[34] Twenty-seven per cent of children falling into the low-income and material deprivation category in 2009/10 had at least one adult family member who was disabled.[34]

Particular groups are also over-represented among families experiencing persistent poverty – living below 60 per cent of median equivalised net household income in three out of the last four years before housing costs. Statistics from the DWP from the 'low income dynamics' dataset shows that, between 2005 and 2008, 38 per cent of children in workless households, and 23 per cent of children in lone parent families, experienced persistent poverty, compared with 12 per cent of all children.[40] Risks are particularly apparent for the children of teenage mothers, as well as for the mothers themselves. Using data from the MCS, Mayhew and Bradshaw reported in 2005 that teenage mothers were over three times more likely to live in poverty than mothers in their thirties.[21,41] Mothers living in poverty are more likely to give birth to low birth weight babies; a factor which is associated with poorer long-term health and educational outcomes.[1] The 2010 Teenage Pregnancy Strategy acknowledges that the infant mortality rate for babies born to teenage mothers is 60 per cent higher than for babies born to older mothers.[42]

The health of the mother is also adversely affected: teenage mothers have three times the rate of postnatal depression of older mothers; are at a higher risk of poor mental health for three years after the birth; and are less likely to finish their schooling, with the consequent risks of unemployment.[42]

There is additional evidence that income has a direct impact on parenting and on children's health and wellbeing. Yeung and colleagues posit that a low family income may be detrimental to children's development because of its association with parents' non-monetary capacities, including their emotional wellbeing and interactions with their children.[43] Hardships are hypothesised to increase maternal emotional distress which, in turn, is associated with an increase in harsh parenting practices. Research conducted in 2007 concluded that '[H]olding constant other types of parental capital, income is strongly associated with the types of maternal psychological functioning that promote self-esteem, positive behaviour and better physical health in children.'[44]

Between 2003 and 2011, the average cost of raising a child from birth to 21 years increased by 55 per cent from £140,389 to £218,024.[45] The most expensive ages for raising a child are between five and 10 years, when children are regularly growing out of clothes and shoes.[40] Costs also vary regionally: in 2011 the cost of raising a child in the north east was £202,383, compared with £239,535 in outer London.[45] These burdens are inequitably borne by mothers. Dixon and Margo have shown that women who have children at younger ages and are low skilled seriously reduce their lifetime earnings: the 'fertility penalty' – the difference between the average lifetime earnings for a childless, low-skilled women compared with a low-skilled woman with two children – is £334,000.[46] The comparable figure for a high-skilled woman is £19,000. As Dixon and Margo acknowledge, this difference not only reduces a women's social mobility, it also makes child poverty considerably harder to reduce since child poverty is the result of living in households with low income.[46]

It is clear that large numbers of children are living in households on less than adequate incomes and that it is families, and particularly lone parents, who are most at risk of falling into poverty. There is a real need to focus attention on mechanisms by which to reduce the financial and other risks for those with children.

3.8   Reducing inequalities in health

This chapter considers the substantial evidence that a number of factors influence health in the early years of life and that these factors may also affect health in later life. There is currently less evidence available on effective interventions that may be utilised to prevent ill health and to reduce inequity. It is on this area that future policy must now concentrate.

The evidence that is available can be used to predict what is likely to succeed where there is no direct evidence of efficacy. A comprehensive approach to this problem is likely to be required and interventions are needed in areas other than health services. The point made throughout the Marmot Review, and reiterated in this chapter, is that laying good foundations during a child's early years is crucial to reducing health inequalities across the life course.[1] Intervention studies in the early years suggest that performance in two basic domains of child development, the cognitive (education) and the social-emotional (parenting) can be modified in ways that should improve long-term outcomes.[47] The interventions identified for particular problems, in many cases, have beneficial effects for a range of problems, and can therefore be said to be of benefit more generally for the health and wellbeing of many young children. Responsibility for the interventions identified frequently cut across the remit of many organisations and Government departments. It is clear that any successful intervention will need a multi-sectoral approach.

There are many interventions that could protect against inequalities both generally and in health. Some interventions have been more robustly evaluated than others: not all projects and services will have the time, money and expertise to evaluate the impact of their work on children's health in sophisticated ways. This chapter does not exclude projects that do not include rigorous evaluations of effectiveness of the sort described above. Many projects may not collect specific outcome data relating to children's health but on theoretical grounds are highly likely to have a beneficial impact on family wellbeing. Projects of this sort are considered and, where evidence of effectiveness has been demonstrated more substantially, this is highlighted.

In terms of factors that could protect against inequalities, the Carnegie Task Force on meeting the needs of young children concluded that the following could be considered 'protective' in early years:

- temperament and perinatal factors (such as full-term birth and normal birth weight): having characteristics that attract and encourage care giving;
- dependable caregivers: growing up in a family with one or two dependable adults whose child-rearing practices are positive and appropriate;
- community support: living in a loving, supportive and safe community can limit the risk to health.[48]

It appears that educational interventions and family support offer the best means yet identified of protecting children from inequalities and therefore for protecting their health. Support can take several different guises, it can be interpersonal or emotional, practical (child care or safe environments) or financial. There is now a considerable body of experimental knowledge which suggests that the effectiveness of interpersonal 'support' depends on the supporters' capacity to enable parents to feel less isolated, less criticised and less vulnerable. Whether the support is effective depends upon the interpersonal skill of the person doing the support; on working in a way that is accepting, encouraging, valuing and empowering.

3.9   Educational interventions

From the late 1990s onwards, the UK saw a significant expansion in the provision of early years education and care. This was based, in large measure, on a clear appreciation that the development of early cognitive ability is associated with later educational success, income and better health but that it is those children from the most disadvantaged backgrounds who are more likely to begin school with lower cognitive, emotional, and social capabilities.[49,50]

The most well-known and researched early years programme to emerge in the UK is Sure Start. At its inception in 1999, Sure Start was an early intervention initiative aimed at developing and enhancing the services provided for households in relatively small, deprived areas in order to improve the health and wellbeing of young children.[51] Recognising that the delivery of health services for children was often fragmented, with responsibility spread across the NHS, social services, schools and the voluntary sector, Sure Start was purposefully designed to bring different support agencies together in one place, to meet children's needs. By 2011, there were more than 3600 Sure Start Children's Centres across England. The centres are aimed at pregnant women and continue supporting women and their children until they reach primary school age. While each centre is autonomous, and designed with the needs of the local community in mind, all centres are expected to provide certain core services. These include: advice on child and family health services; family and parenting support; high quality childcare and early learning; access to specialist services such as speech and language therapy and budgeting advice; and help for parents and carers to access work and training opportunities.[52]

Evaluations of the effectiveness of Sure Start have produced varying results. In 2008, Melhuish and colleagues compared the wellbeing of 5,883 three-year-old children and their families living in Sure Start areas with 1,879 children from non-Sure Start areas; the second group of children was identified from the MCS. Children and families from the Sure Start area showed five beneficial effects associated with living in that area and no adverse effects.[53] These included better social development, with children displaying more positive behaviour and greater independence than those in non-Sure Start areas. The risk of negative parenting was also lower in Sure Start areas while provision of a more stimulating home environment was higher. Families living in Sure Start areas also used more services designed to support child wellbeing than those from non-Sure Start areas.[53]

An earlier study had shown that the effects of living in a Sure Start area 'varied with the degree of social deprivation'.[51] While children from relatively less socially deprived families benefited from living in a Sure Start area, those from relatively more socially deprived families – particularly those headed by teenage mothers, lone parents, or workless households – were adversely affected. The National Evaluation of Sure Start reports that the children of teenaged mothers (14% of the sample) scored lower on verbal ability and social competence and higher on behavioural problems than their counterparts in non-Sure Start areas.[54] Children from workless households (40% of the sample) and children from lone-parent families (33% of the sample) growing up in Sure Start areas scored significantly lower on verbal ability when compared to children from non-Sure Start areas.[54] The findings suggest that early intervention has produced greater benefits for the moderately disadvantaged than for the severely disadvantaged. It should be noted that overall more children and families were affected beneficially than adversely.[54]

When interpreting these results it is also necessary to keep in mind that Sure Start programmes have been in operation for less than a decade in the majority of areas, inhibiting longitudinal evaluative research. The High/Scope Perry pre-school programme began in the Ypsilanti, Michigan, school district, in 1962.[55] The programme identified 123 low income African-Americans, aged three and four years, who were assessed to be at a high risk of school failure. The group was then split; 58 received a high-quality pre-school programme while the remaining 65 did not receive a pre-school programme. Data on both groups was collected annually from ages three to 11 years and again at ages 14, 15, 19, 27 and 40 years. The study found that, at age 40, those who had been through the pre-school programme were more likely to have graduated from high school than the control group (77% compared to 60%).[55] A marked sex difference was also discernible: while 46 per cent of women from the control group finished high school, the figure stood at 86 per cent among females who had attended pre-school.[55] Pre-school graduates, at age 27, were over twice as likely to own their own home, four times more likely to earn a good income and five times less likely to have been in repeated trouble with the law.[56] See **Chapter 7** for a further discussion on Sure Start.

A good general education that provides a programme of personal, social and health education – or 'life preparation' – appears to help young women to avoid early pregnancy. Since the launch of the Government's Teenage Pregnancy Strategy in 1999 the under-18 conception rate has fallen from 46.6 per 1,000 live births in 1998 to 40.5 per 1000 live births in 2008 – a reduction of 13.3 per cent over 10 years.[42] International evidence has shown that sex and relationship education (SRE), together with accessible, young people-centred contraceptive and sexual health (CASH), have the strongest impact on reducing teenage pregnancy rates, both through delaying sexual activity and through increasing the use of contraception.[42] The Government's 2010 Teenage Pregnancy Strategy has placed both SRE and CASH at its core, while at the same time attempting to tackle those factors that increase the risk of teenage pregnancy including poverty, poor educational attainment, and low aspirations.[42]

3.10   Family support

In terms of psychological health, prenatal and infant development programmes have been assessed, with most programmes consisting of home visiting at-risk families.

There is now strong evidence that intervention during a child's early years, particularly through the provision of skilled home visitors, can provide the type of support necessary to improve the health of the child, as well as their cognitive development.[57] In the UK, the HCP is the universal, early-intervention and prevention, public health programme. It offers all families screening tests, immunisations, developmental reviews and information and guidance to support parenting and healthy choices. Recognising that poor health outcomes are experienced by children in the most at-risk families, the HCP has recently increased its focus on vulnerable children and families, to ensure that this group receives a personalised service.[58]

More targeted, specialised support is offered through the Family Nurse Partnership (FNP) Programme in England. This is a preventive programme designed for vulnerable, young, first-time mothers. Through offering intensive and structured home visiting, delivered by specially trained nurses, from early pregnancy until the age of two years, the programme helps young parents to build supportive relationships, adopt healthier lifestyles for themselves and their babies, and provide good quality care. By 2015, the Government aims to more than double the capacity of the programme from 6,000 clients at present to 13,000 clients.[59] Early evaluations of the programme have produced promising results: the most recent, published in 2011, reported that graduates of the FNP were positive about their parenting capacity and their ability to provide a high level of warmth and a low level of harsh discipline.[60] Such factors make a difference. Analysing data from the MCS, Lexmond and Reeves found that parents who are able to combine warmth with consistent control and discipline were more likely to have children who, by the age of five years, had a good attention span, showed concern for other people's feelings, and were confident.[61]

Other reported short-term benefits of the FNP include increased use of contraception, with 84 per cent reporting using birth control six months after giving birth. Of the 850 clients with data, 105 (12%) had given birth to a second child; this is lower than found in the Memphis trial of FNP where the comparable figure was 22 per cent.[60] The number of clients involved in education was also encouraging: more than one-quarter were enrolled in education or training after their child's birth, half of whom had not been in education at the start of the programme.[60] More anecdotal evidence also suggests that children's behaviour, communication and language skills were all improving. It is anticipated that firmer evidence will be provided by the forthcoming randomised control trial of the FNP, which will provide the proper basis from which to judge the outcomes of the programme.[60]

Programmes designed to reduce the incidence of child abuse and neglect have also shown some success. A growing body of evidence indicates that interventions aimed at improving parental disciplinary practices and sensitivity can measurably lower abusive behaviour and improve family wellbeing.[62] The Incredible Years programme teaches parents to replace physical discipline and punishment with more positive, effective methods for managing unwanted behaviour. Versions of the programme have been rolled out in a number of OECD countries. An evaluation of its effects on families in Eastern Canada found that mothers who maltreated their children learned how to be more constructively involved with, and care about, their children.[63]

The Nursing Family Partnership (NFP) – as practised in the United States – has been repeatedly shown to be one of the most effective programmes in reducing child abuse. A randomised controlled trial in Elmira, New York (n=400) reported a 56 per cent fall in emergency department visits for accidents and poisonings during the second postpartum year among families who were provided with a nurse-home visitor throughout pregnancy and until the child was two years of age when compared with the control group.[64] A subgroup of nurse-visited women, including single, low-income, teenage mothers who were identified to be at the highest risk, had 80 per cent fewer incidents of verified child abuse and neglect, although this was not shown to be statistically significant (p=0.07).[64]

The Incredible Years programme also meets the National Institute for Health and Clinical Excellence (NICE) guidelines for parenting programmes for the effective treatment of conduct disorders in non-abusive families. The National Academy for Parent Practitioners notes that less than 10 per cent of over 150 known approaches currently used in England have good evidence of effectiveness.[65] Such programmes also vary greatly in terms of the content and quality of their materials, the sophistication of training available for practitioners, and the delivery of the programme.[65] This is particularly important given that the quality and consistency of delivery has been identified as crucial to the effectiveness of parenting support programmes.[1]

Despite some promising results, evidence of what works in reducing child maltreatment and improving parenting practices remains limited, particularly when compared with other paediatric public health programmes.[62] It is clear that there is a need for long-term personal contact with at risk families. Current spending on early intervention is low: national estimates have put prevention spending at 4 per cent of total health spending.[66] The OECD reports that for every £100 spent on early childhood (0 to five years) in the UK, £135 is spent on middle childhood (6 to 11 years) and £148 is spent on late childhood (12 to 17 years).[67] Intervention does not always have to be costly. A BMA report, published in 2011, highlighted evidence that improving health and wellbeing during a child's early years can be inexpensive: when children are cuddled, talked to regularly and read to daily, they thrive emotionally and improve their intelligence quotient (IQ) score.[13] The challenge for the state is how to encourage these types of changes. The overriding message in a 2011 independent report to Government on early intervention is that effective programmes have positive socioeconomic returns.[68] The total cost of inaction – of failing to invest in early years intervention programmes – could mean that the UK economy misses out on returns of an estimated £486 billion over 20 years.[69] As the Committee on Economic Development explained over 25 years ago, 'improving the prospects for disadvantaged children is not an expense but an excellent investment, one that can be postponed only at much greater cost to society'.[70]

3.11   Recommendations

- Research into methods to reduce the impact of social inequalities in child health and wellbeing should continue. Where examples are found of initiatives that can make a difference, these should be rapidly rolled out. Examples such as Sure Start should be considered and the elements that made some programmes effective copied into all programmes and made universally available, with particular efforts made to ensure that all populations are reached, including the traditionally hard to reach. This will require a commitment to invest in the development and maintenance of Sure Start and other programmes.
- Pilot programmes of interventions should be implemented, assessed and rolled out if effective. Interventions, for example, to ensure a higher percentage of children are ready for school at school starting age, should be undertaken. Where positive results are seen, the activity or intervention should be widely promulgated and implemented in areas with the same problem. All research-implementation cycles should be subjected to surveillance to measure efficacy.
- Investment in improving the quality of social and other housing is essential to improving health and wellbeing of children and adults. Addressing the causes of fuel

poverty is a key component. Local Government must make health and wellbeing a priority within its housing policy, and report annually on progress to achieving a housing stock that is conducive to the health of housing occupants.
- Health and local authorities should contribute to the work area, and press government for action once an agreed figure is available.
- Community and family support schemes require ongoing investment to reduce adverse impacts on child health and wellbeing. Local and national governments must be helped to understand that interventions may take time to have an effect, and that consistent and reliable funding must underpin evidence-based interventions.
- The high levels of all types of poverty experienced in the UK, including by children, are unacceptable. Society in the UK should expect its Governments to take more effective action to reduce the social, and therefore the health inequalities, currently experienced. Work on the MIHL should inform Government's policy on benefit reform. Health professionals should lobby actively on ensuring a healthy living basis to minimum income protection.
- Partnerships between community, family and educational support schemes should be encouraged.

Chapter 4: Nutrition

Dr Anthony Williams & Ms Grace Foyle

Children need nutritious food for proper growth and development.
The Food Commission, 2000[1]

Appreciation of the links between early life, nutritional status and health in later life has grown considerably since *Growing up in Britain* was published in 1999. The scientific evidence linking early diet to lifelong physical and mental health has strengthened considerably.[2] The implications of these findings, for the current and future economic welfare of societies, are clear, and thus government policies that bear upon the nutrition of parents and their young children have increasing importance.

Growing up in Britain envisaged a range of interventions at the individual, community and macro-economic levels. Although many of the suggestions made have since been incorporated in policy, implementation has often been incomplete and therefore ineffective. It is timely to review the current nutritional health of young children, the impact of policy change and the gaps that still need to be addressed.

4.1   The nutritional needs of children aged 0 to five years

The years between 0 and five are demanding for the developing child – years in which they acquire many physical, social and psychological structures for life and learning. Unfortunately, many 0 to five year olds are not being aided in these tasks by healthy and balanced nutrition: the problem is most acute for those children who are born into and live their early years in poverty.

There is no doubt about the health benefits of breastfeeding during early infancy. All current guidelines, including those from the DH, recommend exclusive breastfeeding for the first six months after birth. The diet of the early years of life needs to be relatively more 'nutrient dense' than the middle years. This is because the physical requirements for nutrients must be met within a relatively small number of calories and generally small quantities of food.

Complementary feeding (colloquially known as 'weaning') begins when semi-solid food starts to be given in addition to milk. The DH advises that at about six months, babies are ready to be moved onto a mixed diet. The 'weaning' period is not only important because of the need to introduce nutritional variety and replenish iron stores; it is also a critical period within which to introduce and accustom infants to the experience and taste of different foods. There may be an important imprinting function, making this the ideal time to introduce particular foods such as vegetables and fruits. There is evidence that the pace at which foods are introduced in the second six months of infancy may affect food preference behaviour throughout life.[3] Inappropriate weaning practices are common[4] and need to be addressed by education and the input of health professionals. Families with lower educational attainment and of lower social class particularly need such support.

4.2   Fetal nutrition

A balanced diet during pregnancy helps to protect the mother's health and to control her level of weight gain. Current UK recommendations for diet before and during pregnancy are given in **Appendix 3**. The embryo and fetus receive all their nutrients directly from the mother. It is important that she achieves nutritional status adequate to support her pregnancy prior to conception and maintains this throughout. Unbalanced nutrition will also cause metabolic and hormonal changes in the mother. In animal models this can affect the allocation of stem cells, embryonic and placental lineages, and have long-term effects on offspring growth and health. In humans, maternal diet and body composition affect the growth of the early embryo, making a focus on diet before pregnancy as important as that during pregnancy. Later in gestation, when fetal growth is maximal, undernutrition leads to a range of adaptive responses such as redistribution of blood flow in the fetal body and changes in the production of fetal and placental hormones that control growth.[5]

These responses may include changes in placental transport function, an area of research about which we currently know relatively little.[6] Even without changes in overall fetal body size, the growth of certain organs such as the heart and kidney can be altered. Thus, even fetuses of normal birth size may have mounted adaptive responses to unbalanced nutrition and are therefore phenotypically altered. If the nutritional challenge is too great or too prolonged for these adaptive responses to cope, eventually slowing in overall fetal body growth must result, leading to low birth weight. In late gestation, this growth restriction is likely to be asymmetrical, with the head being less affected than the body.

Chapter 8 considers, in greater detail, the impact of fetal nutrition on health in later life and the developmental origins concept.

4.3   Young infants: the first six months

The contribution of breastfeeding to health

It is beyond doubt that breastfeeding improves the health of babies and their mothers even in an industrialised country like the UK. Breast milk provides all the nutrients required at this age, in a form that is hygienic and easy to digest. The protein, carbohydrate and fat profiles are unique to breast milk and differ in many ways from other animal milks.[7] Breast milk also contains a range of bioactive components, including anti-microbial and anti-inflammatory factors, digestive enzymes, hormones and growth factors.[8]

The BMA's 2009 report *Early life nutrition and lifelong health*[9] highlights the importance of breastfeeding and raises concerns about the need to increase breastfeeding rates in the UK – including addressing the inequalities in breastfeeding between socioeconomic groupings. Many of the themes from the 1999 report are revisited, establishing current thinking about the relationship between early life nutrition and later health; to what degree inequalities in nutrition still exist; and what factors are influential in determining consumption patterns. Concerns about the future health of children have grown further since the 2009 publication. Public health initiatives should focus attention on the importance of maternal and infant nutrition, in relation both to poor and unbalanced diet and to excessive energy intake. This is true in both high-income countries such as the UK and also in low-and middle-income countries.

Systematic reviews of the international literature have indicated that infants who are not breastfed are at greater risk of acute gastrointestinal and respiratory tract infection during the early months of life.[10] UK hospitalisation data, from 2007, have confirmed this.[11] Later in life, infants who are not breastfed are more likely to be obese and are disadvantaged in cognitive attainment.[12,13] Mothers who do not breastfeed are at increased risk of later breast cancer.[14,15] One difficulty with interpreting the literature is strong confounding by social class, educational attainment and smoking, particularly in the UK where these remain very prevalent influences (this is discussed in further detail in the following paragraphs).[16,17] Another difficulty is that the effects of breastfeeding are graded and strongest among those who are exclusively breastfeeding, yet exposure to exclusive breastfeeding can be difficult to quantify and is not clearly accounted for in many studies.

During the early years, particularly the first 12 months, the pattern of weight gain shown by infants who are exclusively or predominantly breastfed differs from that seen in formula-fed infants.[18] This observation underlies the international multicentre study of growth in healthy breastfed infants which led to the publication of the 2005 World Health Organization (WHO) international growth standard. In 2007, the UK adopted this[19] and new UK-WHO growth charts were launched nationally in 2009. This development is conceptually important because it clearly signals breastfeeding and the pattern of growth associated with it as normative descriptors of infant health.

The initiation of breastfeeding in the UK
The national Infant Feeding Survey (IFS) is conducted every five years; the latest data are from 2010[16] (see **Box 4.1**). These reports provide a wealth of information about variations in feeding practice, and factors that influence the type of milk and duration of milk feeding. They also detail trends in feeding over time. In the UK, exclusive

breastfeeding is recommended up to the age of six months. The IFS shows, however, that 1 per cent of mothers are exclusively breastfeeding at six months. Current guidelines are to introduce solid foods from six months, to provide a varied diet that includes starchy foods, fruit and vegetables and meat and fish, and to encourage the use of home-prepared rather than commercial baby foods (see **Appendix 4**).

The IFS shows that there are strong relationships between the mother's socioeconomic status and educational attainment and breastfeeding prevalence – these factors are associated with both initiation rates and breastfeeding duration. In the UK Gateshead Millennium Baby Study (1999/2000), 84 per cent of mothers with higher education initiated breastfeeding compared with 25 per cent of mothers with no educational qualifications.[20]

Box 4.1: The UK IFS 2010 findings on breastfeeding[16]
- Initial breastfeeding rate increased from 76 per cent in 2005 to 81 per cent in 2010 in the UK (83% in England, 74% in Scotland, 71% in Wales and 64% in Northern Ireland).
- Across the UK, 69 per cent of mothers were exclusively breastfeeding at birth in 2010. At one week, less than half of all mothers (46%) were exclusively breastfeeding, while this had fallen to around a quarter (23%) by six weeks.
- Almost three-quarters of mothers (73%) had given their baby milk other than breast milk by the age of six weeks. This proportion rose to nearly nine in ten (88%) by six months.
- Almost half (49%) of all mothers who had prepared powdered infant formula in the last seven days had followed recommendations for making up feeds, for example, using boiled water (allowed to cool to 70°C). This is a substantial increase since 2005 when 13 per cent did so.

Breastfeeding rates in the UK are much lower than in many European countries – for example, 90 per cent of babies in a nationally representative sample studied in Norway were exclusively breastfed from birth, and high rates were still present at one, four and six months.[21] The proportions of mothers still breastfeeding at four months and six months were 44 per cent and 7 per cent respectively. There were also strong negative associations with the Townsend score, a measure of deprivation based on residential postcode.

The 2010 IFS, encouragingly revealed a rise in the proportion of women initiating breastfeeding ('incidence'), accompanied by a rise in the proportion of women breastfeeding at later stages in the first year ('prevalence').[16] There have been marked increases in regions of the UK (particularly Scotland and Wales) where the incidence and prevalence of breastfeeding has historically been lower than England. Encouragingly, increases among younger women and those in lower social class groups were also noted, though clear geographical, educational and socioeconomic inequalities remain. For example, the 2010 statistics for England show that among managerial and professional classes, 90 per cent of mothers initiated breastfeeding, compared to 71 per cent of those who had never worked. Similarly 91 per cent of those who completed their education beyond the age of 18 initiated breastfeeding, compared to 63 per cent of those who left school at the age of 16 or under.[16]

Analysis of the 2005 statistics reveals that, in contrast to the increase in initiation, the proportion of women who stop breastfeeding at each stage of the survey has not changed since 1975 (see **Figure 4.1**). Nationally, 40 per cent of women stop breastfeeding in the early weeks when the rate of discontinuation is highest (see **Box 4.2**).

Box 4.2: Reasons why mothers do not breastfeed or cease breastfeeding early[22]

A 2006 focus group study in the UK[22] suggested further detail of the reasons women may not breastfeed or why they stop breastfeeding early. These were as follows.

- The attitude of other people – women felt that breastfeeding in public was unacceptable and embarrassing, while bottle feeding was accepted by everybody and in all places. A lack of places to breastfeed out of sight restricted women's ability to get out of the house. This may be a bigger issue for low-income women, who may not have the option of breastfeeding in the car. Some women reported breastfeeding in public toilets as the only option. Women wished that cafés and shops could provide places to breastfeed with some privacy.
- Attitudes of family and friends – some women said that even family and friends found it 'repulsive' to be in the same room when they were breastfeeding. Some grandparents thought it excluded them from having the chance to feed the new baby. It was clear that the opinion of family and friends was a stronger influence than that of health practitioners.
- Lack of knowledge – women vaguely knew that breastfeeding was supposed to be beneficial, but they could not name any benefits, and were not convinced about them. In the study only one woman had learnt at school about benefits of breastfeeding; most did not hear about it until they were pregnant. Feeding was not well covered in antenatal classes.
- Lack of professional support – women experienced difficulty in trying to establish breastfeeding but were unwilling 'to bother the midwife'. Bottle feeding seemed easier.
- Experience – breastfeeding seemed difficult and painful, and many women experienced problems, ranging from getting the baby latched on, sore nipples, and disturbed sleep. Women, especially adolescents, complained of a lack of freedom to travel/socialise/work.
- Worry about baby's weight gain – women said that health visitors were 'always worried about weight gain'.

Although some women in this study mentioned the benefits of breastfeeding – including feelings of wellbeing and relaxation during feeds, convenience (less washing up), and less expense, it is clear that there are significant barriers for women in the UK which impact on their choice to breastfeed.

Figure 4.1: Data from the consecutive UK quinquennial surveys of infant feeding on the proportion of mothers who stop breastfeeding by the time the baby is six weeks old

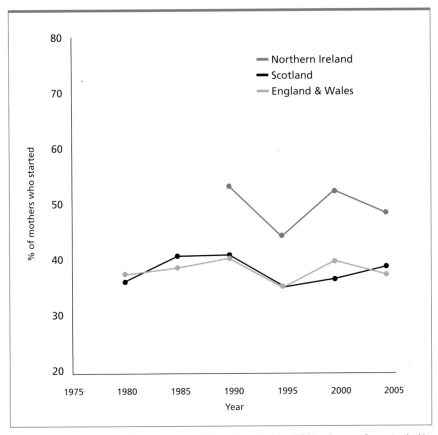

Source: Compiled by Dr Max Davie (Consultant Paediatrician, Mary Sheridan Child Development Centre, Lambeth).

This pattern of infant feeding contrasts sharply with that observed in countries where breastfeeding is more prevalent (see **Figure 4.2**). The reasons women stop breastfeeding during the early weeks are well characterised (see **Table 4.1**). A belief that there is 'insufficient milk', nipple pain and breast pain account together for the majority.[16] It is clear that women do not stop by choice alone, as 63 per cent of those who stop in the early weeks say that they would like to have breastfed for longer had they been able.[16] These problems could be prevented by more effective provision of breastfeeding support around the time of birth and during the early weeks.[17] It is noteworthy too that lower social class and lower educational attainment correlate strongly with early discontinuation.[23] This may well indicate inequality in the ability to access early support services. These high discontinuation rates suggest that early breastfeeding support in the UK is ineffective and needs to be intensified, particularly after discharge from hospital. Focusing provision of trained support at this stage, when rates of discontinuation are highest, is likely to yield considerable health gains.[2,17]

Figure 4.2: Patterns of breastfeeding in Norway[21] and the UK[16]
British mothers discontinue breastfeeding (or lose exclusivity) as a consequence of early formula introduction whereas Norwegian mothers introduce non-milk complementary foods much later.

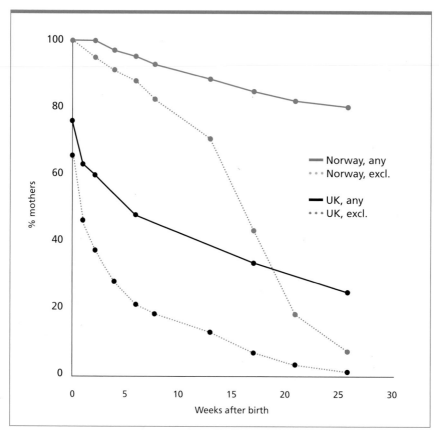

Source: McAndrew F, Thompson J, Fellows L et al (2012) *Infant feeding survey 2010*. London: The Information Centre; Lande B, Anderson LF, Baerug A et al (2003) Infant feeding practices and associated factors in the first six months of life: the Norwegian infant nutrition survey. *Acta Paediatrica* 92: 152-61.

Table 4.1: Reasons given by mothers in the UK for stopping breastfeeding by baby's age when breastfeeding ceased, 2010

	Total	Baby's age when breastfeeding ceased					
		Less than 1 week	1 week, less than 2 weeks	2 weeks, less than 6 weeks	6 weeks, less than 4 months	4 months, less than 6 months	6 months, less than 9 months
		%	%	%	%	%	%
Insufficient milk	31	22	34	35	39	34	23
Baby would not suck/rejected, would not latch on	19	27	23	22	14	13	17
Painful breasts/nipples	12	22	19	17	10	6	4
Baby feeding too often/constantly/ every x hours/ hungry baby	10	5	7	11	13	13	8
Breastfeeding took too long/was tiring, too demanding	8	5	8	8	11	9	4
Returned to work/college	6	0	0	0	4	13	20
Mother ill/on medication that prevented breastfeeding	6	7	9	7	5	5	4
Domestic reasons (coping with other children/relatives)	5	4	6	6	7	6	2
Unweighted bases	5816	1052	348	1107	1355	855	870
Weighted bases	5699	886	376	1117	1345	815	875

Base: All Stage three mothers who stopped breastfeeding during survey period (responses mentioned by 5% or more in 2010 show n).

Source: McAndrew F, Thompson J, Fellows L et al (2012) *Infant feeding survey 2010*. London: The Information Centre. Reproduced with the permission of The Information Centre.

Interventions to encourage breastfeeding

There is strong evidence that UNICEF 'Baby Friendly' accreditation of maternity providers increases the incidence and the prevalence of breastfeeding, notably from a cluster-randomised study performed in Belarus.[24] Within the UK, the number of units accredited as 'Baby Friendly' has risen over the last decade, particularly in Wales and in Scotland where national data show that the incidence of breastfeeding has risen substantially.[16,25,26] It is not clear, however, whether UNICEF 'Baby Friendly' accreditation reduces the proportion of mothers who discontinue breastfeeding. Postnatal care guidance from NICE recommended that 'All healthcare providers (hospitals and community) should implement an externally evaluated structured programme that encourages breastfeeding, using the Baby Friendly Initiative (BFI) as a minimum standard'.[27] This recommendation appears to have substantially increased the number of healthcare providers applying for UNICEF 'Baby Friendly' accreditation.

Systematic reviews have identified interventions and desirable qualities of support that women need to enable them to breastfeed.[28] Ideally support should be delivered across the perinatal period, both antenatally and postnatally. It should be proactive, as women who are experiencing problems may not ask for help even when it is available. Successful breastfeeding requires close support during several weeks after birth, including help from family and healthcare personnel. The 2006 NICE *Postnatal care guidance*[27] and subsequent Guidance on *Improving the nutrition of pregnant and breastfeeding mothers and children in low-income families*[29] made a number of recommendations directed to improving the quality of breastfeeding support in the UK but there has not been a national audit of implementation. Anecdotal evidence suggests that implementation is patchy and at a national level still generally lacking.

There is a need also, to increase the competency of health professionals in delivering breastfeeding support and there have been important professional developments in this area. For example, the UNICEF UK BFI now accredits modules teaching breastfeeding in undergraduate courses of nursing and midwifery. The University of York and Humberside NHS Region, have also collaborated to develop a distance learning course providing modules at master's level open to all health professionals. These are important initiatives that will better equip the NHS workforce to deliver breastfeeding support and remain up to date with the expanding evidence base in this area.

A 2012 report from UNICEF concludes that investment to increase and sustain breastfeeding rates will also provide a rapid financial return on investment.[30] There are large costs to the health service of treating diseases that are associated with not breastfeeding. The savings associated with not having to treat gastrointestinal and lower respiratory tract infections, acute otitis media and necrotising enterocolitis in infants would yield considerable cost savings.[31] When a broader view is taken, and cases of breast cancer, Sudden Infant Death Syndrome, poor cognitive development and early years' obesity are included, additional cost savings accrue correspondingly.[31]

Breast milk substitutes

If mothers cannot, or choose not to, breastfeed, there is a range of commercially available formula milks designed as total substitutes for breast milk during the baby's first year. They are the only safe alternatives to breast milk and infants can grow and develop normally on these feeds. The content of infant formula is tightly regulated and must meet compositional criteria required by statute in the Infant and Follow-on Formula Regulations.[31] These regulations also govern the labelling and marketing of infant formula. This is important, firstly to ensure that parents who have elected not to breastfeed receive accurate practical and factual advice on the use of infant formula, independently from commercial interests. Secondly, this ensures that the promotion of breast milk substitutes does not undermine breastfeeding. Although it is 30 years since ratification of the International Code of Marketing of Breastmilk Substitutes,[32] it remains debatable whether European and national legislation adequately incorporates all its Articles.

It is imperative that mothers who are not breastfeeding receive practical instruction on the safe reconstitution and use of infant formula, particularly since advice changed in 2006 in response to reports of infantile *Cronobacter* (formerly *Enterobacter sakazakii*) infection through contamination of powdered formula.[33] Studies in this area have consistently shown that many mothers do not reconstitute powdered formula properly, generally tending to err towards over-concentration of the feed.[34] Recommendation 14 of NICE Public Health Guidance 11, asked commissioners and managers of maternity and children's services, to ensure that mothers have access to a qualified health professional. This will ensure that they are informed about the use of infant formula from a source free of commercial influence. Health professionals must also have access to independent scientific and factual information on the composition of the many branded formulas available, so that they can advise mothers. This need has recently been met by publications from the BFI and the *Caroline Walker Trust*.[35] *First Steps Nutrition Trust* also provides evidence-based information and resources about the importance of good nutrition from pre-conception to five years.[36] The UK BFI standards require Trusts to demonstrate that mothers who elect to formula feed their baby are shown how to make up a bottle of infant formula before they are discharged from the hospital unit. The Baby Friendly standards also proscribe promotion and marketing of breast milk substitutes through the healthcare system.

European legislation, introduced in May 2011, has permitted the use of health claims in marketing of infant formula.[37] It is uncertain what impact this may have on the sales of infant formula and, in particular, whether it may encourage the use of infant formula over breastfeeding. The philosophy that underpins the justification of a health claim on infant formula is questionable: infant formula is unique as a dietary product that supplies the entire nutrient intake during a vulnerable period of development. A health claim may be justified if sufficient scientific evidence exists to link the addition of an infant formula ingredient to an improvement in physiological function. On the basis that no infant should be deprived, there would be a strong case for the ingredient in question to be a statutory compositional requirement of the Infant and Follow-on Formula Directive.[38]

4.4   Infant feeding six to 12 months

The DH recommendations on breastfeeding and on the introduction of solid food were revised in 2003,[39] in the light of recommendations from WHO[40] and the UK's Scientific Advisory Committee on Nutrition (SACN).[41] Current UK policy is set out in **Box 4.3**. It is recommended that complementary feeds are introduced from the age of six months onwards, and that infants progress onto foods consumed by the rest of the family by around one year. The optimal diet for infants at this stage is not known, and is certainly not 'innate knowledge' for parents. Detailed guidelines are available on suitable foods at every stage (see **Appendix 4**). Key recommendations are a varied diet, adequate energy density, high-quality (preferably animal) protein sources, and fresh fruit and vegetables.

Examination of the 2010 IFS data,[16] suggest that while feeding practices are changing, most mothers in 2010 were not following the DH guidelines, since three-quarters of mothers (75%) had introduced solids by the time their baby was five months old. This suggests that the revised advice from the DH has been associated with a marked reduction in the proportion of mothers introducing solid foods before four months of age. There has been a marked trend towards mothers introducing solid foods later in 2010 compared with 2005. In 2005, 51 per cent of mothers had introduced solid foods by four months, but by 2010, it had fallen to 30 per cent. This change seems likely to benefit infant health.[17]

> ## Box 4.3: DH Infant Feeding Recommendation (2003)
> Breast milk is the best form of nutrition for infants
>
> - Exclusive breastfeeding is recommended for the first six months (26 weeks) of an infant's life.
> - Six months is the recommended age for the introduction of solid foods for infants.
> - Breastfeeding (and/or breast milk substitutes, if used) should continue beyond the first six months, along with appropriate types and amounts of solid foods.
>
> All infants should be managed individually so that insufficient growth or other adverse outcomes are not ignored and appropriate interventions are provided.

Source: Department of Health (2003) Infant feeding recommendation. London: Department of Health. Reproduced with the permission of the Department of Health.[39]

During the second six months of infancy, infants will readily accept a widening range of new tastes and textures; this tendency has accordingly been termed 'neophilia'. Empirical studies have shown that breastfed infants accept new foods more readily than those who were not breastfed. This may be because they have been previously exposed to these flavours through breast milk. It is important that parents capitalise on this tendency and diversify the infant diet aiming to achieve provision of three meals a day, with snacks between meals, by the age of one year. There is clear evidence that family eating habits govern the types of food provided for infants and young children.[42] Those families that pursue dietary habits characterised as prudent (or 'healthy') are more likely to offer their children diets high in vegetables and fruit; these tend also to be families from more privileged social groups who also smoke less frequently and consume less alcohol. This suggests a role for more individual counselling, both peer and professional, during the period of complementary feeding and current research is evaluating delivery to less privileged families through Sure Start centres.

Infant feeding and the mother's return to work

In the UK, the proportion of women in employment has increased considerably in recent years and about 50 per cent of women with pre-school children are in paid work outside the home. Working mothers often return to work early after having a baby and can have difficulty maintaining breastfeeding if not supported by their employers. This may discourage working mothers from breastfeeding at all. Strategies to support working mothers to continue with breastfeeding are needed. There is a clear need to re-examine the extension of statutory maternity leave and to improve the availability and quality of childcare close to the mother's workplace. The Health and Safety Executive has issued guidance for prospective parents, setting out their rights in relation to breastfeeding on return to work[43] and this is supplemented by a DH information leaflet directed at both employees and employers that provides practical information on topics such as expression and milk storage.[44]

Recommendation 20 of NICE Public Health Guidance 11, highlighted the need for continued support for breastfeeding in pre-school settings and accompanied this with guidance on the safe storage of expressed breast milk (Recommendation 12).[45] The School Food Trust, in its 2010 report to the DfE, *Laying the table*, also stressed the need to ensure that pre-school settings support the implementation of the DH infant feeding guidance.[46]

4.5   Support for parents of young children in low-income families

National programmes introduced within the UK to address inequalities in the health of young women and children may have an important impact on nutrition. The Healthy Start scheme was introduced in 2005, following a review of the Welfare Food Scheme (WFS) in 2000 by the Committee on Medical Aspects of Food and Nutrition Policy (COMA). The review recommended that pregnant women should be given vouchers for a wide range of foods and identified the need for health professionals to give general dietary advice during pregnancy, emphasising the importance of breastfeeding. The aim of Healthy Start is to reduce inequalities in nutrition for women and children. The scheme provides food support, professional advice and support to pregnant women and mothers of young babies and children from disadvantaged backgrounds. Unlike the WFS before it, the vouchers can be exchanged for fresh or frozen fruit and vegetables in addition to milk and infant formula. Beneficiaries are also entitled to Healthy Start vitamin supplements for mother and child until the age of four years. Early evaluation of the scheme in Devon and Cornwall suggested that women who were recipients of Healthy Start were buying more fruit and vegetables than they were before the scheme began.[47] Further follow-up will be needed to confirm whether these beneficial effects on fruit and vegetable uptake are observed on a wider scale and maintained in the longer term. The evaluation did not examine overall uptake of the scheme, nor were any nutritional outcomes measured. A survey of health professionals was also carried out: interviews with a small sample of health visitors and midwives suggested that most professionals interviewed were aware of the scheme and how to apply for it. Knowledge about some elements of the scheme remained low, however, and the authors of the evaluation concluded that coverage of training to prepare for Healthy Start had been somewhat patchy. Evaluation at national level is needed to assess uptake of the scheme and to examine its impact on the nutrition of women and young children. Other public health programmes that are directed at families with young children including Sure Start and Children's Centres, also have the potential to bring about improvements in maternal nutrition and infant feeding practices. See **Chapter 3** for a more detailed discussion on the impact of Sure Start and Children's Centres.

Alongside these changes, new vitamin preparations suitable for mothers (pregnant or breastfeeding) and children were also introduced. These should be available free of charge to families eligible for vouchers under the Scheme. Recommendation 3, one of five key priorities of NICE Public Health Guidance 11,[29] specifically pointed out the important role these have, particularly in the prevention of vitamin D deficiency, further encouraging ready availability through community pharmacies. The NICE guidance also suggested that they should be made available through pharmacies for purchase by families not eligible for Healthy Start benefits. Unfortunately there have been numerous problems with the production and distribution of these supplements, which have compromised their potential contribution to public health.

Growing up in Britain pointed out the need to ensure that 'nutritional education is combined with practical advice… accompanied by quasi-cash incentives to purchase healthier foods'. The reformulation of the WFS as 'Healthy Start' could achieve this objective, and an evaluation is in progress. This should resolve current uncertainties about uptake and use of vouchers, implementation of related NICE guidance and the distribution of Healthy Start vitamin supplements. Additional information should be provided through the ongoing Diet and Nutrition Survey of Infants and Young Children (four to 18-months of age), which commenced in 2010.

4.6 Nutritional status of young children aged one to five years

The National Diet and Nutrition Surveys (NDNS) historically have been the major indicators of population nutritional status in the UK. The last survey relating to children from $1^1/_2$ to $4^1/_2$ years of age was published in 1995 and related to data collected in 1992/3, almost 20 years ago.[48] *Growing up in Britain* drew attention to a number of adverse indicators, including the high percentage of food energy derived from fat (particularly saturated fat), high intakes of sodium and non-milk extrinsic sugars, coupled with low intakes of iron, fruit and vegetables, starches and non-starch polysaccharides (NSP). The BMA's 2005 report *Preventing childhood obesity* highlighted the impact childhood obesity can have on children's current and future health.[49]

More recent national data are few but early results from the NDNS rolling programme show some encouraging trends over the last 15 years.[50] Although the sample studied is small (at this early stage of the rolling programme), toddlers showed increased mean intakes of iron and zinc (probably attributable to increased consumption of meat), and increased consumption of fruit, vegetables and NSPs. The use of whole milk continued to dominate over skimmed milk but the proportion of energy derived from fat also declined slightly. The consumption of oily fish remained very low in this group (<10%) but 9 per cent of toddlers were consuming a fish oil supplement. Overall, 19 per cent of toddlers were consuming a dietary supplement in some form. Further NDNS data are awaited, as are data from the ongoing NDNS of Young Children (4 months to 18 months of age), who had not been surveyed for many years.

Obesity

The rapid increase in the number of obese people in the UK represents a major public health challenge that requires urgent action. Obesity is among the leading health indicators that most influence morbidity and mortality in the UK. It is strongly associated with multiple chronic conditions, including heart disease, high blood pressure, arthritis, diabetes and some cancers (eg breast and prostate).[51-54] It is also commonly associated with indigestion, gallstones, sleep apnoea, stress, anxiety and depression.[54] Addressing this key public health concern requires a comprehensive, cross-government strategy that promotes individual behaviour change across society as a whole, and seeks to remove or mitigate unhealthy and unhelpful influences on behaviour. Central to this are policies that will create an environment that supports and sustains healthy eating and physical activity. A coordinated approach is required to increase the popularity, understanding and acceptance of such policies among the general public. Parental obesity, high birth weight, formula feeding and rapid weight gain during infancy are strong early life indicators of risk for later obesity.

In the last decade, a number of population-wide policy measures have been directed at reducing the prevalence of obesity but they have not gone far enough. In addition to those measures, incorporated in the 2011 obesity strategy there is a need to recognise that a range of interventions to support and promote behaviour change are required. Personal responsibility and 'nudge' need to be reinforced with regulatory approaches that help people make healthy choices. Such an approach is supported by the Nuffield Council on Bioethics 'ladder of interventions', which assesses whether a public health policy is proportionate and justifiable.[55] This position is also supported by the BMA's 2012 paper *Behaviour change, public health and the role of the state – BMA Position Statement*.[56] It also reflects the conclusions of the 2011 House of Lords Science and Technology Committee inquiry into behaviour change, which found that non-regulatory measures used in isolation, including 'nudges', are unlikely to be effective.[57]

The significant negative influence business has on the development of effective, evidence-based strategies to tackle the obesity crisis is extremely concerning. This is evident with the Government's responsibility deal on food.[58] At its heart is a fundamental conflict of interest. While the food industry has a role to play, this should be when a strategy is in place and regulations are being implemented. It is essential that Government moves away from partnership with industry and looks at effective alternatives to self-regulation to ensure that there is a transparent and effective policy development process.

There has been an alarming rise in the levels of obesity among children in the UK and, as highlighted in the 2005 BMA Board of Science report *Preventing childhood obesity*,[49] more recent predictions anticipate this trend will continue.[59] Advertising and marketing are key factors which can affect dietary choices and attitudes to food, particularly among young people.[60] Existing safeguards included in the Audiovisual Media Services (AVMS) Directive, which prohibit product placement in children's programmes, are ineffective. According to Ofcom figures, 71 per cent of children's viewing is outside dedicated children's programming.[61] Research by Which? in 2008 found that 16 of the 20 programmes on the commercial television channels most popular with children were not covered by Ofcom's regulations to protect children from unhealthy food marketing.[62]

The DH's Change4Life campaign, introduced in 2009, is described as the marketing component of the Government's response to the rise in obesity.[63] The campaign aims to inspire a societal movement in which everyone who has an interest in preventing obesity, including government, business, healthcare professionals, charities, schools, families or individuals, can play their part. The campaign has been found to increase awareness among mothers regarding the need to improve their children's dietary habits.

The National Child Measurement Programme (NCMP) is an important element of the Government's work programme on childhood obesity, and is operated jointly by the DH and the DfE. The NCMP was established in 2006. Every year, as part of the NCMP, children in Reception (aged four to five years) and Year Six (aged 10 to 11 years) are weighed and measured during the school year, to inform local planning and delivery of services for children, and to gather population-level surveillance data to allow analysis of trends in growth patterns and obesity. The NCMP also helps to increase public and professional understanding of weight issues in children and is a useful vehicle for engaging with children and families about healthy lifestyles and weight issues. To encourage engagement, parents can request their child's results from their primary care trusts (PCTs). Results from the 2010/11 school year report show that in Reception, over one-fifth (22.6%) of the children measured were either overweight[a] or obese. In Year Six, this rate was one-third (33.4%).[64]

There is an apparent paradox in the high prevalence of obesity among young children and a reported mean energy intake below the estimated average requirement (EAR).[48] This may possibly be explained by two factors. Firstly, under-reporting of energy intake is an acknowledged feature of all dietary surveys. Secondly, the EAR for young children was in the past derived by factorial estimation. More recent data derived using doubly-labelled water methodology have shown that the factorial method overestimated the

---

a   For population surveillance purposes, overweight is defined as a body mass index (BMI) exceeding the eighty-fifth percentile of the UK1990 BMI Reference. Obesity is defined by a BMI exceeding the 91st centile. These definitions differ from those used clinically, which apply to the ninety-first and ninety-eigth centiles respectively. 'Underweight' signifies a BMI < second centile on the same reference.

true energy requirements of this age group. The EAR for young children has accordingly been revised downwards by some 20 per cent from that previously set by COMA.[65,66]

Very few interventions specifically directed at reducing the prevalence of obesity among children aged under five years have been evaluated systematically,[67] though there have been several public health initiatives in the UK. Some have already been mentioned in this chapter, including promotion and support of breastfeeding (particularly encouraging exclusive breastfeeding), the postponement of solid foods from the early months of life, and the adoption of a growth standard for the very young (0 to four years) based on the weight gain of breastfed infants first offered complementary foods at a mean age of 5.4 months.

Further initiatives have included education and training in the prevention of obesity for those working with young children (Healthy Exercise and Nutrition in the Really Young [HENRY]) and marketing of healthy eating and exercise to parents through the 'Start for Life' Initiative (which was suspended in 2010). The 2006 NICE guidance on prevention and treatment of obesity,[68] also made specific reference to steps which may be helpful in the prevention of obesity in the very young. These were principally that childcare settings should minimise sedentary activities during play time, and 'provide regular opportunities for enjoyable active play and structured physical activity sessions', and that they should 'implement Department for Education and Skills, Food Standards Agency and Caroline Walker Trust guidance on food procurement and healthy catering'.

Early years settings: opportunities to encourage 'eating well'

A very large number of young British children attend formal day care placements. A 2009 survey of organised childcare found that 2,442,100 childcare places were offered by over 100,000 providers.[69] In 2009, nearly three million children were attending childcare and early years settings. The majority of places in full and sessional day care are taken up by children under five years of age (97% and 98% respectively).[69] Since September 2010, all three and four year olds have been entitled to 15 hours of nursery education each week. By 2014/15 this should be extended to every disadvantaged two year old – approximately a six-fold increase in current provision. A 2006 pilot evaluated the effect on the most disadvantaged two year olds of free entitlement between 10 and 15 hours of childcare. The pilot showed that 90 per cent of disadvantaged families took up their whole entitlement to such free placements.[70] These observations suggest that early years settings constitute an environment in which children and families could be engaged very effectively in learning about healthy eating and so set lifelong habits.

It is important in realising these opportunities to recognise the huge diversity in the nature of provision. It ranges from childminders caring for small numbers of children in their own homes, through voluntary provision in church or village halls, to formal and

permanent provision by commercially or state-funded providers (see **Figure 4.3**).
This diversity presents challenges to the education and training of the workforce, to
procurement and to provision of food which meets consistent, adequate and healthy
nutritional standards. In order to inform its recent revision of the Early Years Strategy,
the DfE commissioned the School Food Trust to report on these issues and provide
practical recommendations to the review of Early Years Strategy conducted by Dame
Clare Tickell.[71] This task was accomplished by the Advisory Panel on Food and Nutrition
in Early Years which set out eleven recommendations in its report *Laying the Table*.[46]
Laying the Table highlighted the continuing need to provide adequate amounts of
healthy and nutritious food in early years settings. The report recommended that all
early years settings integrate the aims of achieving healthy eating and learning through
food by applying or adapting their policies and practice on health, wellbeing and
education. This approach should involve parents and children. In order to achieve these
objectives it is important that food and drink provision remains a statutory component
of the DfE's Early Years Strategy.

Figure 4.3: Number of early learning and childcare places by type of
provider, 2009

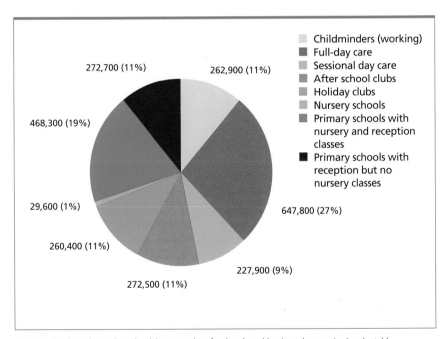

Source: School Food Trust (2011) *Advisory panel on food and nutrition in early years. Laying the table.*
Recommendations for national food and nutrition guidance for early years settings in England. London: School
Food Trust. Reproduced with the permission of the School Food Trust.

An important practical issue historically, highlighted in *Growing up in Britain*, and demonstrated in national[72] and local studies, has been the variability in the suitability of food served to young children. *Laying the table* set out clear practical food-based guidance within a nutrient framework that would enable an improvement in standards. The report demonstrated how carers with little training in nutrition could assemble attractive and palatable daily menus for young children that meet their nutritional requirements.

This task built on work previously completed by the Caroline Walker Trust[73,74] and has since been supported by further practical materials developed by the Trust,[75,76] which incorporate menus and photographic illustrations of appropriately sized portions. It was suggested that these materials should be made as widely available as possible, particularly to parents. *Laying the table* also pointed out the need to support better the early years workforce by enabling training, particularly in the area of diet and nutrition. It called for all local authorities to have access to a suitably qualified professional who can, if required, offer advice on interpreting the guidance within the context of individual settings. This should be a registered public health nutritionist or dietitian who has experience of working within the sector. This harmonises with Tickell's finding that: 'Repeatedly people reinforced the importance of an experienced, well-trained and supported workforce, and the international evidence supports this. Indeed, there is strong evidence that under-qualified and under-supported staff have a detrimental impact on outcomes for children'.[71] This theme was also stressed by the Marmot review in 2010.[77]

4.7   Micronutrient deficiency

In the 1995 NDNS, the intake of most micronutrients was satisfactory but significant exceptions were vitamin A, vitamin D (a Reference Nutrient Intake (RNI) is set for children aged three years or younger), iron and zinc. In keeping with these observations there was clear biochemical evidence of low vitamin D and iron status.

Vitamin D deficiency

The exact population prevalence of vitamin D deficiency globally is debated because there is a current lack of agreement between authorities over the biochemical definition of 'deficiency'. The most widely adopted biochemical indicator of status is serum 25-OH vitamin D concentration and within the UK a level of <25nmol/l (or <10ng/ml) is by consensus regarded as the threshold indicating risk of deficiency. Increasingly, levels between 25 and 50nmol/l are regarded as indicating 'insufficiency', as levels may drop to below the 'deficiency' threshold within the winter months when ultraviolet-B (UVB) irradiation through sunlight (required for skin synthesis of vitamin D) is absent.

In the NDNS, the proportion of young children (under six) with serum 25-OHD level <25nmol/l was relatively low (approximately 2%) though about 10 per cent showed levels <40nmol/l. This low population prevalence however belies a much higher prevalence among ethnic minorities.[78] In recent years, there have been numerous reports that the number of young children in the UK presenting with rickets is rising. Although these have been principally case series and not based on population data, there has been increasing concern among professionals. These have been recognised in a number of documents, most recently a position statement of the SACN,[79] which reiterated the importance of ensuring that all pregnant and breastfeeding women are advised to consume a daily supplement of 10µg (400IU) vitamin D. This has been long-standing policy in the UK, as has the advice that breastfed infants over the age of six months receive a daily supplement of vitamin D that is continued through the early years of childhood. Where the mother's status in pregnancy is uncertain (for example because she did not consume a daily supplement), or where the infant is from a high-risk population group, supplements should be started from birth. Infants who are receiving formula as their main drink during the second half of infancy should not require a supplement, as infant formula (and follow-on formula) is fortified with vitamin D. A daily supplement should be taken when the infant progresses to liquid cow's milk, at about one year of age.

Despite promulgation of this advice in several policy documents, including the COMA review of the WFS[80] and the NICE public health guidance on maternal and child nutrition,[45] uptake has been poor. There have been a number of barriers which include poor professional understanding and knowledge of policy, lack of public awareness, and limited availability of suitable, low-cost vitamin D supplements. In its review of the WFS, COMA recommended that the entitlement to free vitamin supplements should be broadened beyond low-income groups and extended to groups showing high prevalence of deficiency, regardless of family income. This was not implemented in Healthy Start. The NICE maternal and child nutrition guidance (Recommendation 3) also set out a number of steps intended to improve compliance, including the suggestion that the low-cost 'Healthy Start' supplements for infants, children and women should be made available through community pharmacies. Despite this, low availability has been a key issue. At the root of this problem have been interruptions in manufacture and low profit margins, which have made the sale unattractive to retail pharmacists.

In 2011, the SACN embarked on an extensive review of the vitamin D status of the British population. This will explore some key areas including the biochemical characterisation of deficiency in the population, relationships between sunlight exposure, vitamin D intake and status, and the potential role of strategies such as fortification of foods in increasing population intake.

Iron deficiency

The 2010 SACN report *Iron and health*,[81] highlighted the relatively high prevalence of iron deficiency (6%, based on serum ferritin) among children aged $1^1/_2$ to $2^1/_2$ years, based on data from the NDNS. Further analysis of the NDNS data revealed the greatest prevalence of iron deficiency anaemia (haemoglobin <110g/l and/or serum ferritin <10μg/l) is found in children from low-income households, and from those in which the head of household is unemployed or receiving benefits. Children of mothers with low educational attainment or those who were not breastfed were at increased risk of iron deficiency anaemia. The dietary factors most strongly correlated with iron deficiency were high intake of cow's milk and milk products, and low intakes of meat, fruit and vegetables.[82] Children from ethnic minority groups, particularly those of South Asian origin, are at greater risk than white British children.

Iron deficiency in young children is of particular concern because it is associated with delay in cognitive or language development. The long-term consequences of this association are, however, unclear and confounding by sociodemographic factors makes attribution of causality unwise. There is no clear relationship between elemental iron intake and iron status in this age group but iron deficiency generally marks a diet that is unbalanced and low in quality, limited in haem iron, fruit and vegetable content but high in milk and milk products. Where milk intake is high, the replacement of some by fresh fruit and vegetables, as envisaged through implementation of Healthy Start would be expected to have a desirable impact on the prevalence of deficiency. There are some signs of progress towards achieving this aim in that the most recent NDNS findings (2008/09 rolling programme; see above) indicate that meat, fruit and vegetable intakes (and so iron and zinc intakes) have increased in this age group.

Iodine deficiency

Iodine deficiency is the primary cause of preventable mental retardation and brain damage, having the most devastating impact on the brain of the developing fetus and young children in the first few years of life.[83] Iodine deficiency also increases the chance of infant mortality, miscarriage and stillbirth.[84] Pregnant women, lactating women, women of reproductive age, and children younger than three years of age are considered the most important groups in which to diagnose and treat iodine deficiency because iodine deficiency occurring during fetal and neonatal growth and development leads to irreversible damage of the brain and central nervous system and, consequently, to irreversible cognitive impairment.[85,86]

The International Council for Control of Iodine Deficiency Disorders reported in August 2011 that a national study in the UK showed that more than two-thirds of schoolgirls, aged 14 to 15 years, in the UK have low iodine intakes.[87] The authors of the paper concluded there is '...an urgent need for a comprehensive investigation of UK iodine status and implementation of evidence-based recommendations for iodine supplementation'. Analysis of the NDNS dietary data for the SACN showed that intakes of most of the UK population, including children under 10 years of age, are acceptable but almost one in five girls aged 11 to 18 have an intake below the LRNI. This is associated with a strikingly lower milk intake among this population group, cow's milk being the principal contributor of iodine in the UK diet.[88] The UK is now in the top 10 iodine-deficient countries (based on national median urinary iodine concentration (UIC)<100µg/l in children) with the greatest numbers of school-age children with insufficient iodine intake (UIC<100µg/l).[89]

4.8   Teeth and fluoridation of water

Dental caries (tooth decay) is a major oral health problem in most industrialised countries, with children an especially vulnerable group. The WHO *World oral health report* (2003) reported that dental caries affected 60 to 90 per cent of school children and the vast majority of adults worldwide.[90]

The prevalence of poor dental health has well-defined links to socioeconomic factors and geographical location. While the average caries incidence may have fallen, dental health inequalities are widening, with tooth decay continuing to represent a significant public health threat in socially deprived areas. Children in non-fluoridated underprivileged areas of the UK are more likely to experience decayed, missing or filled teeth (DMFT) than those in either affluent, or similar, but fluoridated areas.[91]

Fluoride is naturally present in all water supplies at varying levels of concentration. Its potential for benefiting oral health was first identified in the 1930s, and it is now used widely in toothpastes and mouth rinses to help prevent dental caries. Many authorities worldwide artificially fluoridate their water supplies, to either improve the oral health of the population as a whole or specifically target deprived areas to help combat inequality in dental health.

The BMA's 2009 briefing paper on fluoridation of water, concluded that it is a cost-effective public health strategy for reducing tooth decay in a population. Fluoride has been found to be highly protective against dental caries, and there is no convincing evidence of any adverse risk to human health by the introduction of water fluoridation.[92-98] Through targeting of areas with a high prevalence of tooth decay, artificial water fluoridation is an effective strategy for reducing dental health inequalities.

4.9   Recommendations

Early infant feeding

The number of women initiating breastfeeding has increased substantially since 1999. Little or no impact has been made on the proportion of women who discontinue in the early weeks. This demonstrates that parents' choice is not adequately supported by the healthcare system and also illustrates substantial inequalities in the accessibility of support services.

- There is a need to invest in practical help from trained supporters – health professional or from the mother's peer group. The importance of this has been highlighted in several position statements and policy documents but implementation is still very poor.
- Investment in UNICEF 'Baby Friendly' accreditation of acute Trusts and community providers needs to be maintained in order to ensure that the recent progress made, in increasing breastfeeding initiation, is not lost. Such investment is likely to prove cost-effective within a short time scale.[30]
- There is a clear need to re-examine the extension of statutory maternity leave and to improve the availability and quality of childcare close to the mother's workplace.
- Thirty years after the publication of the International Code on Marketing of Breastmilk Substitutes, there remain gaps in the legal framework controlling the marketing and promotion of breast milk substitutes in the UK. The attachment of health claims to products such as infant formula and follow-on formula may exploit these and there is a need to monitor the impact of this development.

Later infant and young child feeding

- The promotion, protection and support of breastfeeding, coupled with appropriately paced diversification of the diet to encourage acceptance of a wide range of healthy foods, is fundamental to the prevention of obesity in later life.
- The foods that parents introduce to their children reflect their own dietary preferences and lifestyle, implying that changing behaviour necessitates engagement with whole families rather than merely offering advice on children's diets.
- This means engaging with families in a range of environments including retail outlets, early year's settings, children's centres and Sure Starts.
- Promotion of activity and identification of safe play space is also an important objective.

Generic issues

Lack of policy awareness among professionals and carers is a recurring theme in infant and young child nutrition.

- There is a need to ensure that the workforce has more access to specialised and contextualised advice, and that it can access suitable training.
- Competencies at an appropriate level related to infant and young child nutrition should be clearly defined core components of training for all professionals who care for young children and work with their parents.

Access to services may lie at the root of many inequalities in infant and young child nutrition. While the introduction of Healthy Start promised to engage health professionals with parents from the earliest stage of pregnancy, it is unclear whether this strategy has proved effective in improving parents' dietary and infant feeding practices.

- Uptake of the scheme, use of the vouchers and availability and consumption of the vitamin supplements need to be monitored and reviewed.

- The financial value of the benefits offered under the scheme requires review and this will become a more pressing issue as the cost of food increases in coming years.
- Diversifying the number, and improving the quality of 'drop-in' services available through Sure Start and Children's Centres may also improve access to services capable of fulfilling the range of functions required to support breastfeeding, complementary and young child feeding.

Appendix 5 summarises some of the key nutritional concerns and recommendations from *Growing up in Britain*; it sets against each, the steps that have been taken and those that still need to be addressed.

4.10   Conclusions

Since the publication of *Growing up in Britain*, a number of policy initiatives have been implemented and there is some evidence of improvement in the nutritional health of young children in the UK. In particular, UNICEF BFI accreditation and progress towards implementation of NICE Public Health Guidance recommendations has been associated with striking increases in the proportion of women initiating breastfeeding. The greatest increases have been seen where incidence has historically been low. There is also evidence of an increase in breastfeeding initiation among lower socioeconomic groups. It is important that these efforts continue to be supported.

Disappointingly, this progress with initiation of breastfeeding has not been matched by a reduction in the proportion of women who discontinue breastfeeding in the early weeks of the baby's life. This remains unacceptably high (approximately 40% of those who start). Local health providers need to address this as a matter of urgency, by implementing recommendations from the NICE Public Health Guidance 11 and ensuring that the soluble and preventable problems causing women to stop early are more effectively addressed. The NICE Public Health Guidance 11 calls for the proactive delivery of trained breastfeeding support in the early days and weeks of the baby's life.

When women choose not to breastfeed, or discontinue breastfeeding, it is important they have access to independent advice about the appropriate use of breast milk substitutes. This should come from a suitably trained health professional and be free of commercial conflict of interest. Regulation of the manufacture, promotion, distribution and supply of breast milk substitutes should continue to be governed by European and UK legislation, which requires review to ensure that the principles of the International Code are upheld in the interests of infant health.

Implementation of the Healthy Start scheme has provided opportunities for health professionals to engage more closely with parents, advising on healthy diets for both themselves and their children. The impact of the scheme, however, is currently under review. More training of health professionals in nutrition may be needed to maximise the opportunities that the scheme provides. It is evident that the distribution of vitamin supplements within the scheme is patchy and nationally inadequate. This has a cost in the high current prevalence of vitamin D deficiency and rickets among infants and young children, particularly in black and ethnic minority groups.

Rapid weight gain in infancy and early childhood are antecedents of obesity in later childhood. The introduction of the UK-WHO 0 to four growth standard has been an important step in aiding the recognition of a healthy pattern of early growth. There remains a need to improve the quality of food provided for young children in day care settings attended by the majority of under-fives. The introduction of practical guidance by the School Food Trust is an important development in this context. This may, however, require a review to accommodate reappraised guidance on the energy requirements of young children published in 2012.

Chapter 5: Child maltreatment: moving towards a public health approach

Dr Jenny Woodman (PhD) & Professor Ruth Gilbert

> *Child abuse casts a shadow the length of a lifetime.*
> Herbert Ward

Since 1999, when this report was last published, there has been increasing recognition of the role that a public health approach can play in tackling child maltreatment. Calls for a public health approach to child maltreatment – a strategy that aims primarily to reduce risk factors for maltreatment – have been based on four main arguments:[1-3] the right of children to be protected from harm in the first place; the frequency of child maltreatment, which, if all occurrences were notified, would overwhelm child protection systems; the inaccuracy of identification systems, which miss the large majority of maltreated children; and fourth, the effectiveness and cost effectiveness of intervening to prevent child maltreatment compared to intervention once child maltreatment has occurred.

In this chapter, we review the evidence to support a public health approach and trace its faltering development in healthcare and children's social care services over the last decade. Education and child care services are also critical to the prevention, as well as recognition of and response to, child maltreatment, but their role is beyond the scope of this chapter.

5.1 Definitions

Public health approach

A public health approach can be defined by a four-step process. Defining the condition in the population, determining the risk factors for the condition, developing interventions to address the risk factors and thereby reduce the frequency of the condition, and lastly implementing and monitoring the effectiveness of the intervention on a population basis.[4] For child maltreatment, a public health approach means focusing on reducing the risk factors that give rise to maltreatment, rather than on maltreatment once it has occurred. A public health approach, therefore, translates as a preventive approach, which can act on risk factors at all levels of the ecological model of maltreatment:[5] whole society, neighbourhood, family, parent and child. Depending on the risk factors being addressed, preventive interventions may be universal (eg legislation), or targeted (eg parent training). A further distinction commonly used in public health is between primary prevention, preventing occurrence of the condition in the first place, and secondary prevention, preventing recurrence once the condition has occurred. This distinction is less useful in the field of child maltreatment. Maltreatment lies on a spectrum of harmful parent-child interaction and is often hidden, making it hard to be certain whether intervention is preventing occurrence or recurrence.

Child maltreatment

Child maltreatment encompasses any acts of commission or omission by a parent or other caregiver that result in harm, potential for harm, or threat of harm to a child, even if harm is not the intended consequence. Four forms of maltreatment are widely recognised – physical abuse, sexual abuse, emotional abuse, and neglect – which frequently coexist (see **Table 5.1**). Increasingly, witnessing intimate partner violence is also regarded as a form of child maltreatment. The impact on children of witnessing domestic abuse is examined in the 2007 BMA report *Domestic abuse*. Neglect and emotional abuse are, by definition, persistent problems, manifest by harmful parent-child interactions, whereas physical and sexual abuse and witnessing intimate partner violence are events, which may be covert.[6] More than 80 per cent of maltreatment is perpetrated by parents or parent substitutes, apart from sexual abuse, which is most frequently perpetrated by acquaintances or other relatives.[6]

Table 5.1: Definitions of child maltreatment***

	Definition	Comment
Child maltreatment*	Any act of commission or omission by a parent or other caregiver that results in harm, potential for harm, or threat of harm to a child. Harm does not need to be intended.	In the USA, 82 per cent of substantiated cases were perpetrated by parents or parent substitutes.[7]
Physical abuse*	Intentional use of physical force or implements against a child that results in, or has the potential to result in, physical injury.	Hitting, kicking, punching, beating, stabbing, biting, pushing, shoving, throwing, pulling, dragging, shaking, strangling, smothering, burning, scalding, and poisoning. Seventy-seven per cent of perpetrators are parents, according to US figures for substantiated physical abuse.[3,7]
Sexual abuse*	Any completed or attempted sexual act, sexual contact with, or non-contact sexual interaction with a child by a caregiver**	**Penetration:** between the mouth, penis, vulva or anus of the child and another individual.
		Contact: intentional touching, directly or through clothing, of the genitalia, buttocks or breasts (excluding contact required for normal care).
		Non-contact: exposure to sexual activity, filming, or prostitution. For substantiated cases in the US in 2006, 26 per cent of perpetrators were parents and 29 per cent a relative other than a parent.[7] Parents form a smaller percentage (3 to 5%) of perpetrators of self-reported sexual abuse.[8]

Continued overleaf.

	Definition	Comment
Psychological (or emotional) abuse*	Intentional behaviour that conveys to a child that he/she is worthless, flawed, unloved, unwanted, endangered or valued only in meeting another's needs. In the UK, the definition includes harmful parent-child interactions which are unintentional: 'the persistent emotional ill-treatment of a child such as to cause severe and persistent adverse effects on the child's emotional development'.[9]	Can be continual or episodic, for example triggered by substance misuse. May include blaming, belittling, degrading, intimidating, terrorising, isolating or otherwise behaving in a manner that is harmful, potentially harmful, or insensitive to the child's developmental needs, or can potentially damage the child psychologically or emotionally. In the UK, witnessing intimate partner violence is classified as psychological abuse.[9] Eighty-one per cent of substantiated cases in the US were perpetrated by parents.[7]
Neglect*	Failure to meet a child's basic physical, emotional, medical/dental, or educational needs; failure to provide adequate nutrition, hygiene or shelter; or failure to ensure a child's safety.	Failure to provide adequate food, clothing or accommodation, not seeking medical attention when needed, allowing a child to miss significant amounts of school, failure to protect a child from violence in the home or neighbourhood or from avoidable hazards. Parents make up 87 per cent of perpetrators of substantiated cases in the US.[7]
Intimate partner violence	Any incident of threatening behaviour, violence or abuse (psychological, physical, sexual, financial or emotional) between adults who are, or have been, intimate partners or family members, regardless of sex or sexuality.	Most frequently the perpetrator is the man in heterosexual couples, but there is growing recognition of violence inflicted by females.

*Definitions are based on Centres for Disease Control and Prevention report 2008, with modifications in italics.[10]

**Includes substitute caregivers in a temporary custodial role (eg: teachers, coaches, clergy, and relatives).

***US data have been used for this table as the best available data. It is important to note that the detail and extent of routinely collected social care data is poor in England.

5.2   The frequency and nature of maltreatment

Broad agreement across high and middle income countries on what constitutes child maltreatment has paved the way for improved tools for measuring its occurrence. One new development since the 1990s has been the growing use of validated self-report or parent-report survey tools as an alternative to child protection agency information for measuring child maltreatment.[11-17] These surveys have highlighted the fact that child maltreatment is common: between one in 25 to one in 10 children are exposed each year in the UK.[6,18,19] This is far more than are receiving child protection services at any one time. Approximately 3 per cent of children each year are classified as a child in need and receive social care services, and four per 1000 are on a child protection plan in England – mainly for neglect or emotional abuse.[20] Data from child protection agency activity are therefore poor indicators of actual maltreatment. Agency activity is driven more by capacity and policy directives than by actual occurrence of maltreatment.[21]

Self-report and parent-report studies have advanced our understanding of the type of children affected by maltreatment. We now know that, far from being a problem that mainly affects young children, child maltreatment is highly prevalent in adolescents.[19,22,23] We also know that children exposed to one type of maltreatment are often exposed to other types over time.[24,25] The same children are frequently exposed to other forms of victimisation – such as violence, bullying or sexual abuse – by peers or strangers, which can be just as harmful.[26,27] Further advances in our understanding of child maltreatment since the 1990s come from long-term follow-up studies of maltreated children. These have shown that child maltreatment (whether reported to child protection agencies or self-reported) is often a chronic condition with long-term consequences, such as increased risks of poor mental health, obesity or alcohol abuse, and involvement in violence and criminality, which start in childhood and adolescence and persist into middle age.[6] The impact of childhood and adolescent maltreatment on mental health is also examined in the 2003 BMA report *Adolescent health*.[28]

Numerous, population-based studies have defined a range of environmental, parent and child risk factors for child maltreatment.[6] Poverty, unemployment, poor housing and a lack of social support are all related to an increased risk of maltreatment.[6] Parent risk factors include mental health problems, drug and alcohol misuse, intimate partner violence and parents' own exposure to maltreatment or their lack of experience of positive parenting in childhood; all increase the risk of inadequate or abusive parenting or of harmful parent-child interaction.[6] Child risk factors include disability, behaviour problems and chronic disease. These risk factors often coexist and interact, adding stresses and demands on parents who may already have limited parenting capacity, family support and financial resources. It is easy to understand how this combination of adversity for the parents and child can lead to some children experiencing episodes of maltreatment or chronic failure of adequate parenting, which manifest as neglect or emotional abuse.

Major consequences flow from these advances in the understanding of child maltreatment. The first is the fact, underpinned by self-report and parent-report studies, that child maltreatment involves a range of severity that reaches far into the 'normal' population. Maltreatment is not inflicted only by unimaginably vicious or neglectful parents but occurs as part of a spectrum of parenting behaviour, ranging from optimal to severely abusive (see **Figure 5.1**).

Figure 5.1: Distribution from optimal to abusive parenting and representation of policy to reduce child maltreatment

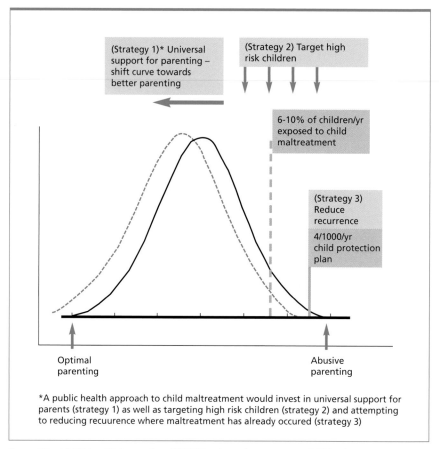

(Strategy 1)* Universal support for parenting – shift curve towards better parenting

(Strategy 2) Target high risk children

6-10% of children/yr exposed to child maltreatment

(Strategy 3) Reduce recurrence

4/1000/yr child protection plan

Optimal parenting

Abusive parenting

*A public health approach to child maltreatment would invest in universal support for parents (strategy 1) as well as targeting high risk children (strategy 2) and attempting to reducing recuurence where maltreatment has already occured (strategy 3)

Source: Gilbert R, Widom CS, Browne K et al (2009) Burden and consequences of child maltreatment in high-income countries. *The Lancet* **373**: 68-81. Reproduced with the permission of the authors.

The second consequence is the realisation that most maltreated children do not come to the attention of child protection agencies most of the time. Numerous studies have shown that professionals (including paediatricians) refer to child protection services only a minority of the children whom they suspect are being maltreated.[21] Reasons include uncertainty about the diagnosis, lack of confidence that referral will do more good than harm, and concerns about the capacity of services to respond.[21] Even when children are investigated and followed up by child protection agencies because of child maltreatment, such input is usually short term. The large majority of child protection plans last less than a year and one-fifth last less than three months.[20] Most children remain with their family (only 0.2% of the child population became a 'looked after' child in 2010/11),[29] and these children's lives do not necessarily improve after social care investigation or intervention.[21,30] The implication is that even children with confirmed maltreatment spend most of their childhood outside the scrutiny of child protection services. Third, to address the widespread occurrence and serious long-term consequences of maltreatment, strategies need to shift from an emphasis on immediate child safety and forensic assessment to determine culpability, to interventions likely to reap the greatest benefits for children, the adults they will become, their families and wider society. Consideration of the most effective and cost-effective long-term strategies has driven the call for a public health approach focused on reducing risk factors such as early evidence of harmful parenting.

Fourth, along with the focus on a public health, preventative approach, there has been growing use of robust methods, such as randomised controlled trials, to evaluate the effectiveness of interventions for child maltreatment.[31] These evaluations have found that few in-home interventions are effective for preventing recurrence of maltreatment, especially not for neglect.[31] The most striking finding, however, is how few randomised controlled trials have been done, despite the harms and costs associated with child maltreatment.[31,32] There have been no randomised controlled trials, for example, comparing out-of-home with in-home care on the child's safety, health, achievements, and quality of life. More evidence is available for prevention. Targeted interventions to prevent maltreatment appear to be more effective and cost effective than child protection once maltreatment has occurred.[3,33-35] The need for the shift in emphasis to prevention was advocated in the 1963 Children and Young People Act, reiterated in the Children Act 1989 and in research in the 1990s, and again recently in the Munro report (see **Figure 5.2** and **Table 5.2**).[33] A preventive, public health approach to child maltreatment is slowly gaining momentum, but effective translation into practice has been patchy.

Figure 5.2: Timeline of child protection policy in England

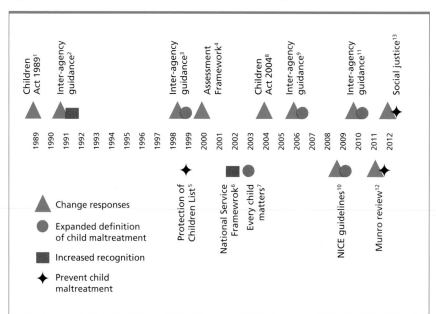

Source: Adapted from Gilbert R, Fluke J, O'Donnell M et al (2012) Child maltreatment: variation in trends and policies in six developed countries. *The Lancet* **379**: 758-72.

Table 5.2: Key to children's social care policy timeline in Figure 5.2

	Date	Policy	Significance
1	1989	Children Act.[36]	Emphasised balance between protecting children from abuse and protecting families from unnecessary and unwarranted intrusion by the state. Introduced concept of 'likely' significant harm as threshold for statutory action by local authorities to protect children from abuse (section 47). Set out statutory duty for local authorities to provide services to children 'in need' and their families (section 17). Created statutory responsibility for all professionals to refer concerns about child abuse and neglect to an agency with power to investigate and intervene (social services, police or National Society for the Prevention of Cruelty to Children (NSPCC)).
2	1991	*Working Together under the Children Act 1989: A guide to professional arrangements for Interagency Cooperation for the protection of Children from Abuse* Guidance on professional roles and responsibilities.[37]	Update of 1988 *Working Together*. Focused on identifying children likely to suffer significant harm and how and when to carry out an investigation (section 47 Children Act). Part eight contained expanded guidance on 'case reviews' (now known as 'serious case reviews'), first introduced in the 1988 Working Together.
3	1999	*Working Together to safeguarding children: A guide to Inter-agency Working to safeguarding and Promote the Welfare of Children.*[38]	Update of 1991 *Working Together*. Focus broadened from child protection (section 47 Children Act) to also include safeguarding and promoting children's welfare (section 17 Children Act). Published in the context of the 'refocusing debate', which emphasised the importance of family support services for children in need, alongside child protection services for those likely to suffer significant harm.

	Date	Policy	Significance
4	2000	*Framework for the Assessment of Children in Need and their Families.*[39]	Primarily a practice tool for professionals, which was designed to help determine whether a child was in need or likely to suffer significant harm and to determine appropriate family support services.
5	2000	Protection of Children List.	The Protection of Children Act (1999) required recording of individuals disqualified from working with children.
6	2000	NSF.[40]	Aimed to establish clear standards for promoting the health and wellbeing of children and young people and for providing high-quality services that meet their needs. Set child protection services in the wider context of services to safeguarding children and promote child welfare.
7	2003	*Every Child Matters: Change for Children.*[41]	The ambitious ECM agenda was framed in terms of supporting all children. It conceptualised children on a spectrum, ranging from those needing only universal services to those needing specialist services, such as child protection. The programme aimed to integrate universal, targeted and specialist services so that child protection and safeguarding were not isolated from services to meet the needs of all families. The guidance aimed to promote prevention while also strengthening protection.
8	2004	Children Act.[42]	The updated Children Act placed 'a duty to cooperate' on all services and required all local authorities to replace Area Child Protection Committees with Local Safeguarding Children Boards. It also created a statutory duty for agencies, including health, to make sure they had made arrangements to safeguard and promote the welfare of children.

	Date	Policy	Significance
9	2006	*Working Together to safeguarding children: A guide to Inter-agency Working to safeguarding and Promote the Welfare of Children.*[43]	The Working Together guidance was revised in response to the public inquiry report by Lord Laming into the high-profile death of Victoria Climbié as a result of maltreatment from her carers. It offered the first detailed definition of 'safeguarding' and supported the ECM agenda.
10	2009	NICE guidelines: *When to Suspect Child Maltreatment.*[44]	Evidence-based guidance for health professionals on recognising and responding to child maltreatment. Guidance was given on the characteristics and features that should prompt professionals to 'suspect' maltreatment and 'consider' maltreatment. 'Suspected' abuse, with high levels of certainty and severity, should be referred to social care. Action following 'considered' maltreatment, where severity or certainty is not high enough to reach thresholds for social care referral but maltreatment cannot be ruled out, was outside the scope of the guidelines. NICE, however, recommends discussion with colleagues, information sharing and further examination.
11	2010	*Working Together to safeguarding children: A guide to Inter-agency Working to safeguarding and Promote the Welfare of Children.*[45]	The revised guidance was a response to The Laming Report 2009 *The protection of children in England: a progress report;* a report on the implementation of Laming's previous recommendations following high-profile cases of child death from maltreatment, including that of Peter Connolly. Includes further detail on children who may be particularly vulnerable and need safeguarding and incorporates changes to 'Serious case reviews' recommended by Lord Laming (2009). Includes interactive web-based version.

	Date	Policy	Significance
12	2011	*The Munro review of child protection: final report – a child-centred system.*[33]	This Munro review was commissioned by the new Coalition Government in 2010. It calls for greater emphasis on professional judgement and less target-driven, protocolised activity in social care. The report, and particularly the Government's response, acknowledges the role of healthcare professionals in managing children who are below the threshold for referral to social care for child protection, but details are lacking on how this role should be implemented and supported.
13	2012	*Social Justice: Transforming Lives.*[46]	The Social Justice Strategy prioritises a preventive approach for Government policies for the family. Under this strategy, there will be resources allocated to universal services to improve parenting and extension of free nursery places for all children, as well as targeted interventions to help families already identified as vulnerable. The main premise of the strategy is that work will improve individual and family health and welfare. This strategy should be seen in the context of other cuts and changes to tax and benefits. Forecasts suggest that there will be net disadvantage to families and child poverty will rise.
14	2012	General Medical Council (GMC) guidance: *Protecting Children and Young People: the responsibility of all doctors.*[47]	This guidance emphasised the responsibility of all doctors to bear children or young people in mind, even those professionals who did not routinely come into contact with children or young people. It reassures doctors that they will be able to justify their actions if a complaint is made against them to the GMC, so long as their concerns were honestly held and reasonable. Although the focus is largely on the sharp end of social welfare problems (child protection), nods to a broader approach are seen in the emphasis on understanding and recognition of risk factors for maltreatment

	Date	Policy	Significance
			and awareness of supportive community services, such as those run by voluntary groups, to which patients may be referred. Like the 2009 NICE guidance, there is little detail about the types of intervention or approaches that health professionals should use for vulnerable or maltreated children.
15	2012	Health and Social Care Act 2012.[48]	Under the Health and Social care Act 2012, responsibility for safeguarding was transferred from PCTs to clinical commissioning groups (CCGs) and commissioning boards (CBs). The Care Quality Commission (CQC) will be jointly responsible with The Office for Standards in Education, Children's Services and Skills (Ofsted) for ensuring that safeguarding duties are adequately discharged and will monitor safeguarding provision via biennial inspections. The CQC is currently drawing up an inspection framework for 2013.

Source: Gilbert R, Fluke J, O'Donnell M et al (2012) Child maltreatment: variation in trends and policies in six developed countries. *The Lancet* **379**: 758-72.

5.3 Preventive policies

The curve in Figure 5.1 represents a simplified view of parenting from optimal, which few of us achieve, through to harmful, abusive parenting. Leaving aside arguments about how parenting (on the *x* axis) could be measured and whether it would be symmetrically distributed, the diagram can help to explain the theoretical impact of a public health approach to improve parenting. The theory states that universal, whole-population strategies for improving levels of parenting would shift the curve to the left.[49] This could improve parent-child interaction a small amount on average for the whole population, potentially impacting on behaviour, depression, self-esteem, school achievement, obesity and other outcomes related to less than optimal parenting. A small shift for the population overall would, in theory, also shift many of those in tail of the distribution on the right, out of abusive parenting (see Figure 5.1).

Examples of whole-population, universal strategies likely to shift patterns of parenting, include legislation against smacking, reducing child poverty, and improving support for parents. It should be noted that UK law permits parents to smack children as long as it does not leave a mark, but there is widespread opposition to this policy, with campaign groups demanding that the UK follows the Swedish example and bans all physical chastisement of children. There is general agreement among researchers that babies should not be smacked, and that children who are smacked are more likely to be aggressive and have poor emotional regulation. Smacking is not more effective than non-physical forms of discipline, and it is clearly linked with poorer outcomes. It demonstrates to children that problems can be solved by physical aggression rather than in non-violent ways (see **Chapter 7** for a more detailed discussion).

Empirical evidence of the effectiveness of these approaches is difficult to obtain. The best example comes from Sweden, where repeated self-report and parent-report studies over four decades have shown a decline in the reported prevalence of physical abuse. Pinpointing which interventions caused these changes is very difficult. In practice, multiple factors are likely to have contributed. Much of the decline pre-dated legislation banning smacking (1979), against a background of rising provision of universal pre-school child care, maternal employment, and generous maternity and parental leave.[6,50] One Swedish author cites the social contagion effects of information about how children should be cared for – disseminated through early daycare settings, and reinforced by other parents – as responsible for the rapid adoption by immigrant families of the Swedish approach to child discipline.[51] Such methods might not work so well in a more class-segregated society, such as the UK.

Government policy initiatives since 1989 are summarised in Table 5.2. From 1997 until the new Coalition Government took over in 2010, the UK Government adopted elements of a public health, risk-reduction approach, improving child wellbeing and reducing maltreatment through investment in universal support for parents. Following Tony Blair's pledge to end child poverty, three strands of policy were developed (for further details on the Labour Government's (1997 to 2010) policies to eradicate child poverty see **Chapters 2 and 3**). Investment in universal child care provision, increased financial support for families, and initiatives to make work pay. As a result, child poverty fell steeply in absolute terms between 1999 and 2010 (with a plateau between 2004/5 and 2008).[52,53] These policies were coupled with infrastructure targeted at deprived families with young children, with services centred on Sure Start schemes based in Children's Centres.[52] For school-age children, the children's fund, introduced in 2001, stimulated a variety of local projects that aimed to minimise the negative effects of child poverty and social exclusion (for further details on child poverty and Sure Start schemes see **Chapter 3**).[54]

Establishing whether these initiatives had a direct effect on child maltreatment is hard, as measures of maltreatment experienced by children, as opposed to professional responses to child maltreatment, are not routinely collected in the UK. Better data would be provided by repeated self-report studies of maltreatment in the past year.

Some evidence of a decline is provided by comparing national surveys in the UK done by the NSPCC in 1999[55] and 2009.[56] These showed some decline in harsh physical punishment or violence and in verbal aggression but not in neglect.[56] These data, however, reflect exposure to maltreatment throughout childhood and are strongly affected by recall of recent events by the 18 to 24 year olds surveyed. They are not good measures of change across all age groups. Past-year data were not collected in the earlier study, but the foundation has been laid for future follow-up studies to determine changes, compared with the 2009 survey.

In policy documents, the new Coalition Government has given early intervention and preventive approaches a central role in its *Strategies for reducing family poverty, improving child wellbeing and reducing maltreatment* (see **Figure 5.2**; **Table 5.2**). With current reforms to tax and personal benefits and cuts to public spending, there is some scepticism about how this approach will work in practice.[53]

5.4   Preventive healthcare
Primary care services
Public services, particularly in health and education, can play an important role in preventing child maltreatment. Such universal services are able to take a population-wide approach to identifying and targeting high-risk families. Within healthcare services, 90 per cent of contacts take place in primary care.[57] Primary care is the main universal service for the whole family and virtually all children are registered with a GP. The service is run by skilled family practitioners trained in developing and maintaining therapeutic relationships with patients facing a range of health and psychosocial issues.

Knowledge of the epidemiology of child maltreatment makes clear what a pivotal role GPs could have. First, children in the UK present to primary care frequently. On average, children under five years old consult five times a year with their GP[58] and about one in 13 children have seen their GP in the last two weeks.[59] Second, the primary care team has insight into risk and protective factors for child maltreatment and the functioning of the family through caring for the mother and siblings, and often for the father and extended family. They are, therefore, well placed to monitor and respond to domestic violence, depression, drug or alcohol abuse, and signs in family members of stress, trauma or failing parenting. A Danish study found that half the neglected children reported by GPs were first identified through consultations for health problems in the parents.[60]

Third, GPs hold a continuous healthcare record for the child as well as for other family members. Although patients are not always seen by the same GP and may be seen by other members of the primary healthcare team, such as a practice nurse, the record of concerns and past problems is contained in the patient's record. No other services have such longitudinal insights across multiple family members. Fourth, as child maltreatment is often a chronic condition, merging with other forms of victimisation, the primary care team can play a key role in anticipating stressors for vulnerable families and initiating support or therapeutic services. Fifth, research consistently shows that a substantial proportion of maltreated children (or members of their family) have chronic medical problems or disability.[61] The primary care team can play a critical role in addressing health problems on an ongoing basis. This continuity of care is particularly important for the most vulnerable families, who may spend periods of time being monitored and supported by children's social care services (eg on a child protection plan), but who may nevertheless require ongoing support, possibly throughout childhood, with a focus on health needs.

Although the pivotal role of the GP has been acknowledged by policy makers in practice,[33,62-66] there is still contention and mismatched expectations about the role and responsibilities of the GP's involvement in child protection.[67-70] In addition, GPs' abilities to proactively pursue concerns about child maltreatment have been reduced by relocation of health visitors from GP practices into children's centres, where they work alongside social workers and early years' service providers such as Sure Start.[21,71] Primary care is not yet maximising its potential for a strong preventive role in child maltreatment.

In contrast to the UK, primary care paediatricians in the US, the equivalent of GPs in the UK with paediatric training, have a more recognised role in responding to child maltreatment and, in some areas, operate a preventive role.[21,34,62,72] One approach, evaluated in a cluster randomised controlled trial – the Safe Environment for Every Kid (SEEK) study – involved teaching doctors about risk factors for child maltreatment, participation of a social worker in clinics, and use of a parent questionnaire to screen for substance misuse in the family, maternal depression, major stress and intimate partner violence.[73] At the two-year follow-up, intervention practices showed modest but significant improvement in their targeting of family problems.

Lessons about a preventive approach to child maltreatment for UK primary care could be taken from the areas of domestic violence and mental health, which are also sensitive and hidden conditions with thresholds for statutory intervention.[74-76]

Paediatric services

The past decade has been troubled for paediatricians involved in child protection in England, with the result that development of a preventive approach has been limited. Although the GMC reports that complaints against paediatricians which are related to child protection are rare,[47] surveys of paediatricians suggest that these type of complaints are common.[77] Against a backdrop of two high profile cases of disciplinary action and prosecutions of paediatricians for their conduct in child protection cases, fear of complaints have risen and interest in specialising in child protection has declined.[77,78] On a more positive note, coordination of child protection has improved with establishment of named doctors and nurses for child protection and a local strategic role carried out by the designated doctor for child protection. The evidence base has also improved, particularly on the accuracy of markers of physical or sexual abuse.[21,79-82] Paradoxically, these developments have reinforced the forensic role of paediatricians and emphasised practices and documentation to support their role in judicial proceedings.[83] Much less official attention has been given to their role in a preventive, public health approach to child maltreatment. Prevention of maltreatment, however, is seen as a core activity for UK community paediatricians, who look after children with disability or behaviour problems.[84]

Part of the reason why paediatric services have not focused on a preventive strategy to child maltreatment is the gap between evidence and practice. Emerging evidence on the epidemiology of maltreatment in the community, the chronic nature of neglect and emotional abuse, the inter-relatedness of different types of abuse and victimisation, and their links with chronic illness and disability, parental and environmental risk factors, does not seem to have been translated into services and practice.

Although research tells us that only a small proportion of maltreated children (included physically abused children) sustain a maltreatment-related injury,[85] most policy and training has been focused on recognition of inflicted injury.[83] Even in an acute paediatric unit, the majority of maltreatment concerns arise with medical admissions rather than injury admissions, although these cases are often labelled as psychosocial problems rather than maltreatment.[86] To respond to these non-injury maltreatment concerns, clinicians need skills in questioning and listening to children and parents. They also need to understand factors affecting parenting capacity and to create opportunities to observe parent-child interaction on repeated occasions.[44]

As with GPs, service configuration limits the paediatrician's preventive role and their ability to respond to risk factors in the family or environment. Action by paediatricians, like other healthcare professionals, is strongly determined by referral pathways and available services laid down by Government or local services. The scope for early intervention is largely limited to referral to children's social services or referral to CAMHS, both with high thresholds for acceptance, or liaison with the GP or with the dwindling workforce of health visitors or school nurses. Barriers to the necessary provision of mental health treatment are examined in the 2006 BMA report *Child and adolescent mental health*. Other options for therapeutic or supportive intervention, such as offering parenting training, support for drug or alcohol abuse in the parents, violence management, or interventions to improve parent-child interaction are not seen as part of the remit of an acute paediatric service. Very often, healthcare professionals simply cannot directly access these services, usually having to go through social services.

For some children, particularly those who are neglected or emotionally abused, maltreatment is a chronic condition. Yet guidance and protocols tend to focus on responding to acute maltreatment events. Less attention is given to long-term management. There is no official framework, for example, for ongoing care or shared care with children's social care services or other providers of interventions.[87-89] For clinicians trying to provide ongoing care, lack of feedback from children's social services is a constant complaint.[21] Anecdotal reports suggest this has not been eased by the development of Common Assessment Framework (CAF) forms, which have proved lengthy and unwieldy for healthcare professionals. Contact with paediatric services initiated by children's social care services, in the form of requests for medicals, tends to be focused on forensic input rather than wider healthcare needs, and applies to relatively few of the children seen by children's social care services.[84]

NICE guidance 2009 and GMC guidance 2012

The 2009 NICE guidance for health professionals has been an important advance in many ways.[44] It provided official recognition of the uncertainty faced by healthcare professionals and the fact that they frequently see children who raise concerns but do not reach the threshold for referral to children's social care services.[44] The guidance defined 'alert features' for recognition at two levels: suspect and consider. Suspected maltreatment should lead to referral to children's social care services. 'Consider' reflects a lower level of certainty. The 2009 NICE guidance recommended further action for these children, including discussion with colleagues or follow up with the aim of gathering further information to decide whether to suspect or exclude maltreatment. In practice, a large number of children are likely to remain a concern but below the threshold for referral to social services. A further advance was the emphasis given to non-injury presentations of child maltreatment and the need for skills in assessing parent-child interactions. The scope of the guidance, however, did not include the question of how health professionals should intervene – apart from referral to children's social care services. While a welcome advance, this guidance might have the effect of reinforcing the notion of maltreatment as a problem of 'diagnosis', rather than as one of recognising children who might benefit from intervention.

The recent guidance from the GMC makes a nod towards a preventive approach, by emphasising that all doctors should understand risk factors for child maltreatment and be aware of supportive services to which they can direct families, such as those run by voluntary community groups.[47] It also places importance on recognising and recording problems which may seem 'minor', as a series of these problems may indicate a more serious problem. Recognising 'minor' concern also allows for early intervention, though this is not explicitly mentioned in the GMC guidance. Despite the mention of risk factors and minor concerns, the focus of this guidance lands squarely on child protection rather than wider child social welfare, and the main role of the health professional is still seen as supporting social care services.

Health and Social Care Act 2012
Under the Health and Social care Act 2012, responsibility for safeguarding was transferred from PCTs to CCGs and CBs. The CQC will be jointly responsible with Ofsted for ensuring that safeguarding duties are adequately discharged and will monitor safeguarding provision via biennial inspections of service providers. The 2012 report by the Children and Young People's Health Forum expressed the concern that the safeguarding responsibilities of CCGs, CBs and service providers was not adequately clear and called for a Quality Standard to be developed.[90] The Forum also stated that CQC registration alone was no guarantee that safeguarding duties would be properly discharged.[90] It remains to be seen how the restructuring of the NHS impacts on child safeguarding practice.

5.5 Children's social care services

Today, local authority children's services are responsible for children's social care, which includes both child protection and child welfare. The 1963 Children and Young Persons Act strengthened by the 1989 Children Act, included a broader welfare remit by requiring social services departments to provide services for 'children in need' (see **Figure 5.2** and **Table 5.2**).[91] An initial referral can be made to local social care services for child protection or for welfare needs, such as family dysfunction, parental illness or child disability.

The multiple remits of children's social care services should, in theory, facilitate a preventive approach, with early interventions offered in response to welfare referrals, as well as attending to child protection. And in the last decade some steps towards a more preventive, public health approach are discernible.

Major policy initiatives in the early 2000s, enacted by the 2004 Children Act, explicitly reiterated the earlier preventive focus of Part Three of the Children Act 1989, by requiring local authority social services to work more closely with health services and other local agencies in order to safeguard vulnerable children, meaning intervening to prevent maltreatment or victimisation (see **Figure 5.2** and **Table 5.2**).[41,43,92,93] Safeguarding includes promoting the welfare of children in need – defined by the 1989 Children Act as those whose vulnerability is such that they are unlikely to reach or maintain a satisfactory level of health or development or their health or development will be significantly impaired, without the provision of services. [41,92,93] Safeguarding is a way of targeting the high-risk population, as shown in **Figure 5.1**, who might benefit from targeted interventions.

One source of confusion about safeguarding is the stated aim to prevent maltreatment happening in the first place. This ignores evidence on the chronic nature of child maltreatment and the fact that professionals outside children's social care services are managing, on a daily basis, 'marginally maltreated' children who are already being maltreated, but who do not reach the threshold for referral to social care services.

Because of limited resources, children at risk of significant harm who require formal child protection investigation are prioritised for assessment and services. This system encourages professionals to label children as needing child protection services, which can be intrusive and punitive, less cost effective and less likely to encourage parental engagement, than providing welfare support for a child in need.

A second problem, is the lack of guidance about where the line of intervention should be drawn in the distribution of parenting shown in **Figure 5.1**. The definition of 'child in need' requires an assessment of the child's likelihood of benefiting from intervention. This, in turn, requires information on the risks of failure to develop or thrive in the long term without intervention and the likely effectiveness of the intervention for improving these outcomes. The prognostic and intervention studies required to inform these assessments are not currently available, leaving decisions about who should be targeted to be based on professional judgement and availability of resources, with inevitable variation between local authorities in thresholds for action.

In England, the important ECM policy agenda and associated documents and tools (see **Table 5.2**) effected a shift in rhetoric, broadening language and policy focus from the sharp end of child protection to include children in need of social welfare services and early prevention.[94] A similar shift in policy was seen in the Scottish policy *Getting it Right for Every Child* (2005). In England, however, this rhetoric was not necessarily accompanied by any significant change in practice. Referrals to children's social care services have not climbed steeply, as happened in New Zealand, where broadening of eligibility for welfare interventions and easier reporting methods led to a four-fold increase in notifications and a doubling in the number of investigations.[95] In England, referrals increased only slightly from 4.9 per cent of all children each year in 2002 to 5.6 per cent in 2011, and the proportion of children placed on a child protection plan has remained around 0.3 to 0.4 per cent of all children each year.[96,97] In addition, there has been concern that the conceptual shift needed to successfully implement tools such as the Framework for Common Assessment did not take place.[98] Services have largely focused in recent years on forensic investigation and interventions to ensure child safety in response to confirmed or likely maltreatment. Part of the reason has been the lack of infrastructure and resources to implement a broader preventive remit.[94,99] Another is the ongoing tension between a populist, media-driven focus on culpability – bringing people who harm children to justice – and a focus on improving outcomes for children.[17] The sense of moral outrage about child maltreatment can translate into a preoccupation, even among professionals, with detection and punishment rather than with interventions most likely to improve conditions for children. This tension is illustrated by the string of public inquiries into specific child deaths, which have sometimes extended the finger of culpability beyond parents to social workers and occasionally healthcare.[66,100] Inquiries into individual deaths and national reviews of the 100 or so serious case reviews each year (death or serious injury where maltreatment was a factor) have had an inordinate impact on policy, while scant attention has been paid to population-based research.[101] Of all the reviews into child protection and welfare services conducted by the government, only the most recent (the Munro review, see **Table 5.1**) has not been in response to a child death.[99]

The Coalition Government, which came into power in 2010, commissioned a review into child protection policy and services over the last decade by Professor Munro, with a view to reform.[33] The review reiterated the importance of a preventive, proactive approach, targeted at vulnerable families. The report focused on social care and how the child protection system could be improved through better understanding of the inherent uncertainty and risk in child protection, the need for professional judgement, and the importance of considering the effectiveness of interventions when responding to child maltreatment. The review also recognised the heterogeneity of child maltreatment and the fact that varied responses are needed. One solution proposed, was more scope for localism and innovation, an approach likely to fit well with Government strategy to open up public services to a range of providers. Expanding the research base was mentioned but insufficiently emphasised. Despite the Munro review's focus on prevention and vulnerable families, there has been scepticism that this can be little more than rhetoric in the current climate. Under Coalition policy, there has been a move to focus services (such as Children's Centres and Sure Start) on the sharper end of social welfare need and there have been cuts to resources needed to offer preventive services.[99] Despite the focus on prevention in the Munro review, the title betrays a focus on 'child protection' and the term 'safeguarding' seems to have been dropped.[99] Lastly, there was no vision of investment in robust research for children's social care, similar to the National Institute for Health Research (NIHR) investment in applied research for health, and recently for adult social care, to inform practice across the NHS and social care.

The review did recognise the importance of other public services, schools, primary care and adult mental health services specifically to aid social care in their proactive, preventive approach. Details were lacking, however, about how other public services could intervene early in response to concerns about child maltreatment, when the threshold for child protection investigations has not been reached.

5.6   Future directions

The research evidence favours a shift towards a public health, preventive approach to child maltreatment, away from a forensic approach focussed on immediate safety and culpability. Lessons from epidemiology suggest that prevention involving universal support for families has the potential to have the greatest impact, by shifting the curve towards support for effective parenting.[102] There has been some progress towards universal support for families in the last 10 years but the political rhetoric has failed to meet its potential in terms of service change. This seems likely to continue to be the case in the present political and economic climate.[103,104]

Two areas need urgent development in the future. First, a greater focus on healthcare services for parents as a way of preventing, recognising and responding to child maltreatment. Evidence of such activity is starting to emerge, with official recognition of the potential role of adult mental health services,[33] and trials involving early intervention by clinicians to address parental problems in order to reduce maltreatment.[73,105] Inclusion of GPs in this vision for early intervention needs to be expanded and evaluated in the UK. Proactive, preventive roles for GPs and paediatricians, particularly where child maltreatment is chronic, will require access to social welfare interventions outside the direction of children's social care services. Given that one role of the Local Children's Safeguarding Board is to map local organisations to facilitate help and support for vulnerable children, perhaps this body could play a part in aiding healthcare to access these types of interventions. The recent Munro review emphasised the importance of Local Children's Safeguarding Boards but it is still unclear whether or how their role in relation to healthcare services will be developed as the NHS continues to be reconfigured.[33]

The second area for development is the research agenda. Unless we can provide evidence of effectiveness of preventive interventions on a population basis, the focus is likely to remain on culpability and children's immediate safety where interventions are coercive and sanctioned by law. Early interventions potentially affect many more families, they usually depend on voluntary participation, and they need to be acceptable and helpful. They also need to show benefits outweighing harms, using valid measures of child wellbeing. The same logic needs to be applied to coercive interventions, particularly where early intervention and coercion converge – in the removal of young children from their parents – now more common in England than in most other western high-income countries.[29,50]

As the research base develops, the heterogeneity of child maltreatment and need for diverse intervention strategies is likely to become more apparent. We need to recognise how thin the evidence base is to support the drastic ways we intervene in children's lives and invest to find out what works, when and for whom.

5.7   Recommendations
Policy and research
- Future polices to tackle child maltreatment should take a public health approach and focus on preventive and family welfare services to improve support for parenting. Research evidence suggests that this approach, rather than a forensic approach of diagnosis and establishing culpability, is likely to make most impact on child maltreatment and child welfare.
- Robust population health research should be used to inform policy, rather than enquiries into individual child deaths.

- In the area of child protection,[a] use of routine data and linkage of data from health, social care, the judicial system and education is essential for understanding which professionals are coming into contact with children and patterns of this contact, which children might not have any early or preventive services, where services might be duplicated and which outcomes are linked to input from which services.
- There is an urgent need for randomised controlled trials to evaluate which interventions work and for whom. These studies are needed both for preventive social welfare interventions and for the coercive interventions such as out-of-home care.

Practice
- Healthcare should play a more clearly recognisable role in addressing the health determinants and consequences of child maltreatment.
- Healthcare practitioners should focus on targeting families who stand to benefit from effective interventions to improve parent-child interaction and thereby reduce the risk of child maltreatment and its consequences. Clear guidance is needed on how healthcare professionals can access therapeutic interventions directly, without always going through social care services.
- GPs should be given a more proactive role in the ongoing support, monitoring and management of parents whose health needs increase the risk of harmful parent-child interaction.

---

a   Please refer to the BMA's toolkit on child protection available via the BMA website.

Chapter 6: The child with a disability

Dr Max Davie

Disabled children and young people should enjoy the same rights and opportunities as other children, and should be fully included in every part of society.
Council for Disabled Children, 2008[1]

6.1 Definition of disability

The Disability Discrimination Act (DDA)[a] define a disabled person as a person with 'a physical or mental impairment which has a substantial and long-term adverse effect on his ability to carry out normal day-to-day activities'.[2] The important point about this definition is that it makes no reference to the origin of these difficulties, nor any attempt to exclude particular classes of condition.[b] Children with Asperger's syndrome, or with anorexia nervosa, or with cystic fibrosis are, therefore, all disabled (although may not define themselves as such), and have a right to protection under the Act. This chapter will adopt the DDA definition, as it reflects accurately the medical consensus that disability is a broad category, not limited to what have traditionally been regarded as 'disabled children', ie those with physical and/or cognitive limitations of a developmental nature.

The DDA definition does not have universal acceptance: most prominently, the social model of disability regards disability as a social construct, existing only as a result of the broader society's failure to accommodate difference. This academic debate has generated much heat, but sheds little light. Our purpose in defining disability is, after all, the identification of a population in need of additional assistance, in order to make precisely the kind of accommodation that social theorists advocate.

6.2 The disabled child population

A 2010 study by Blackburn et al examined the prevalence of childhood disability as identified on the FRS.[3] A rate for disability of 7.3 per cent was found, indicating that 952,741 children in the UK suffer from a disability (as defined by the DDA). The study classifies disability by difficulty in classes of activity, not diagnosis. The findings are summarised in **Table 6.1**.

---

a   Please note, the DDA has been superseded by the Equality Act 2010.

b   Some conditions are specifically excluded from being covered by the disability definition, such as a tendency to set fires or addictions to non-prescribed substances.

Table 6.1: Proportions of children with a DDA-defined disability reported as experiencing particular difficulties

Difficulty/ problem experienced	% [95% confidence intervals] of population (weighted)			% [95% confidence intervals] of disabled children (non-weighted)			
	All		Male		Female		P
Mobility	193,950	1.5 [1.3,1.7]	150	20.7 [17.9,23.8]	98	21.1 [17.8,25.3]	0.940
Lifting and carrying	84,759	0.7 [0.6,0.8]	66	9.1 [7.2,11.4]	44	9.5 [7.1,12.5]	0.921
Manual dexterity	107,798	0.8 [0.7,1.0]	93	12.8 [10.6,15.5]	41	8.8 [6.6,11.7]	0.040
Continence	88,748	0.7 [0.6,0.8]	66	9.1 [7.2,11.4]	48	10.3 [7.9,13.4]	0.556
Communication	255,534	2.0 [1.8,2.2]	210	29.0 [25.8,32.4]	106	22.8 [19.2,26.8]	0.022
Memory, concentration, learning	288,203	2.2 [2.0,2.4]	260	35.9 [32.5,39.5]	96	20.6 [17.2,24.6]	<0.001
Recognising physical danger	171,352	1.3 [1.1,1.5]	154	21.3 [18.5,24.4]	55	11.8 [9.2,15.1]	<0.001
Physical coordination	167,585	1.3 [1.1,1.5]	151	20.9 [18.1,24.0]	64	13.8 [10.9,17.2]	0.002
Other	268,427	2.1 [1.9,2.3]	214	29.6 [26.4,33.3]	135	29.0 [25.1,33.3]	0.846
Difficulty if didn't take medication	247,898	1.9 [1.7,2.1]	160	22.1 [19.2,25.3]	141	30.0 [26.3,34.7]	0.452

Numbers add up to more than 7.3 per cent due to multiple impairments.

Source: Blackburn CM, Spencer NJ & Read JM (2010) Prevalence of childhood disability and the characteristics and circumstances of disabled children in the UK: secondary analysis of the Family Resources Survey. *BioMed Central Pediatrics* **10**: 21. Reproduced with the permission of BioMed Central Pediatrics.

The last category will include children with well-controlled chronic disease, who strictly qualify as disabled, even if not experiencing any ongoing impairment (although arguably ongoing medical care does impair their quality of life). Unfortunately, it is not clear how many qualify as having a disability purely on this basis. At least 5 per cent of children in the UK are experiencing impairment of the type described above, and this group will be our subject.

These categories do not give a comprehensive picture of the level and patterns of need. It is, however, important to note that the most prevalent needs are learning (broadly)

and communication. This is supported by studies of the prevalence of disability by diagnosis. No one study, however, collects data across the spectrum of disability in a way that matches UK diagnostic practice. **Table 6.2** offers a summary:

Table 6.2: Prevalence of disability by diagnosis

Condition	Prevalence/1,000
Language disorders	30-50
Severe learning disability	3
Moderate learning disability	20
Dyspraxia/developmental coordination disorders (DCD)	50
ADHD	10-20
Autistic spectrum disorders (ASD)	10
Fetal alcohol syndrome (FAS)	0.3
Syndromes	3 (approximately)
Physical disability (apart from DCD)	1 (approximately)
Profound and multiple learning difficulties	1

Source: Blackburn CM, Spencer NJ & Read JM (2010) Prevalence of childhood disability and the characteristics and circumstances of disabled children in the UK: secondary analysis of the family resources survey. *BioMed Central Pediatrics* **10:** 21. Reproduced with the permission of BioMed Central Pediatrics.

There is an obvious disparity between the 5 per cent figure, given above, and the sum of the prevalence figures given in **Table 6.2**. This may be explained by two factors. Firstly, many children have more than one diagnosis, and secondly, for many of the more common conditions (eg DCD), only a more severe presentation would be likely to fulfil the definition of disability. If only severe ADHD were counted, for example, the prevalence would be around 7/1,000. The condition-specific figures are, therefore, compatible with the Blackburn study.

Table 6.2 provides a picture of a large number of children with relatively 'mild' disability, and a much smaller group of children with profound disability. This is also the case within the diagnostic categories: much of the recent increase in ASD diagnosis has occurred in the higher-functioning population. We have a picture of the pattern of need: a large number of children requiring ongoing help, guidance and support, and a smaller group requiring more intensive intervention. For all groups, such help needs to be coordinated not just within health but also within education and social care.

The variation and overlap within and between diagnoses, require assessment and intervention to be broad and personalised. All aspects of the child need to be examined and addressed, be they physical, cognitive, communicative, emotional or behavioural. Such a requirement, for a group as large as the childhood disability population, places an obvious burden on services.

This burden has increased since 1999, owing to changes in the nature of the population. There is a sharply increasing group with intensive medical needs.[4] This is primarily a result of improved survival rates of premature neonates. Equally, there is an increasing recognition of the prevalence of ADHD, for example, and disabling problems with coordination and motor planning. Given these factors, it is easy to see how demand for child disability services has exploded in the last decade.

6.3   Services: outcomes and shortfalls

In order to examine the question of how services measure up to expectations and standards, and what can be done to improve them, it is necessary to ask the following inter-connected questions:
- what do children and families want from child disability services?
- what are the professional standards that disability services should aspire to?
- how do we measure quality and outcomes in disability?
- how do we organise and commission disability services to achieve quality?
- what are the socioeconomic barriers for families?
- what are the educational barriers encountered by children?
- how do we engage families and stakeholders in change?

6.4   Child disability services

Within child disability services, unlike in other aspects of healthcare, the healthcare professional is very often not treating the condition itself, but making a holistic effort at improving the child's function and quality of life. The problems encountered are very often common to all disability, for example, behaviour, sleep and feeding problems for the child, financial problems in the family, and educational failure in schools. Secondly, the care of disabled children and families is complex, requiring contributions from health, social care and education. Even within health, very often children see a variety of professionals, in primary, secondary and tertiary care, and across community, hospital and mental health settings.

In 2011, the Every Disabled Child Matters (EDCM) campaign published a report[5] compiled from the views of families with disabled children. The report called for:
- efficient services coordinated and communicating with each other
- integrated services, through which families can be guided by key workers
- information about services at a local and national level

- transparency of process when deciding on what can be offered locally
- early identification of difficulties and intervention at an early age.

The extent to which these requirements are being fulfilled will be discussed in further detail in the following paragraphs.

6.5   Professional standards

This area has, in some ways, shown great progress since 1999. The NSF[6] for children was published in 2004, and included a section on disabled children; this followed the original Kennedy Inquiry,[7] and Lord Laming's 2003 report.[8] In 2010, Sir Ian Kennedy[9] published his review of the services provided by the NHS England to children and young people. The review has uncovered many cultural barriers standing in the way of improving services for children and young people. These were created, and operate, at a number of levels, from Whitehall, through regional and local organisations, to contacts between individual professionals, and with children, young people and those looking after them. Sir Ian makes several recommendations for improvement. It is difficult to disagree with Sir Al Aynsley-Green (former Children's Commissioner) when he comments that the UK has 'the world's best-defined standards of health care'.[10]

There is a recurrent feeling of déjà vu whenever a report on children's services is produced. Comparing the 2004 NSF and Kennedy's 2010 report, inter-agency care pathways, multi-agency transition groups, pooled budgets, and urgently improved access to mental health services are recommended by both. We know what ought to happen, but it is apparent, from the available data, that we are not there yet. In contrast, following introduction of the NSF for CHD, there was a rapid and sustained improvement in outcomes in this area.[11] It is reasonable to infer a link with the fact that the recommendations of the NSF for CHD were made compulsory, and money provided to back them up. By contrast, the children's NSF is merely aspirational, with no additional resources attached.

The current NHS funding situation creates the risk of a disproportionate loss of funding to children's services, as the NSF-led adult services have to cope with increased demand and fixed standards. Risk for children with disability is likely to be especially high, as elements of their core care (eg short breaks) extend beyond the health sector to social care and education, where funding is decreasing. There is no easy answer to this difficult situation. The economic situation precludes appeals for increased overall funding, and so given increasing demand, some services will need to be prioritised for funding over others. A clear children and young people's health budget, at both a national and local level, will allow for the balancing of adult and child health priorities to take place in an open and honest manner.

The second factor limiting the implementation of these reports and recommendations may lie in the very nature of the work itself. The cross-cutting multi-agency nature of child disability work may have the side-effect of making the responsibility for delivery of standards unclear. There is no consensus regarding responsibility for the management of behavioural problems in ASD, and professionals from child health, mental health, social care and education all contribute without, in many instances, any one agency taking ownership of the problem. The 2012 *Report of the Children and Young People's Health Outcomes Forum*, highlighted the failures in child health in the UK.[12] It noted that too many health outcomes for children and young people are poor and that, despite important improvements, more children and young people are dying in this country than in other countries in northern and western Europe. The report calls for integration of care around the needs of children, young people and their families. This is fundamental to improving their health outcomes. It also reduces duplication and waste and saves significant sums of public money that can be spent on service improvement. It is particularly important for children and young people with disabilities or at risk of developing disabilities, with long term conditions, with complex needs or with mental health disorders. The most effective commissioning for disabled children, according to the Children and Young People's Health Outcomes Forum, integrates specialist healthcare, community services like NHS therapists and local authority educational support services, special schools and children's social care services.

The need for clarity in relation to 'standards for care' has become much more pressing with the introduction of the Children and Families Bill.[13] This covers children with special educational needs (SEN) or disability, and requires 'local authorities to publish a "local offer" showing the support available to disabled children and young people and those with SEN, and their families'.[14] This would go some way towards satisfying the need for transparency and information, recommended in the EDCM report, although what evidence should be consulted when deriving a 'local offer' is not yet clear.

Clear practical professional guidance and standards will be essential to allow families and professionals to make the 'local offers' consistent, effective and fair. Most progress in this area has been in specific conditions; for example, the NICE guidance on the diagnosis of ASD.[15] Children do not present with diagnoses, but problems, which may not point to a specific condition until quite careful assessment has been performed. To further complicate matters, these conditions overlap, have features and complications in common, and generally confound diagnostic boundaries.

Pre-diagnosis guidance on recognition and assessment of childhood disability, and guidance regarding the types of common but often severe problems that are common to most disabilities, such as sleep, feeding and behavioural disturbance, is essential. Guidance should be evidence based, incorporating research recommendations and setting out quality indicators that can be audited. Similar guidance has been produced by NICE for many clinical situations, and NICE is the obvious body to take on this work, in association with professional groups. The process of producing the guidance would inevitably uncover countless unanswered research questions, acting as a spur to the underdeveloped academic aspects of child disability assessment, and encouraging cross-fertilisation of research across disciplines.

6.6   Quality and outcomes

Child disability services are staffed by dedicated professionals with children's best interests at heart. But this dedication does not always translate into quality of services.

A good-quality service should provide:
- early identification of difficulties and timely multidisciplinary assessment
- access to necessary services for emergent difficulties, untrammelled by organisational boundaries
- coordinated care, minimising disruption to family life
- clear protocols and pathways for the management of particular difficulties
- effective information sharing.

The responsibility for early identification and initial management of difficulties falls to professionals at the 'primary level', for example, health visitors, teachers, and GPs. It is often nursery staff, for example, who first spot speech and language problems and take the initial steps towards remediation. These professionals often lack knowledge, training and support from specialist services. Attention has moved towards inter-agency training and liaison, the HCP is an example of this work,[16] although currently this is limited to the health sector. Given the advantages of early identification and intervention in childhood disability, there seems to be a strong argument for a review of child development content in the curriculum of all professions working with children. Specifically, it is surprising to find that there is no child development in the curriculum of teacher training courses.

Children should have access to the lengthy multidisciplinary assessments offered in tertiary centres, receiving a comprehensive 'gold-standard' assessment of all aspects of their health and development. Given the current funding situation, it seems sensible to open a debate about the balance between spending on assessment and on intervention. To take an example, in some areas, services have introduced a 'consultation' model by which primary-level staff are trained by specialists in basic identification of need and first-line intervention, with only children experiencing continuing difficulties referred on for specialist assessment. This model has been found to be beneficial in DCD.[17] The important point here is that assessment should not be an end in itself, but serve as available and effective intervention.

In relation to access to services, once a diagnosis or formulation of difficulties is established, a management plan is made. This phase of a family's experience of services can be problematic in several ways. Firstly, the management plan is often made without consultation with the family. This may be because services feel they are simply offering what is indicated and available. As the evidence base improves and more protocols become available, there will be pressure on clinicians to manage difficulties 'as per protocol'. Families are then often referred to other agencies both within health and in other sectors, for services that may not be available. Referral is essentially a process by which one professional makes a 'bid' for the services of another, in the hope that this second professional will be able to help the patient. This process is very time-consuming, stressful and too often futile; all of these difficulties increase with 'organisational distance', and most problems occur when referring to external agencies.

Services are frequently poorly coordinated. For children with complex needs, the number of appointments soon adds up and can create considerable disruption. Since the pioneering work of Mary Sheridan in setting up child development centres, there has been a recognition that joint or coordinated appointments are desirable. The EDCM report, however, makes it clear that they are not being achieved. Simply exhorting professionals to coordinate better has not been effective. This is an area deserving more study, but a few suggestions can be made at this point:

- when implementing the new commissioning arrangements set out in the Health and Social Care Act, and implementing payment by results (PbR), joint working should be incentivised
- telemedicine should be harnessed when the opinion of a geographically distant specialist is required
- for children with complex health needs, some follow-up should be delegated from the specialist hospital level to secondary practitioners such as community paediatricians.

The formation of a comprehensive and robust local multi-agency protocol covering a diagnosis or pattern of difficulties can reduce the stress and uncertainty of being referred. A system where a professional is informed by a colleague of the child and family's need for a service, established by robust assessment against agreed norms and criteria, would be better. There might be an agreement, for example, that every child with ASD receives input from speech and language, paediatric follow-up until the age of five years, and an assessment of need by social care. The introduction of 'local offers' may help these protocols to emerge.

Good information sharing between services can prevent the situation, condemned by Kennedy, by which families 'go to multiple appointments to tell the same story'.[18] The barriers to information sharing are multiple for example, a lack of interoperability between IT systems. In her 2012 review of Information Governance, 'Information: to share or not to share?', Dame Fiona Caldicott has highlighted a number of cultural barriers to sharing, for example because healthcare professionals are anxious about compliance with data protection rules. The findings of the Caldicott Review will be published in Spring 2013 and will include recommendations to support and enable appropriate information sharing.

Child disability lacks an orderly, quantitative outcome such as survival rates or complication rates. When we examine outcomes, there are several approaches. The first, outlined by Kennedy, revolves around satisfaction with the process and outcomes of care.[9] He recommends, radically, that this be the sole criterion for measuring the quality of children's services: satisfaction of the family with the process, and satisfaction of the relevant quality indicators, as ensured by professionals. The idea has great potential for simplifying a potentially highly complex and confusing area. Paediatric professional bodies would play a leading role, along with other professional groups, in developing national measures of family satisfaction. This would need explicit support from the DH.

The second approach looks more broadly at the overall quality of life, either of the individual or the family unit, as a whole. An improvement in the quality of the patient's life is the *sine qua non* of medical treatment. The factors underlying quality of life estimation in disability are complex, and the causal chain between high-quality healthcare and resulting improvement may be long, both in the complexity of the process and the time course. In this context, the outcome of the Children's Outcome Measurement Study (CHUMS trial),[19] looking at patient reported outcome measurements (PROMs) in children with disability, will be important in determining the future direction of work in this area.

6.7 Commissioning and organisation of disability services

Given the devolution of political control of the NHS to the individual nations of the UK, it is difficult to give a comprehensive picture of the current organisation of health services for disabled children. The child development centre mode inspired by the work of Mary Sheridan among others, is widely adopted. In this (ideal) model, child development professionals share a building, information system and organisational structure, and work together to deliver the seamless multidisciplinary assessment and management of childhood disability. They are (ideally) joined by professionals from mental health, education and social care, to ensure that management of a child's difficulties can proceed untrammelled by organisational boundaries, towards optimal function for the child. The British Association for Community Child Health (BACCH) has produced a manifesto for community child services, currently in draft, which can be accessed via their website.[20]

As Kennedy made clear in 2010, services are not always designed with children in mind, or with the involvement of children and families.[9] Care is typically commissioned by block contract to services, split along organisational lines which reflect the history of the organisations rather than local need or ease of access.

The Children and Families Bill will in several ways help with the formation of clear 'local offers' and pathways. The Bill makes provision for joint commissioning for children with SEN, which should result in the integrated multi-agency care that children with disability need.

It is not clear to what extent joint commissioning will be supported by organisational integration between services. A 2012 article detailed the barriers and benefits to integration.[21] The article concluded that the large-scale pilot of integrated care services was showing early signs of success for patients and staff, but this is often despite NHS processes not because of them. It is unclear how the changes to commissioning in England will help or hinder this drive to integration. While there has been verbal assurance from Government that integration of care remains a priority, the financial tariff structures and outcome frameworks created by the Bill do not seem to encourage integration, and EU competition law will still apply to a reformed NHS. There are still many unknowns regarding the details of the Health and Social Care Act, including the role and powers of the local health and wellbeing boards.

While most commissioning will be done locally by CCGs, there is provision in the Act for national specialist commissioning. Unfortunately, the early indicators are that these services will be based on diagnosis (eg vein of Galen malformation services) rather than need (eg technology-dependent children), thus creating a 'molecular lottery'. At the time of writing, discussion is ongoing as to how to refine this approach.

The long-awaited application of PbR to disability services (which will need to be funded on a per-patient rather than episodic basis) will provide a spur to the formalising of pathways, as patients can then be funded 'by pathway'. This in turn may lead to the breakdown of organisational barriers, and may also lead to financial incentives towards joint working and fewer appointments for families. How the 'consultation model', mentioned above, fits into this system is unclear and it may be that disability services need to be funded by a hybrid of block contracts and PbR. This is under discussion at the DH at the time of writing, but the 'year of care' currently under trial for adults with long-term-care (LTC) holds greatest promise for funding services for children with disability.

6.8   Socioeconomic barriers

The 2010 paper by Blackburn et al demonstrates the socioeconomic trap that disability sets for families.[3] Having a child with a disability is estimated to increase the family expenditure by 10 to 18 per cent. Median household income, however, was found to be 13 per cent lower in children with a disability. This situation is likely to worsen, given the reduction in tax credits effective from 2011 and the restrictions on Disability Living Allowance (DLA) under the Welfare Reform Act.[22] These are the headlines, but Blackburn digs behind these to the impact on family life and finances. Not only do these families live more impoverished lives, but they are also significantly more indebted than the rest of the population. They are less likely to own their own home, and thus hold no capital with which to decrease the cost of borrowing. Given the long-established link between low socioeconomic status and poor health outcomes, it is easy to see how families become trapped by disability into a cycle of poverty and worsening health. A 2012 report by Contact a Family,[23] made the situation vividly clear: one in six families with disabled children are going without food, and one in five without heating, owing to financial pressures. At this extremity, poverty is unarguably a menace to health, and therefore a concern for the health sector.

As with the problems of poverty generally, there are no easy solutions to this. Action can be taken at individual, local and national levels. Clinicians have a responsibility, as part of a commitment to children's wellbeing, to ensure that families are aware of their eligibility for benefits. Local authorities have a duty to provide easy-to-access benefit advice that is not dependent on meeting any particular threshold, and national bodies, such as the BMA, can demonstrate to Government the false economy of cutting benefits to vulnerable families, whose worsening resultant health will increase the drain on NHS resources.

6.9   Educational outcomes

Three-quarters of children with disability have SEN, and this figure grows with increasing severity of disability. The recent green paper on SEN was highly relevant. It begins by painting a bleak picture of the current educational outcomes for children with SEN. Compared to the general population, more than twice the number young people who have had a statement of SEN are not in education, employment or training at 18, and pupils at school action plus (extra help but no statement) have 20 times the risk of a permanent exclusion from school.

It is not clear that this issue has been addressed by recent developments. The SEN green paper published in 2011, proposed that schools remain financially responsible for excluded pupils, and that they be required to perform a multi-agency assessment prior to exclusion. This requirement has disappeared from the final bill. The Ofsted inspection regime is focused on achievement and good order, not inclusion and welfare.[24] The disproportionate exclusion of pupils with SEN is likely to be unaffected by the Children and Families Bill.

The Bill does seek to address the bureaucratic and frustrating process of obtaining support. The 'local offer' is discussed above. Another major initiative is the replacement of statements of SEN with Education, Health and Care (EHC) plans.[25] These will be introduced for children who would currently receive a statement of SEN. The introduction of these plans will do nothing for those not currently protected by statements, and it is not clear how health and social care budgets will be mobilised under the new plans.

The other challenge for the EHC plans is how to ensure efficient input from the various agencies involved in assessment, so that the change is not merely 'rebranding'. The obvious solution is to integrate the plans with the existing CAF. This system is not mentioned in the Bill, so it seems that the two are to run alongside each other (with inevitable duplication). The practicalities and challenges of delivering such a system will emerge from pathfinder exercises in the coming months.

6.10 Engagement of children, young people and families

There is no area where the dangers of noble words without action are more apparent than in the often-stated commitment to engage 'service users' in service improvement. None of the recommendations of this chapter will be achievable without the views of the families involved, either being consulted or actively advocating on behalf of children with disability. It would be absurd to produce a 'local offer' without the involvement of the families. The views of families will provide insight into difficult problems, such as whether to measure satisfaction with one episode of care, or with the overall process of assessment and management. We would also, by doing so, be respecting Article 12 of the UNCRC.[26]

The move towards requiring public involvement in commissioning is welcome. Commissioners should require that any tender or contract has significant family involvement in its formation. Such an approach may encounter the danger of tokenism, with public involvement a 'box to be ticked'. A more fundamental change may therefore be required.

Kennedy provides us with a useful structure.[9] The key feature of his local service partnerships is that they contain a mixture of professionals, politicians and members of the public, and hold the local children's budget as a whole, independent of organisational boundaries. This is helpful in two ways. It makes 'special interest' groups less influential, and, by mixing professions, it tends to prevent members of the public from feeling 'outranked' by any one group. The idea needs to be explored in more detail, and the CCGs should be implemented with these principles in mind.

6.11 Recommendations
Government should:
- revisit the Kennedy report in the light of the changes planned in the Health and Social Care Act and consider Local Service Partnerships as a vehicle for change, supported by local children's budgets and simplified outcome measures
- ensure that the benefits of the new systems envisaged for the Children and Families Bill are shared by all children with disability
- implement PbR, bearing in mind the chronic nature of difficulties and the benefits of a consultation model

- put child development on the curricula of teaching training courses
- review the impact of Ofsted's assessment framework on inclusion and welfare for children with SEN.

Professional bodies should:
- campaign for awareness regarding the impact of benefit cuts on families of disabled children
- collaborate to produce professional guidance and standards on pre-diagnosis assessment and generic problems, in order to inform the development of local offers
- produce and evaluate outcome measures for childhood disability.

Local authorities and health commissioners should:
- establish local need and work on an offer for childhood disability
- set up local service partnerships to guide the formation of care pathways in disability.

Clinicians in a leadership role should:
- collaborate with local partners to produce care pathways and 'offers' for local disability services
- get involved with local CCGs to ensure appropriate commissioning
- get involved in national work.

All clinicians should:
- ensure that the families they work with understand what services are available, and feel empowered to make their voices heard
- ensure that the families they work with are in receipt of all relevant benefits.

Carers of disabled children should:
- get involved in service improvement.

See **Appendix 6** for a list of websites that are useful for keeping up to date on this complex and rapidly evolving subject.

Chapter 7: Emotional and behavioural problems

Dr Jessie Earle

> *Childhood is not just a preparation for life, it is a part of life.*
> *Notes on an Unhurried Journey*, John A Taylor[1]

Rates of psychiatric disorders in young people are rising.[2] These disorders frequently begin in childhood and are often a source of considerable distress and lost opportunities for the children involved, their families or both. Much is now known about cost-effective prevention and early intervention in the development of emotional and behavioural problems, in order to support a healthier developmental path. The challenge is to develop and implement coordinated and effective primary and secondary preventive initiatives on a widespread and equitable basis, at a time when resource constraints have led to significant reductions in spending on early intervention in the public sector.

7.1   Definitions of mental health
Children's mental health is not simply the absence of mental ill health, but can be described in its own right. The NHS Health Advisory Service definition[3] has been widely adopted.

The components of mental health include the following capacities:
- the ability to develop psychologically, emotionally, intellectually and spiritually
- the ability to initiate, develop and sustain mutually satisfying personal relationships
- the ability to become aware of others and to empathise with them
- the ability to use psychological distress as a developmental process so that it does not hinder or impair further development.

Within this broad framework, and incorporating the developmental nature of both body and mind in childhood and adolescents, mental health in young people is indicated more specifically by:
- a capacity to enter into and sustain mutually satisfying relationships
- continuing progression of psychological development
- an ability to play and learn so that attainments are appropriate for age and intellectual level
- a developing moral sense of right and wrong.

For babies and younger children, infant mental health has been defined as: 'the young child's capacity to experience, regulate and express emotions, form close and secure relationships, and explore the environment and learn. All of these capacities will be best accomplished within the context of the caregiving environment that includes family, community and cultural expectations for young children. Developing these capacities is synonymous with healthy social and emotional development'.[4]

Infants and young children are entirely dependent on their caregivers and context to support their emotional development and mental health. There is a complex interrelationship between the child's individual characteristics, the capacity of parents to provide sensitive and developmentally appropriate care, the support and services available in the wider community, the quality of the physical environment, and the degree to which Government policy is family-friendly.

From this systemic perspective, it is apparent that a variety of agencies, both statutory and non-statutory, will have an interlinking impact on the mental health of young children. This needs to be acknowledged in planning initiatives promoting young children's mental health.

Many young children will experience an impairment in their mental health or emotional wellbeing at some point.[5] One study showed that the prevalence for three year old children was 10 per cent with 66 per cent of parents sampled having one or more concerns about their child.[6] A further study showed that 7 per cent of children aged 3-4 years exhibited serious behaviour problems.[7] For these children, the nature of their problems may be conceptualised in different ways. In addition to the variety of familial and cultural explanations that may be evoked for the child's difficulties, health services, education services and social services will often think about these children using different language and emphasising different aspects of their problems. These differences can breed misunderstanding and inhibit communication. Psychiatrists, for example, tend to distinguish between normal and abnormal groups of children, and think of the abnormal group as having disorders with specific characteristics, treatments and outcomes. They see these disorders as produced by an interaction of biology and environment. Teachers, and others involved in education, tend to use an undifferentiated category of 'emotional and behavioural problems'. They see these as primarily caused by adverse environmental factors, in particular problems in the family context, and perceive them as essentially amenable to improvement through education. Social workers and workers in the voluntary sector, tend to regard labelling children as a stigmatising process which is best avoided, and prefer to explain children's problems in social terms. These descriptions are of course stereotypes, and there will be many exceptions to the characterisations presented. Many GPs and health visitors, for example, often think more like teachers and social workers than typical medical professionals. But the problem of different languages and conceptual frameworks in different professional groups, and between professionals and the families they are working with, is a real one. It inhibits the development of the common understandings and collaborative relationships which are so important across and within the different organisations involved with young children – the NHS, social services, education, and the voluntary sector – and between these agencies and the families accessing their services.

7.2 Identifying young children with emotional and behavioural problems

All infants and young children will display some degree of emotional or behavioural disturbance at various stages in their development, and these relatively transient perturbations are an ordinary part of growing up. It is to be expected that a child will be stressed by the birth of a sibling or the separation involved in starting nursery, though different children will display their feelings to differing extents and in different ways.

For families whose children have more extreme or pervasive emotional or behavioural problems, or where the problems do not resolve despite their parent or carer's efforts, additional assessment or support may be needed from universal services such as health visitors, GPs or nursery staff, or possibly from psychologists or other specialist mental health professionals.

7.3 Common types of emotional and behavioural problems age 0 to five years

Different sorts of emotional and behavioural problems in children aged 0 to five years need to be distinguished from each other, so that appropriate treatment and support can be provided. Persistent emotional and behavioural disturbance in young children may be an early indication of developmental problems, such as autism, speech and language disorders or learning disabilities, and professionals in contact with young children need to be able to identify children who are deviating from the expected developmental trajectory. Early identification allows the possibility of early intervention which can optimise outcomes for the child.

Sleeping problems are common in young children and can cause considerable stress for their families. Approximately 20 per cent of children aged one to three years, and 10 per cent of children aged four to five years, have significant problems settling to sleep and waking at night. Providing support for parents to modify their child's sleep pattern so that they start to sleep better can improve not only the child's sleep, but also the child's daytime behaviour and overall parent-child interactions.

Feeding problems are also common in young children, and include faddiness and selective eating and more severe problems resulting in failure to thrive.[8] An American review found feeding disorders in 25 per cent of children developing normally and 80 per cent of children with developmental delay.[9] UK data from 2009/10 found 19.7 per cent of children entering school were obese.[10] Both biological and environmental aspects should always be considered in the assessment and management of feeding difficulties. More straightforward problems can be managed in primary care, but referral for specialist multidisciplinary assessment will be needed in more complex cases (see **Chapter 4** for a more detailed discussion on feeding).

Tantrums, aggression and non-compliance are part of ordinary toddler development, as young children experiment with autonomy and test parental limits, but some young children have pervasive and protracted behaviour difficulties in excess of those seen in their peers. Behaviour problems that may be seen as outside the developmental norm for this age group include frequent aggressive behaviour in the absence of prosocial behaviour, and aggressive behaviour which appears proactive rather than occurring as reaction to frustration, alongside an overall inflexibility, fearlessness and resistance to control. Approximately 50 per cent of these young children will have persistent behaviour problems and may be diagnosed with oppositional defiant disorder or conduct disorder in later childhood.[11]

Restless, impulsive and excitable behaviour is common in young children, though in some this behaviour may be extreme and some parents may question whether their child has ADHD. Guidelines from NICE recognise the diagnosis in children aged three years and above, where the child has persistent inattentiveness, hyperactivity and impulsiveness that is marked in relation to peers, is present in more than one setting, and causes at least moderate impairment. Diagnosis needs to be made by a specialist, and recommended UK treatment for ADHD in pre-school children is parental attendance on a structured group-based parenting programme.[12] These parenting programmes, which should meet criteria set out by NICE, are also recommended for parents of children with disruptive behaviour problems.

Young children who have been exposed to single or repeated traumatic experiences, either within or outside the family, may show emotional and behavioural disturbances, including distressed reactions to reminders of the traumatic events, repetitive re-enactments in their play, sleep disturbance and developmental regression.[13] Children under five years can be diagnosed with post-traumatic stress disorder (PTSD), though some aspects of the diagnostic criteria are not developmentally appropriate for this age group.

Many young children will be fearful and anxious at times, but most will be successfully reassured and comforted by their parent or carer. Where the child's distress is more sustained, and the parent is struggling with helping their child manage their anxieties, some professional help may be needed to support the parent-child dyad.

A few young children will have such disturbed relationships with their caregivers that they are diagnosed with attachment disorders. Most of these children will have been severely neglected or abused. They may be either extremely withdrawn and inhibited in social situations, or indiscriminately social and disinhibited. There is a distinction between children diagnosed with attachment disorders and the much larger group of children described as having insecure or disorganised attachments towards their caregivers. This latter group are at increased risk of emotional or behavioural problems but do not meet diagnostic criteria for having a disorder.

7.4 Long-term consequences of mental health problems in children aged 0 to five years

There is now good evidence that problems in the early years of childhood may presage problems in adolescence and adult life.[14] A New Zealand longitudinal study of mental health outcomes, showed that restless impulsive three year olds had higher rates of serious persistent antisocial behaviour at age 21, and unduly shy, inhibited three year olds had higher rates of depression at the same age. Three-year-old boys in either group, had an increased risk of alcohol-related problems at age 21, and both groups of three year olds had an increased risk of suicide during adolescence. Another review concluded that children identified as hard to manage at ages three or four years have a high probability (approximately 50:50) of continuing to show behavioural difficulties throughout primary school years and into adolescence.

This review identified the following factors as predictive of behaviour problems that persist from the early years:
- the presence of multiple behaviour difficulties (spread)
- problems evident in different contexts (pervasiveness)
- a distressed and/or dysfunctional family context.

There is also a considerable financial cost of leaving young children's behaviour problems untreated.[15] In one study of 80 children aged three to eight who had been referred to CAMHS with severe antisocial behaviour, it was calculated that mean additional costs of £5,960 had been incurred in one year. These costs are both incurred by the family (including time off from work because of the child's behaviour and repairs to the home following damage), and also by the additional services involved with the child because of their behaviour. Another study followed up children who had been diagnosed with oppositional defiant disorder or conduct disorder at the age of 10 years. By the age of 27, each had cost the public around £200,000, 10 times more than children in a control group.[16] These potentially adverse long-term costs and consequences of emotional and behavioural problems in childhood mean that these merit identification and treatment when problems first emerge. Of course, in addition to these longer-term reasons for addressing emotional and behavioural problems in the early years, children and families also need help with these problems because of the immediate stress and distress that they cause.

7.5 Risk and protective factors for young children's mental health problems

Children's mental health problems are not the product of simple chains of causality. Problems that appear similar may have arisen for very different reasons in different children. In children whose main problem is aggressive behaviour, for example, this may have a number of different causes. For some, their aggression may be linked to their individual characteristics. Children with delayed language development may hit out because their limited powers of communication leave them frustrated. For other children, family issues may be more important. Domestic violence within the family may be echoed by aggression in the children. Yet for others, social issues may have a significant impact. In families where unemployment, poor housing, and financial difficulties combine to preoccupy the adults, there may be little time and energy available for appropriate parenting. For many children with mental health problems, individual, family and social risk factors such as these will interact. In the same way that there is little specificity linking children's mental health problems with single causative factors, in general, there is also a lack of specificity between particular risk factors and particular mental health problems in children.

Single risk factors are less powerfully correlated with mental disorder in children than multiple risk factors. Having a single risk factor very slightly increases the risk of having a disorder, but with two or more risk factors, the risk of negative outcomes increases considerably.

In conceptualising causation in individual cases, it is useful to think of a balance between risk factors and protective factors. Protective factors can reduce the adverse impact of risk factors. A single mother with a low income, for example, may find the support of her extended family helps her cope with her new baby, and protects her from the normal ups and downs of new motherhood becoming chronically problematic. **Figure 7.1** shows some of the risk and protective factors that influence children's mental health.

Figure 7.1: Risk and protective factors that influence children's mental health

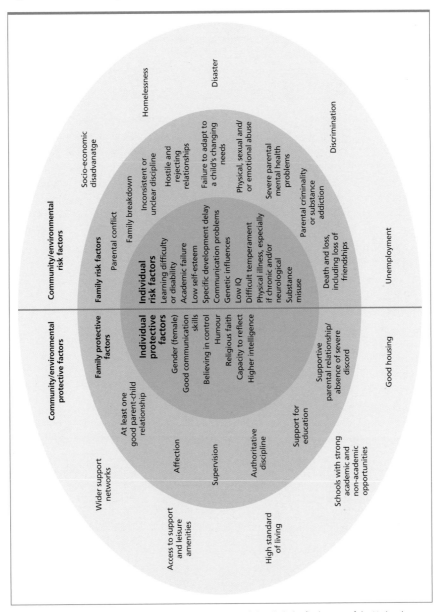

Source: Department of Health (2008) *Children and young people in mind: the final report of the National CAMHS Review*. London: Department of Health. Reproduced with permission from the Department of Health.

Interventions need to focus both on reducing risk factors and on increasing resilience. Resilience is an individual's tendency to cope with stress and adversity. Resilience can be promoted at individual, family and community levels by reducing exposure to risks and adversity, boosting the child's individual resources and the assets in their lives, and mobilising innate adaptational capabilities.

7.6   Individual risk factors
Genetic factors
The old debate over whether particular mental health problems arise because of nature (genetics) or nurture (environment) has been replaced by a much more sophisticated appreciation that genes and environment act in a way that is mutually interlinked. A child's genetic inheritance may contribute a vulnerability that, in combination with environmental adversity, can result in mental health problems. Replicated findings have shown that those children who have a genetic variant which produces lower levels of monoamine oxidase A (MAOA) enzyme have higher rates of conduct disorder, antisocial personality, and criminality when exposed to physical maltreatment.[17] Other children, however, who also have lower levels of MAOA enzyme but who are not exposed to physical maltreatment, do not have higher rates of these problems in later life.[17] The gene variant producing lower levels of MAOA is only a vulnerability factor for adverse outcomes if children with this variant are also exposed to physical maltreatment. In a similar way, children with other genetic variants, in combination with adverse environmental conditions, are predisposed to later depression and suicide.

The idea that children are genetically predisposed to be more or less vulnerable to environmental stressors has been expanded to suggest that children are genetically predisposed to be more or less sensitive to environmental influence, both good and bad. This has been characterised in terms of 'daffodil' children who are genetically resilient in the face of adversity, and 'orchid' children who are genetically vulnerable to environmental adversity but also respond exceptionally well to positive aspects of their environment. One Dutch study involved an intervention to promote parental sensitivity in toddlers with high levels of behaviour problems, and studied the relative responsiveness to the intervention in children with different genetic susceptibility to behaviour problems.[18] The group of children with the high-risk genetic variant, who would be most vulnerable to adverse circumstances, in fact responded most positively to the supportive intervention.

In the future, interventions may be tailored to the specific genetic profile of individual children, but in the meantime, reducing adverse environments and promoting high-quality parenting are likely to reduce the numbers of children whose genetic vulnerabilities manifest in later mental health problems or other negative outcomes.

Disability

Psychiatric disorders are two to four times as common in children with learning disabilities, with 30 to 50 per cent of them having a diagnosable mental disorder. Autism and ADHD are more common in children with learning disabilities than in children without learning disabilities. Psychiatric disorders, however, may be difficult to detect in children who have reduced verbal communication, and professionals may find it hard to distinguish between the features of the learning disability and the features of the mental disorder.

Children with physical disabilities are also at increased risk of psychiatric disorders, particularly where their disability involves brain damage. **Table 7.1** shows relevant results from an epidemiological study of 10 and 11 year olds.

Table 7.1: Increased risk of psychiatric disorders in children with physical disabilities – results from an epidemiological study of 10 to 11 year olds

Children with:	% with psychiatric disorder
• no physical disorder	7
• physical disorder not affecting the brain	12
• idiopathic epilepsy	29
• cerebral palsy and allied disorders IQ>70	44

Source: Goodman R & Scott S (1997) *Child psychiatry*. Oxford: Blackwell. Reproduced with the permission of Wiley-Blackwell.

Other disabilities in children have also been shown to be associated with increased rates of psychiatric disturbance, including severe hearing loss and marked language delay or impairment. The increased rates of mental health problems in children with disabilities is in some cases related to brain damage, and in others is linked to the psychosocial disadvantages experienced by some children with disability. Many children will have both a biological and psychosocial vulnerability to mental health problems. For families, it is often the behaviour problems, like chronically disturbed sleep or aggressive outbursts, which are the hardest aspects of their child's problems to deal with.

The families of the babies which have disabilities evident at birth, and also those whose children's disabilities become apparent at a later stage, need a comprehensive range of support, which may involve health, education, social and voluntary services. Improving the early detection of emotional and behavioural problems in children with disability and the effective management of these problems involves developing greater awareness of good practice and better coordination of services.

Individual resilience

Some individual characteristics promote resilience in children. These include intrinsic qualities such as easy temperament or high IQ.[19] Other individual attributes such as secure attachments, positive self-image, effective interpersonal skills, cognitive skills and the development of special talents, can be nurtured through good parenting and high-quality pre-school provision.

7.7   Family risk and protective factors

Family size

Children from larger families are at increased risk of mental health problems, with 13 per cent and 18 per cent of four- or five-children households respectively having mental health problems, in comparison with 8 per cent of two-children households.[20] Children from large families are twice as likely to develop conduct disorder and become delinquent than children from smaller families. Such children are also more likely to have delayed language development, lower verbal intelligence and lower reading attainment, and to experience less parental supervision and more sibling aggression, all of which may contribute to their behaviour problems.

Family structure

The Millenium Cohort study has tracked almost 15,500 UK children born in the year 2000 and has examined family structure and its influence on emotional and behavioural problems at the age of five years. Children either born to mothers in cohabiting relationships where the parents had separated, or born to solo mothers who had not married the natural father, had three times as many behaviour problems in comparison to children born in stable married families.[21] Taking into account maternal depression and family poverty reduced the difference in the level of behaviour problems between the different types of family structure, but it remained statistically significant.[21] Similar levels of emotional problems were found across all types of family structure, once maternal depression and differences in income were taken into account. Children raised in families where the parents are lesbian or gay are not at increased risk of emotional or behavioural problems.

7.8   Parental risk factors

Parental mental ill-health

Parental mental disorder is associated with increased rates of mental disorder in children.[22] This is often assumed to be because the parent's mental disorder disrupts effective parenting, but may also be because of a shared genetic vulnerability between parent and child, or because the child is exposed to many other environmental adversities such as poverty, poor housing and isolation, which are often features of life for those with chronic mental illness. The types of disorder that children develop do not correspond exactly to those experienced by their parents, though there is a tendency for young children of depressed mothers to show apparent symptoms of depression, and an association between personality disorder in a parent and conduct disorder in children. Parents with mental illnesses may be consistently or periodically affected, and their parenting can be severely or only mildly affected.[23] Where they are unable to parent effectively, the effect on their children can be buffered by the presence of another adult, or the other parent, who can take on the main caregiving role as necessary, ideally with minimum disruption to the children's normal routines.

For children aged 0 to five years, one important category of parental mental illness that has been the subject of much research is postnatal depression. This affects approximately 10 per cent of mothers. Many mothers with postnatal depression find it difficult to provide sensitive and responsive care for their infants, and observational studies have shown behavioural, emotional and cognitive changes in the infants of these mothers.

Fathers may also experience some degree of depression after the birth of a child, and this has been shown to be associated with adverse emotional and behavioural outcomes in their children at the ages of three to five years, and an increased risk of conduct problems in boys.

Parents who abuse drugs or alcohol

It is estimated that there are between 200,000 and 300,000 children in England and Wales where one or both parents have serious drug problems, and between 780,000 and 1.3 million children affected by parental alcohol problems. Drugs and alcohol can adversely affect the developing fetus.[24] In 2007, the BMA published a guide for healthcare professionals on fetal alcohol spectrum disorders (FASD).[24] The guide considered the adverse health impacts of alcohol consumption during pregnancy and the particular problem of FASD. The child's parenting and home situation may also be unstable and chaotic, leaving younger children particularly vulnerable.[25] Parental abuse of drugs or alcohol is associated with higher levels of behavioural and emotional problems in children.

Parental conflict, separation and divorce

Children are at an increased risk of mental health problems where there is parental disharmony and also where parents divorce or separate, but there is considerable variation in how different children react. Divorce or separation is also often accompanied by conflict and by a reduction in economic security, and the impact of these different stressors on children's lives can be hard to disentangle. Each family situation is different and no universal recommendation can be made about whether parents in conflict should stay together or split up. Immediately after divorce or separation, children's levels of distress increase, but after a while, most children adjust to the new circumstances, and may be less stressed than children whose parents remain together in a high-conflict situation. For families facing divorce or separation, the young children will benefit from minimal disruptions to their usual routine, a simple explanation of what is happening, and reassurance that it is not their fault.

Domestic violence

Exposure to domestic violence increases the risk of children developing emotional and behavioural problems.[26] Young children in particular are dependent on their parents to provide safety and security, and this is fundamentally undermined by violence in the home. Infants and young children exposed to domestic violence may be excessively irritable or distressed, regress in their language development or toilet training and have sleep disturbances or separation anxiety. Parents often underestimate the impact of any violence on the children, but a survey has found that in 90 per cent of domestic violence incidents children are in the same room or the next room. Forty to 60 per cent of children exposed to domestic violence also experience direct emotional, physical or sexual abuse themselves. Witnessing or experiencing violence as a child is associated with greater use or tolerance of violence as an adult, with an intergenerational transmission rate of about 30 per cent. The BMA's 2007 report *Domestic abuse* examines how children who are exposed to violence in the home may suffer a range of severe and lasting effects.[27] The BMA's report is intended to lead the way in encouraging the healthcare professions to raise awareness of the problem and makes recommendations for tackling domestic abuse.

Parent-child interactions

It is often the quality of parenting and parent–child interactions in a family, as they tackle the normal or exceptional problems of their child's development, which differentiates between a vulnerable child who develops mental health problems and a vulnerable child who achieves his or her potential. A family's capacity to parent effectively will be intimately connected to the levels of support and stress they experience. How parents raise their children is influenced not only by how they were raised themselves and who they become, but also by the everyday circumstances of their lives, and the resources to which they have access. Statutory and voluntary services can play an important role in helping parents provide a nurturing environment for their children.

Antenatal effects

Parenting begins before birth and the developing fetus can be affected by smoking, drugs (including alcohol), poor nutrition and excessive maternal stress or anxiety.[25,28] Smoking in pregnancy increases the risk of low birth weight, with its attendant problems. In 2004, the BMA published a guide for healthcare professionals on the impact of smoking on sexual, reproductive and child health in the UK.[29] The report considered active and passive smoking by both men and women, and summarises the impact on sexual health, conception and pregnancy, as well as effects on the reproductive system. If the developing fetus is regularly exposed to heroin, cocaine or large amounts of alcohol, a variety of adverse effects have been reported, including short and long-term difficulties with modulating arousal, activity level and attention. These deficits can make parenting difficult, and where the parent is still involved in substance misuse, they may already have reduced resources for the task of parenting. Pregnancy may, however, act as a trigger for behavioural change, inspired by concern for the developing fetus. Advice, sensitively given, may help pregnant mothers reduce their alcohol intake, stop smoking, and stop using other drugs.

Excessive maternal stress and anxiety have also been shown to be linked with emotional and behavioural problems in the fetus, with the children of the most anxious 15 per cent of mothers having double the risk of emotional or behavioural problems compared with the children of the less anxious mothers. From birth onwards, parents develop a repertoire of practical parenting skills, derived from their own experience of being parented, advice from kin and community networks, and social and cultural norms.

Parent-infant interaction and attachment patterns

The quality of parents' interaction with their babies and young children is known to influence children's expectations about relationships not only during childhood but also in later years.[30] Having parents who can sensitively discern and respond to their baby's communications and help the baby regulate their emotional states will help the baby develop the capacity to recognise their own emotions and a sense that intimate relationships can be a source of comfort at times of stress. Research in neurobiology and neurophysiology is making links between babies' physiological states and neurobiological development and the quality of the caregiving context in which they are growing up, and there are some indications that abusive interactions can have long-lasting physiological or neuroanatomical effects on the child's developing brain.

A parent's capacity to respond to their child, particularly when the child is fearful or distressed, will inform the quality of the attachment that the child forms with them.[31] This attachment relationship forms a blueprint for later intimate relationships.[31] Attachment theory, as proposed by Bowlby and modified since, has stimulated an extensive body of research, much of which has implications for young children's mental health.[32] Bowlby's clear exposition of the importance of facilitating young children's developing attachments to their main caregivers has underpinned many important developments in childcare practice for those aged 0 to five years. Young children are no longer admitted to hospitals without their parents. Nurseries and daycare facilities (in principle at least) use key-workers with whom children are encouraged to develop special relationships, and adoptions are, where possible, completed while children are young.

Children's attachments can be classified in four ways; secure, insecure avoidant, insecure ambivalent and disorganised, and a child may have a different attachment pattern with each of their parents. Securely attached infants perceive their caregiver as a reliable source of comfort and safety in stressful situations, whereas infants with insecure or disorganised attachments do not, and use various different strategies to manage their distress on their own. Children with insecure avoidant attachments appear to be undisturbed by stressful events like separation from their parent, but in fact heart rate monitoring would show that they are physiologically highly stressed.[31] Children with insecure ambivalent attachment are intensely distressed by stressful situations but find it difficult to be soothed by their parent.[31] Children with disorganised attachments do not have a coherent attachment strategy but may use a mixture of proximity seeking, avoidance and resistance, or appear fearful of their carer.

Insecure attachments are associated with increased rates of emotional and behavioural problems especially in families facing other adversities, whereas secure attachments serve a protective function. Children classified as having disorganised attachments often come from families which face marked socioeconomic adversities, or they are often the victims of maltreatment. These children are at greatly increased risk of having pre-school behaviour problems, though it is likely that their disorganised attachment status is only one element in an array of risk factors to which they have been exposed.

There is evidence that in 70 per cent of cases, infants will develop the same pattern of attachment towards their parent as their parent has towards their own attachment figures, suggesting that ways of responding at times of stress are passed unconsciously from generation to generation. Interventions designed to reduce insecure and disorganised attachments and increase attachment security are focused on increasing parents' understanding of children's emotional states and attachment needs and often on helping parents develop a new perspective on their own attachment history.

Parenting style
Research into parenting has looked at what sorts of parenting style is most effective in promoting children's emotional wellbeing. One model developed by Maccoby and Martin identified four styles with different outcomes for the future mental health and functioning of children along two different dimensions, level of demand/control versus level of acceptance/rejection.[33]

1. Authoritarian parenting
Children growing up in authoritarian families, with high levels of demand and control but relatively low levels of warmth or acceptance, tend to be less socially skilled, do not internalise standards of good behaviour and have lower self-esteem. Some of these children may appear subdued; others may show high aggressiveness or other indications of being out of control.

2. Permissive parenting
Children growing up with indulgent or permissive parents, who are warm but provide low levels of demand and control, also show some negative outcomes, and by adolescence tend to be more aggressive, immature, irresponsible and lacking in independence.

3. Neglecting parenting
Neglecting parents provide neither warmth and acceptance nor adequate demand and control. Their children tend to show disturbances in their relationships with peers and with adults. At adolescence, youngsters from neglecting families are more impulsive and antisocial, less competent with their peers, and much less achievement oriented in school.[34]

4. Authoritative parenting
These parents provide high levels of both control and warmth, setting clear limits but also responding to the child's individual needs. Their children typically show higher self-esteem, and are more independent, are more likely to comply with parental requests, and may show more altruistic behaviour as well. They are self-confident and achieve greater educational success.

The limitation of this type of classificatory approach to parenting is that it can appear to play down the impact of contextual and child factors. It is important to stress that parent-child relationships are not simply the result of the adult's parenting style. Children with difficult temperaments will tend to elicit authoritarian parenting, while children with easier temperaments will be easier to parent in an authoritative way. In some stressful circumstances, parenting is almost inevitably disrupted. There is plenty of evidence, however, that parents who are warm and affectionate, in the context of clear, firm limit-setting, will have a positive impact on their children's mental health, and that authoritative parenting can mitigate the adverse effects of other stressors.[35] These general principles are the basis for a wide variety of parent education initiatives.

Physical punishment
There is considerable debate about the effectiveness and longer-term impact of physically punishing children. The legal framework in the UK permits parents to smack children as long as it does not leave a mark, but there is widespread opposition to this policy, with campaign groups demanding that the UK follow the Swedish example and ban all physical chastisement of children. Smacking is not more effective than non-physical forms of discipline, and it demonstrates to children that problems can be solved by physical aggression rather than in non-violent ways (see **Chapter 5** for a more detailed discussion on smacking).[36]

Child maltreatment
Physical abuse, sexual abuse, emotional abuse and neglect will often cause behavioural and emotional disturbances in babies and young children, as well as mental health problems and other adverse outcomes in adolescence and adult life. Young children who are being or have been emotionally abused, may have a whole range of mental health problems, including defiance and aggression, withdrawal, lack of interest in learning and disturbed relationships with adults.[37] Sexually abused young children may

become involved in sexually explicit play with their friends or be sexually provocative with adults. Many, but not all, abused children will have longer-term physical and mental health problems.[38] A proportion (around 30%) of adults abused as children will go on to abuse their own children. The focus of child protection must not only be on identification of existing abuse, but also on family support to reduce the likelihood of abuse occurring in the first place. See **Chapter 5** for further, more detailed, discussions on child maltreatment.

7.9   Non-parental care
Child care
For many parents, finding child care while they work is a necessity. This may be provided in various ways within and outside the home, such as by members of the extended family, childminders, nurseries, nannies and au pairs. Research into the effects of non-parental daycare on babies and young children has produced mixed results. High-quality early intervention studies have shown clear social, cognitive and academic benefits for economically disadvantaged children. An American longitudinal study looking at the impact of different types of early child care, found that higher-quality care was associated with small but significant improvements in cognitive and academic performance.[39] Longer hours of care, especially in the first year of life and in daycare centres rather than with childminders, was associated with later higher rates of problem behaviours.

Good-quality daycare is characterised by high staff–child ratios, individualised rather than institutionalised care, effective key-worker systems, good staff-parent communication, emotionally warm interaction that is sensitive to the child's verbal and non-verbal signals and cues, and the provision of varied and stimulating activities within a structured day. Similar features can be used to evaluate the quality of other non-parental care arrangements such as childminders or nannies. Public health guidance on the promotion of cognitive, social and emotional development of vulnerable children through early education and childcare is currently being developed by NICE.

Fostering and adoption
For adults who were fostered long term, adopted, or brought up in an institution, following neglect or abuse from their birth parent, the personal and social outcomes are most favourable among those who were adopted and least favourable among those brought up in institutions, with those in long-term fostering in an intermediate position. All these groups of children are at increased risk of mental health problems. A large 2003 English survey of children aged five to 10 years in local authority care, found 42 per cent had a mental disorder, compared to 8 per cent of children living in private households. The widespread belief that early adoption is much more likely to be successful, because the child will benefit from stable early relationships with the adoptive parents, remains broadly true, but research shows that later adoptions can also work well. There is a trend to place children, where possible, with extended family, and

also for open adoptions, with contact between the adoptive and biological families.[40] The psychological impact of open adoption has yet to be fully researched and the debate about cross-cultural adoption continues. Fostering and adoption are more likely to work for the mutual benefit of carers and children, where care is taken in establishing the initial placements, and the families have specialised support and help available when they need it.[40]

Those children who have typically spent their early years in poor-quality institutional care will tend to have long-term problems with social functioning, even when adopted into more favourable circumstances, though adoption is likely to be the best available alternative for them.

7.10   Social risk and protective factors
Socioeconomic disadvantage
Poverty is associated with a higher risk of both physical and mental illness across the lifespan, and also with premature death. Children in the poorest households are three times more likely to have a mental illness than children in the best off households. Conduct disorder (severe behaviour problems) is three to four times more common in poor families from poor neighbourhoods. Social class differences in rates of behaviour problems emerge early and are well established by the age of three years. It has been suggested that it may be the extremes of inequality in British society and the impact of social exclusion rather than just having a low income in itself which has a particularly negative effect on families and children. Poverty is usually only one of many challenges facing disadvantaged families, who may also have to cope with poor housing or homelessness, unsafe environments, inadequate local amenities and poor nutrition. How well a family manages to function, in the face of chronically debilitating problems like these, will influence how far socioeconomic adversity impacts on their children's mental health. These chronic adversities are characteristically (but not exclusively) associated with inner-city life. Black and minority ethnic families and children may experience similar complex constellations of disadvantage and racism, often compounded by poor access to culturally sensitive services.[41] Consequent reluctance to access services may result in any mental health issues becoming more severe before assessment and support can be provided. Refugees, with the additional psychological stress of an enforced move to a unfamiliar society, and an uncertain future, are also likely to live in conditions of multiple adversity, with a consequent impact on their children's mental health. In some families, multiple stresses and low income may be reflected in the children developing behavioural and emotional problems.[42]

Housing and homelessness
There is evidence that inadequate housing is associated with an adverse effect on children's mental health.[43] Overcrowding has been identified as a variable which, alongside other risk factors, is associated with increased rates of psychiatric disorder in

children. Homeless families have also been identified as a group with particular mental health needs that are often unmet. A longitudinal study of homeless families found high levels of mental health problems in homeless children and their mothers, which persisted in a substantial minority after re-housing (for further details on the relationship between housing and child health see **Chapter 3**).

Social isolation and social support

The birth of a baby, especially a first child, involves a considerable number of social and psychological adjustments on the part of both parents. This transition can be facilitated by the support of kin and community networks, which can have a protective effect.

Developing a social support structure, often among parents themselves, or using volunteers, is a prominent feature of many initiatives intended to improve parenting skills and children's health. But it is important to remember that parents are active participants in the creation of their own social environments, and those parents most likely to abuse or neglect their children may be least likely to develop and utilise community support networks. These parents will need long-term multidisciplinary professional support to develop and maintain their parenting skills. Short-term interventions at key times with vulnerable groups can also be worthwhile. A follow-up study of mothers at high risk for low birthweight babies, who had had a programme of social support in pregnancy, found at follow-up when the children were aged seven years, that there were fewer behaviour problems among the children and less anxiety among the mothers in the intervention group.

7.11 Interventions to reduce mental health problems

The importance of intervening early with families to promote mental health and wellbeing is widely recognised, in order to meet young children's mental health needs, minimise risk factors and set them on successful developmental trajectories. Too often, disadvantage and parental problems impact on young children's emotional development and mental wellbeing with potentially lifelong consequences, as one negative experience paves the way for another. These disadvantaged children then become the parents of the next generation, and may reproduce their own poor experiences of parenting with their own children. Much is known about the risk factors in children, families and the environment that lead to subsequent mental health problems and other poor outcomes. The complex interaction of these risk factors can be mitigated by integrated interventions, which have both mental health benefits and demonstrable longer-term economic benefits, as the financial burden on society of later mental health and social problems is reduced. The benefits of investing to interrupt cycles of disadvantage are recognised across the political spectrum, yet early intervention initiatives are not yet universally in place.

Frameworks

Health services and social services in the UK use two similar but not identical frameworks to organise their work in promoting young children's mental health. The two frameworks are described in **Boxes 7.1** and **7.2**.

Box 7.1: Four-tier framework for CAMHS

The majority of children with emotional and behavioural problems will receive interventions at tier one or two.

Tier one: Primary or direct contact services

Workers in this tier include GPs, health visitors, voluntary sector workers, social workers, nursery workers, etc. These workers influence children's mental health as an aspect of, rather than the primary purpose of their work. They may be involved in aspects of mental health promotion, explicitly or otherwise, and are well placed to identify and help many children with mental health problems, or their families, without referring them to specialist services. They can be supported in doing this more effectively through training and supervision.

Tier two: Interventions offered by individual specialist child and adolescent mental health professionals

In this tier, individual professionals with specialist mental health training may work directly with young children and their families, or supervise and train those in tier one. These individuals may have a variety of professional qualifications in, for example, psychology, psychiatry, social work, and psychotherapy. A community psychiatric nurse or a psychotherapist offering supervision to health visitors and children's centre staff, a psychiatrist providing regular consultation in a special needs nursery, or a clinical psychologist running a clinic for sleep and behaviour problems are examples of ways in which tier two professionals might be involved in promoting mental health in 0 to five year olds. Children's primary mental health workers with a specific remit to provide consultations and outreach work in tier one are working in many parts of the UK. Psychologists working in child development clinics also provide a specialist service at this level for young children, especially those with developmental delay and associated behavioural problems. An adult psychiatrist may provide a perinatal service identifying and treating mothers with perinatal mental health problems.

Tier three: Interventions offered by teams of staff from specialist CAMHS
Professionals in this tier may have similar backgrounds to those in tier two, but work in coordinated multidisciplinary teams with referred families, rather than as lone professionals. They offer integrated multidisciplinary assessment and management. Young children with severe behaviour problems or attachment issues may be assessed and treated in tier three settings. Unless particular teams have a special interest relating to younger children and their families, much work at tier three may be focused on school-age children and adolescents.

Tier four: Very specialised interventions and care
Work in this tier involves multidisciplinary teams treating highly specific and complex problems, including, for example, services for children with severe eating disorders, or the assessment and treatment of young children with complex presentations following abuse. For older children and adolescents, tier four interventions include inpatient and day patient provision.

This tiered framework described in **Box 7.1** is classified according to the training and configuration of the professionals providing the service, linking to the complexity of need in the children. Within children's services more widely, interventions are classified on a spectrum, based on the complexity of the child's needs, as presented in **Box 7.2**.

Box 7.2: Classification of children's services
Universal services work with all children and young people. They promote and support mental health and psychological wellbeing through the environment they create and the relationships they have with children and young people. They will be equivalent to tier one services in the CAMHS framework.

Targeted services work with children and young people with specific needs – for example, learning difficulties or disabilities, school attendance problems, family difficulties, physical illness or behaviour difficulties. Child and adolescent mental health professionals working at tier two work with targeted groups such as children in a school who have emotional or behavioural problems. Some CAMHS multidisciplinary tier three teams will also work at a targeted level with children with more complex specific needs such as looked after children.

Specialist services work with children with complex, severe or persistent needs. This includes children and young people in tier three and four CAMHS services, as well as those in specialist educational settings, care homes intensive foster care and secure settings.

Policy context

In the first few years of the 21st century, the emotional wellbeing and mental health of young children was addressed within a comprehensive policy context set out within the NSF for Children, Young People and Maternity Services and the ECM Framework underpinning the Children's Act of 2004. Emotional wellbeing and mental health was seen as just one aspect of promoting children's healthy development and positive contribution to society. The emphasis throughout was on holistic support for children's needs and the needs of their families, provided by agencies and services working together in an integrated way. This theme was developed by the CAMHS review of 2008, which underlined the need for flexible joined-up working between agencies, adequate training on mental health and emotional wellbeing for all staff working with children, plus the availability of good-quality information on mental health and psychological wellbeing for children, young people and their carers.[44] The Families at Risk review in 2008, which underpinned the Think Family strategy,[45] focused on the need for integrated interagency interventions for families with multiple problems and adversities, in order to break the cross-generational cycle of disadvantage, which was estimated to affect about 140,000 of the 13.8 million families in England.

Following a change of Government in May 2010, the new mental health strategy,[46] applicable across the lifespan, has focused on choice for service users, increased use of outcome measures, and increased local control of public finance. At the end of 2011, a Troubled Families Unit was established within the Department of Communities and Local Government, to focus on 120,000 families with multiple problems (whose children are at increased risk of emotional and behavioural problems and other adverse outcomes). The plan is for this to fund 40 per cent of local authorities' costs in intervening intensively with these families, payable only once certain defined positive outcomes have been achieved. The Government also plans to provide nursery places for 260,000 disadvantaged two year olds.

Although early intervention is recognised as important, widespread public spending cuts have severely curtailed the early intervention services available for children and families. A 2011 NSPCC review, found predicted cuts in children's social care spending averaging 24 per cent between 2010/11 and 2011/12, with seven councils planning to cut children's social care budgets by 40 per cent.

Information sources

Families need to be able to access reliable information about children's emotional wellbeing or mental health problems, and this need is more pressing as support services are being cut. Many families, children and young people will access information and support from friends or family and via the internet. Young Minds and the Royal College of Psychiatrists are examples of organisations with websites that provide information on mental health issues for parents and young people; the Understanding Childhood website provides downloadable information sheets on the problems of young children in particular. Reality TV focusing on the management of behaviour problems is a source of information for many parents. Health visitors will provide basic information for all new parents, and identify those who may need more intensive interventions and support.

Those working with babies and young children also need access to information about best practice in order to provide quality services. The Early Years Foundation Stage Framework provides standards which providers of education and care to children aged 0 to five years are expected to follow. The importance of developing a positive sense of self, good social relationships and a basic understanding of emotions is recognised as an essential foundation for emotional wellbeing and successful learning. Other useful sources of information for staff working with young children include websites such as the Centre for Excellence and Outcomes in Children and Young People's Services (C4EO), which draw together research and best practice examples from statutory and voluntary sector service providers.

Service provision

Interventions to promote young children's mental health are delivered by a range of agencies, including health services, social services, education services and the voluntary sector. These are integrated to varying extents in different parts of the UK. In the first decade of the 21st century, some local authorities developed pooled budgets and integrated management systems to develop early intervention programmes in their localities, but this is not universal. Nottingham has a strategic planning partnership bringing together public, private, community and voluntary sector agencies, committed to developing a comprehensive early intervention programme. This involves 16 different but complementary early intervention projects and programmes at antenatal, perinatal, early years and school age stages of the life-cycle, targeted at those individuals and families who are very likely to have difficulties without effective interventions. Some of these programmes and projects are among those described in the follow paragraphs.

Sure Start and children's centres

The Sure Start programme, launched in 1998, at a cost of £500 million, was a 10 year anti-poverty programme which targeted all families with a child under four years living in more than 500 of the most disadvantaged communities in the UK.[47] It was an innovative programme, in that it aimed to have a beneficial impact on a whole area, not on a smaller group of targeted individuals. Sure Start Local Programmes (SSLPs) were expected to provide five core services: outreach and home visiting; support for families and parents; good quality play/early learning/childcare; healthcare for children and parents; and support for children (and their parents) with additional needs and disabilities. These programmes were given relative freedom in how they delivered these services and met the limited targets set by the Government.

The SSLPs that were more successful were those with better leadership and clearer objectives, where there was a specific focus on identifying and involving the most disadvantaged families. Because of the diversity of provision in local Sure Start programmes, and an expansion and change in the programme when SSLPs were changed into Children's Centres in 2006, research into the outcomes of Sure Start has been extremely complicated. The National Evaluation of Sure Start Team has been following up children and families living in SSLP areas and comparing them with similar children and families being followed up in the Millenium Cohort Study who do not live in SSLP areas.

Positive findings in the 2010 evaluation (of five year olds), show that parents in SSLP areas had greater life satisfaction, engaged in less harsh discipline, and provided a less chaotic and more cognitively stimulating home environment. More of the parents in SSLP areas who had been out of work when their children were aged three years were in work once their children were five years, in comparison with similar families from non-SSLP areas. Although these positive findings might be expected to promote emotional wellbeing and mental health for young children in areas where there were SSLPs, the evaluation did not find any reduction in children's behaviour problems. Another issue which was problematic in some SSLP areas was ensuring that the families who could most benefit from Sure Start services received a service. There is a need for specifically targeted services for groups with particular needs, like teenage parents or parents with significant mental health problems alongside universal or area-based services like Sure Start (for further details on child poverty and Sure Start schemes see **Chapter 3**).

Perinatal/infant mental health services
Early identification and treatment of mothers with postnatal depression or other postnatal mental health problems is likely to ameliorate the negative impact on their child's development, though further research is needed in this area.[48] Perinatal services are patchy across the UK, with some areas served by multiagency perinatal networks including midwives, health visitors, adult psychiatrists, social workers and child and adolescent mental health workers, but many providing partial services in a much less integrated way. Parents from black and minority ethnic backgrounds may have particular difficulties accessing support and treatment.

Support for families with infants and toddlers
All children born in the UK have a health visitor allocated at birth, who is well placed to identify those families that will need targeted support to mitigate risk factors and promote emotional wellbeing. Health visitors are in a position to identify parents with postnatal depression or other problems and help them seek treatment, and to advise over any difficulties, such as with feeding, sleeping and behaviour. There are a number of programmes in use in certain parts of the country to provide a structured framework for additional support, such as the Solihull Approach, which combines psychotherapeutic

and behavioural concepts and encourages parents to contain and reflect on their own and their babies' emotions, respond sensitively to their babies' communications, and use behavioural techniques to shape their babies' behaviour.

Family Nurse Partnerships

The FNP Programme is a Government funded programme involving two years of regular structured home visiting for first-time teenage mothers during pregnancy and the child's infancy. Family nurses, who may have a midwifery or health visiting background, build supportive relationships with the mothers and help them to adopt healthier lifestyles, care for their babies well, and promote secure attachments. The programme is running in over 50 areas in the UK and due to expand to offer 13,000 places by 2015. The programme is based on the NFP programme which originated in the USA. The NFP has been extensively evaluated and has been shown to have a number of positive benefits, including reduced levels of child abuse and better emotional and language development, plus fewer subsequent pregnancies and less reliance on benefits. The programme is subject to rigorous evaluation in the UK, with initially promising results. A randomised controlled trial is due to report in 2013. If the US findings are replicated, this programme has the potential to have a beneficial impact on the emotional wellbeing of this particular high-risk group of children (see **Chapter 3** for further details on the FNP programme).

Parenting programmes

After thorough review of the evidence, the NICE guidance recommended that structured parenting programmes should be offered to parents of children aged 12 years or under whose children have severe behaviour problems, and also offered as first-line treatment in ADHD.[49,50] The aim of these programmes is to support parents in relating to their children in ways that promote a warm and nurturing relationship, with appropriate limit setting, and help parents avoid negative interactions with their children. The guidance emphasises that these programmes should be delivered by experienced facilitators who adhere to a specific programme whose efficacy has been demonstrated through randomised controlled trials. The programmes should be based on social learning theory and aim to enhance parent-child relationships, with role-play and homework tasks to help the parents develop confidence and learn new skills. There is not much research into the effectiveness of parenting programmes where children are under three years of age, but the research that exists suggests that these programmes improve the emotional and behavioural adjustment of younger children at least in the short term.[5]

One widely used and well-evaluated structured group-based parenting intervention is the Incredible Years series of parenting programmes.[51] The original programmes focused on children aged three to 12 years, but programmes for parents of babies and toddlers are now also available. The programmes involve looking at video examples of parent-child interactions as a basis for discussion and role-play.

Another well-evaluated intervention is The Triple P Positive Parenting Programme.[52] This provides a multilevel framework that allows parents to access different types and intensities of assistance in a stepped approach. Level one involves dissemination of media messages about positive parenting. Levels two and three involve short interventions in primary care, focused on the management of specific problem behaviours. Level four involves more extensive parenting programmes which cover a range of problem behaviours, delivered to individuals or in groups, often with telephone support. Level five programmes are intended for families where parental problems such as depression also need to be addressed. The Pathway programme is designed for parents at risk of maltreating their children, and includes sessions on anger management, and a focus on changing any negative attributions that parents may have about their children.

Children and Young People's Improving Access to Psychological Therapies (IAPT) is a Government-funded project that is providing additional training across the UK in evidence-based interventions, including the delivery of structured parenting programmes for parents of three to 10 year olds. Although structured parenting programmes are available in many parts of the UK, they are not universally available, and not all the parents who could benefit are able to access them.

Video interaction guidance
All evidence-based parenting programmes emphasise the need to build and maintain a warm and nurturing relationship between parent and child, so that the child feels recognised as an individual, loved and supported. This is the basis on which limit setting and discipline can then be established. Where there are tensions or problems in the parent-infant or parent-child relationship, video-based interventions like video interaction guidance can enhance parental ability to perceive and respond to the child's communications in an attuned and sensitive way. This delicate communicative dance is promoted by filming the parent and child together in an enjoyable activity and then reviewing clips of attuned interaction with the parent to develop their skills and confidence in building a positive relationship with their child. Research has found that video-feedback techniques, especially where the focus is on reinforcing and extending sensitive interactions, has a positive effect on parenting skills and parental attitudes towards the child, as well as beneficial effects on the child's development.[53]

7.12   Current situation and future prospects
Although a great deal is now known about the causes of emotional and behavioural problems in young children, and how they can be ameliorated, the availability and accessibility of effective interventions remains very patchy in the UK. After almost a decade of increased funding and more integrated development of children's services, the recession has brought widespread cuts, alongside increasing poverty and family stress. Despite some new initiatives in early intervention and some limited funding for interagency work focused on families with multiple problems, in general young children

and their families will have more challenges to their emotional wellbeing and less support available than in recent years. Although there is good evidence that early intervention can reduce levels of emotional and behavioural problems and prevent later problems that are both distressing and expensive to manage, the political will to fund a sustained and comprehensive programme of early intervention is not currently evident. Radical changes to the commissioning of children's services and increased emphasis on competition between providers will make the provision of coherent interagency networks of services for families with young children increasingly difficult to provide. The impact of these enormous organisational upheavals alongside an expectation to make financial savings will fall disproportionately on the most disadvantaged children and families. There is a risk that the limited funding available will increasingly be diverted from early intervention programmes into more pressing crisis management. Although the argument for the benefits of early intervention to promote young children's emotional wellbeing has been convincingly made, it has not yet been won. More needs to be done to persuade the public and the Government that young children with emotional and behavioural problems deserve to receive adequate and timely support and assistance. This is needed not only to alleviate their distress, but also to minimise the adverse impact on their subsequent development. The early years provide a unique opportunity to promote young children's resilience and wellbeing, reduce the potential for later mental health problems, and minimise the development of entrenched negative behaviours and their subsequent costs to society. It is crucial that this opportunity is not missed.

7.13   Recommendations

- Severe adversities and maltreatment in infancy and the early years can have a lifelong impact on a child's brain development, physiological reactions to stress and later mental and physical health. Devoting resources to supporting families with young children can potentially prevent a proportion of these adverse outcomes, with benefits both for the individual children and in avoiding later financial and other costs for society.
- Many of the risk factors for mental health problems in children are often found in association with each other. Poverty, poor housing, domestic violence, parental mental ill health and drug abuse may cluster together in families, and have a negative effect on children that is multiplicative rather than additive. As less money is spent on social services, family support and health care, it is important that it is targeted towards effective services that are accessible to those most in need.
- Inequalities in access to mental health services need to be addressed. Interpreters need to be available, staff need to be trained to be culturally aware, staff need to be flexible in how and where services are offered.
- As the coordinating role of social services and the local education authority is reduced, with more emphasis on services provided by a range of voluntary and statutory providers seeking funding in competition with each other, maintaining interagency networks remains important if holistic and integrated care is to be provided to families with complex needs.

- The current focus on outcomes-based evaluation of services is an opportunity to learn more about what works to improve children's emotional wellbeing and mental health. Similarly, the introduction of CAMHS PbR planned for 2014 will help to encourage clarity about the focus of CAMHS interventions. It is important that both these changes to practice do not become bureaucratic exercises where form-filling and data collection interfere with the development of creative relationships between families and professionals.
- There is good evidence that providing structured parenting programmes based on social learning principles for parents whose children aged three to eight years have severe behaviour problems, is an effective intervention with the potential to divert children from negative developmental trajectories that are distressing to them, their families and their neighbourhoods and expensive to society. Some programmes, like Triple P, are designed in a stepped sequence according to the level of need that a particular family might have.
- There is emerging evidence that promoting parents' attunement to their child's communications, using video-based techniques, can develop parental skills and help troubled parent-child relationships get back on track.
- Parents and staff working with young children need to be able to distinguish between normal and abnormal developmental trajectories so that, when necessary, appropriate referrals can be made for specialist assessments and interventions.
- Sufficient specialist CAMHS staff should be available in each locality for assessments and interventions to be offered in a timely manner.

Chapter 8: Fetal origins of adult disease

Professor David Barker

The rewards of good health care in childhood, especially health promotion and preventative interventions, are unique because the benefits may last a lifetime and maybe passed onto future generations.
House of Commons Health Select Committee, 1997[1]

Not only do unfavourable conditions during life in the womb and in childhood affect health in childhood, they also predispose to increased risk of disease in adulthood. The research that points to this link began as a means of explaining the geographical inequalities in the rates of CHD in the UK. These differences cannot be explained by known risk factors such as obesity and smoking. In areas where there are high death rates from cardiovascular disease, there were high infant death rates in the past. This suggests that influences that have an adverse effect on infant health have persisting adverse effects in adult life.

8.1 The programming theory of health

Adverse influences during fetal and infant life, importantly malnutrition, change the structures, hormonal and metabolic processes of the body for life. This phenomenon is known as 'programming'.[2] In animals it is surprisingly easy to produce lifelong changes in the physiology and metabolism of the offspring by minor modifications to the diet of the mother before and during pregnancy.[3-5] The steep rise in CHD in the UK during this century has been associated with rising prosperity, but the poorest people in the least affluent places have the highest rates of the disease. These differences in CHD are a major contributor to the socioeconomic inequalities of life expectancy in the UK and are discussed in more detail in **Chapter 3**. The geographical distribution of neonatal mortality (deaths before one month of age) in England and Wales in the early years of the twentieth century closely resembled the distribution of death rates from cardiovascular disease today.[6] At that time, most neonatal deaths were attributed to low birthweight. An interpretation of this geographical association is that harmful influences that act in fetal life, and slow fetal growth, permanently programme the body in ways that predispose to cardiovascular disease in later life.

The large geographical and social class differences in fetal and infant growth which existed in the UK when today's generation of middle-aged and elderly people were born, were reflected in the wide range of infant mortality. In 1921 to 1925, infant mortality ranged from 44 deaths per 1,000 births in rural west Sussex to 114 per 1,000 births in Burnley.[7] The highest rates were generally in northern counties where large manufacturing towns had grown up around the coal seams, and in impoverished rural areas such as north Wales. They were lowest in counties in the south and east, which have the best agricultural land and are historically the wealthiest. A series of Government inquiries on child and maternal mortality from 1910 onwards, prompted by revelations of the poor physique of military recruits, showed how these differences in infant mortality were related to differences in the nutritional state, physique and health of young women, and in infant feeding practices, housing and overcrowding.[8]

In fetal life, the tissues and organs of the body go through what are called 'critical' periods of development, which may coincide with periods of rapid cell division. 'Programming' describes the process whereby a stimulus or insult at a critical period of development has lasting effects. Rickets has, for a long while, served as a demonstration that malnutrition at a critical stage of early life leads to persisting changes in the body's structure. Only recently have we realised that some of the persisting effects of early undernutrition become translated into pathology, and thereby determine chronic diseases, including cardiovascular disease, type II diabetes, osteoporosis, obesity, asthma and certain forms of cancer in later life.[2,4] That this has gone unremarked for so long is perhaps surprising, given the numerous animal experiments showing that undernutrition in utero leads to persisting changes in blood pressure, cholesterol metabolism, insulin response to glucose, and a range of other metabolic, endocrine and immune functions known to be important in human disease.[3-5]

8.2   The placenta

A baby's birthweight depends not only on the mother's nutrition but also on the placenta's ability to transport nutrients to it from its mother. The placenta seems to act as a nutrient sensor regulating the transfer of nutrients to the fetus according to the mother's ability to deliver them, and the demands of the fetus for them.[9] The weight of the placenta, and the size and shape of its surface, reflect its ability to transfer nutrients. The shape and size of the placental surface at birth has become a new marker for chronic disease in later life.[10] The predictions of later disease depend on combinations of the placenta size and shape of the surface and the mother's body size. Particular combinations have been shown to predict CHD,[11] hypertension,[12] chronic heart failure,[13] and certain forms of cancer.[14] Variations in placental size and shape reflect variations in the normal processes of placental development, including implantation, growth and compensatory expansion.[10] These variations are accompanied by variations in nutrient delivery to the fetus.

8.3   Undernutrition in utero

The human fetus adapts to undernutrition by metabolic changes, redistribution of blood flow and changes in the production of fetal and placental hormones that control growth.[15] Its immediate response to undernutrition is catabolism; it consumes its own substrates to provide energy.[16] More prolonged undernutrition leads to a slowing in growth. This enhances the fetus' ability to survive, by reducing the use of substrates and lowering the metabolic rate. Slowing of growth in late gestation leads to disproportion in organ size, since organs and tissues that are growing rapidly at the time are affected the most. Undernutrition in late gestation may, for example, lead to reduced growth of the kidney, which develops rapidly at that time. Reduced replication of kidney cells in late gestation will permanently reduce cell numbers, because after birth there seems to be no capacity for renal cell division to 'catch-up'.[17]

Maternal nutrition and its long-term effects on health and wellbeing are explored in detail in the 2009 BMA report *Early life Nutrition and lifelong health*.[18]

Animal studies show that a variety of different patterns of fetal growth result in similar birth size. A fetus that grows slowly throughout gestation may have the same size at birth as a fetus whose growth was arrested for a period and then 'caught up'. Different patterns of fetal growth will have different effects on the relative size of different organs at birth, even though overall body size may be the same. Animal studies show that blood pressure and metabolism can be permanently changed by levels of undernutrition that do not influence growth.[5] Preliminary observations point to similar effects in humans. Such findings emphasise the severe limitation of birthweight as a summary of fetal nutritional experience.

While slowing its rate of growth, the fetus may protect tissues that are important for immediate survival, the brain especially. One way in which the brain can be protected is by redistribution of blood flow to favour it.[19] This adaptation is known to occur in many mammals but in humans it has exaggerated costs for tissues other than the brain, notably the liver and other abdominal viscera, because of the large size of the human brain. Metabolic fetal adaptations may result in the baby sacrificing muscle growth and being born thin.[20]

It is becoming increasingly clear that nutrition has profound effects on fetal hormones, and on the hormonal and metabolic interactions between the fetus, placenta and mother on whose coordination fetal growth depends.[16] Fetal insulin and the insulin-like growth factors (IGF) are thought to have a central role in the regulation of growth and to respond rapidly to changes in fetal nutrition. If a mother decreases her food intake, fetal insulin, IGF and glucose concentrations fall, possibly through the effect of decreased maternal IGF. This leads to reduced transfer of amino acids and glucose from mother to fetus, and ultimately to reduced rates of fetal growth.[21] In late gestation and after birth, the fetus' growth hormone and IGF axis take over from insulin, and play a central role in driving linear growth. Whereas undernutrition leads to a fall in the concentrations of hormones that control fetal growth, it leads to a rise in cortisol, whose main effects are on cell differentiation.[15] One current line of research aims to determine whether the fetus' hormonal adaptations to undernutrition tend, like many other fetal adaptations, to persist after birth and exert lifelong effects on homeostasis and hence on the occurrence of disease. Undernutrition during pregnancy can affect both placental size and body size of the baby at birth, and recent research has shown that both of them can predict health in later life (see also **Chapter 4**).

8.4   Cardiovascular disease
Cardiovascular disease and body size at birth
The early epidemiological studies on the intrauterine origins of CHD and stroke were based on the simple strategy of examining men and women in middle and late life whose body measurements were recorded at birth. The birth records on which these studies were based came to light as a result of a systematic search of the archives and records offices of the UK – a search that led to the discovery of three important groups of records in Hertfordshire, Preston and Sheffield. The Hertfordshire records were maintained by health visitors and include measurements of growth in infancy as well as birthweight. In Preston and Sheffield, detailed obstetric records documented body proportions at birth.

Sixteen thousand men and women born in Hertfordshire during 1911 and 1930 were traced from birth to the present day. Death rates from CHD fall two-fold between those at the lower and upper ends of the birthweight distribution (see **Table 8.1**).

Table 8.1: Death rates from CHD among 15,726 men and women according to birthweight

Birthweight pounds*	Standardised mortality ratio	Number of deaths
≤ 5.5 (2.50)	100	57
- 6.5 (2.95)	81	137
- 7.5 (3.41)	80	298
- 8.5 (3.86)	74	289
- 9.5 (4.31)	55	103
> 9.5 (4.31)	65	57
Total	**74**	**941**

*Figures in parentheses are kilograms.

Source: Osmond C, Barker DJP, Winter PD et al (1993) Early growth and death from cardiovascular disease in women. *British Medical Journal* **307**: 1519-24. Reproduced with the permission of the British Medical Journal.

A study in Sheffield showed that it was people who were small at birth because they failed to grow, rather than because they were born early, who were at increased risk of disease.[22] The association between low birthweight and CHD has been confirmed in studies of men in Uppsala, Sweden,[23] and Caerphilly, Wales,[24] and among 80,000 women in the USA who took part in the American Nurses Study.[25] An association between low birthweight and prevalent CHD has also recently been shown in a study in South India.[26]

Cardiovascular disease and body proportions at birth

The Hertfordshire records, and the American Nurses and Caerphilly studies, did not include measurements of body size at birth other than weight. The weight of a newborn baby without a measure of its length is as crude a summary of its physique as is the weight of a child or adult without a measure of height. The addition of birth length allows a thin baby to be distinguished from a stunted baby with the same birthweight. With the addition of head circumference, the baby whose body is small in relation to its head, which may be a result of 'brain-sparing' redistribution of blood flow, can also be distinguished. Thinness, stunting and a low birthweight in relation to head size are the result of differing fetal responses to undernutrition, and other influences, and they have different consequences, both immediately and in the long term.[22]

In Sheffield, death rates for CHD were higher in men who were stunted at birth.[27] The mortality ratio for CHD in men who were 47cm or less in length was 138 compared with 98 in the remainder.[27] CHD in South India was also associated with stunting.[26] Thinness at birth, as measured by a low ponderal index (birthweight/length³), is also associated with CHD.[28] **Table 8.2** shows findings among men born in Helsinki, Finland during 1924 and 1933. Death rates for CHD were related to low birthweight.[28] There was, however, a much stronger association with thinness at birth. Men who had a low ponderal index had death rates that were twice those of men who had a high ponderal index (see **Table 8.3**).

Table 8.2: Hazard ratios for CHD in 3641 Finnish men born during 1924-1933

Birthweight kg*	Number of men	Hazard ratios	Number of deaths
≤2.5 (5.5)	145	1.13	11
- 3.0 (6.6)	557	1.23	44
- 3.5 (7.7)	1328	1.46	133
- 4.0 (8.8)	1165	1.11	88
> 4.0 (8.8)	446	1.00	30
p value for trend adjusted for gestation = 0.05			

*Figures in parentheses are pounds.

Source: Forsen T, Eriksson JG, Tuomilehto J et al (1997) Mother's weight in pregnancy and coronary heart disease in a cohort of Finnish men: follow-up study. *British Medical Journal* **315**: 837-40. Reproduced with the permission of the British Medical Journal.

Table 8.3: Hazard ratios by thinness at birth (ponderal index) for CHD in 3641 Finnish men born during 1924-1933

Ponderal index at birth (kg/m³)	Number of men	Hazard ratios	Number of deaths
≤25	724	2.07	82
- 27	1099	1.75	106
- 29	1081	1.33	80
>29	722	1.00	41
p value for trend adjusted for gestation <0.0001			

Source: Forsen T, Eriksson JG, Tuomilehto J et al (1997) Mother's weight in pregnancy and coronary heart disease in a cohort of Finnish men: follow-up study. *British Medical Journal* **315**: 837-40. Reproduced with the permission of the British Medical Journal.

Cardiovascular disease and infant growth

Information routinely recorded in Hertfordshire included the infant's weight at the age of one year. In men, failure of weight gain during the first year of life predicted CHD and stroke independently of birthweight.[29] **Table 8.4** shows that among men who weighed 8.0kg or less at one year of age, rates of CHD were twice those among men who weighed 12.2kg or more. The highest rates of the disease among men and women were in those who had both low birthweight and low weight at one year of age.[30]

Confounding effects of childhood circumstances

These findings suggest that influences linked to fetal and infant growth have an important effect on the risk of CHD and stroke. People whose growth was impaired in utero and during infancy are likely to continue to be exposed to an adverse environment in childhood and adult life. Some have argued that it is this later environment that produces the effects attributed to programming.[31] There is strong evidence against this. The associations between birthweight and CHD are little changed by allowing for lifestyle in later life.[25] Paths of fetal growth, however, determine vulnerability to the effects of an adverse lifestyle. Low income, for example, is only related to CHD among men who were thin at birth.[32]

Table 8.4: Death rates from CHD in 10,141 men according to weight at one year

Weight (pounds)	CHD			All cardiovascular disease			All other causes			Lung cancer			All causes	
	Standardised mortality ratio	95% confidence interval	No. of deaths	Standardised mortality ratio	95% confidence interval	No. of deaths	Standardised mortality ratio	95% confidence interval	No. of deaths	Standardised mortality ratio	95% confidence interval	No. of deaths	Standardised mortality ratio	95% confidence interval	No. of deaths
At birth:															
≤ 5.5 (n = 458)	102	76 to 134	51	96	74 to 122	65	90	70 to 115	67	116	70 to 181	19	93	78 to 110	132
6-6.5 (n = 1317)	83	68 to 99	118	80	68 to 94	155	76	65 to 89	162	64	43 to 92	30	78	70 to 87	317
7-7.5 (n = 2991)	82	72 to 92	266	80	72 to 89	353	79	72 to 88	383	75	59 to 93	80	80	74 to 86	736
8-8.5 (n = 3166)	75	67 to 85	266	79	71 to 87	377	77	68 to 85	401	79	64 to 97	92	78	72 to 83	778
9-9.5 (n = 1505)	56	45 to 68	97	61	51 to 72	144	74	64 to 85	190	57	40 to 81	33	68	61 to 75	334
≥ 10 (n = 704)	66	50 to 86	55	69	54 to 86	78	79	64 to 96	97	94	61 to 138	26	74	63 to 86	175
At 1 year:															
≤ 18 (n = 559)	105	82 to 133	68	101	81 to 124	89	77	61 to 97	74	98	61 to 149	21	89	76 to 103	163
19-20 (n = 1702)	83	71 to 97	158	84	73 to 96	217	92	82 to 104	261	89	67 to 115	56	88	81 to 97	478
21-22 (n = 3288)	85	76 to 95	305	86	78 to 95	420	78	71 to 86	415	73	58 to 90	86	82	77 to 88	835
23-24 (n = 2754)	65	57 to 75	201	66	59 to 75	277	68	60 to 76	309	58	44 to 75	59	67	62 to 73	586
25-26 (n = 1359)	65	53 to 79	98	66	55 to 78	135	79	68 to 92	178	92	68 to 123	46	73	65 to 82	313
≥ 27 (n = 479)	42	26 to 63	23	46	32 to 64	34	77	59 to 99	63	66	34 to 115	12	62	50 to 76	97
Total (n = 10141)	76	71 to 81	853	77	72 to 81	1172	78	74 to 82	1300	75	67 to 85	280	77	74 to 80	2472

Source: Osmond C, Barker DJP, Winter PD et al (1993) Early growth and death from cardiovascular disease in women. *British Medical Journal* **307**: 1519-24. Reproduced with the permission of the British Medical Journal.

Processes linking fetal growth and coronary heart disease
In studies exploring the mechanisms underlying the association between CHD and birthweight, the trends have been found to be parallelled by similar trends in two of the major risk factors – hypertension and non-insulin dependent diabetes mellitus (see **Table 8.5**).[33,34]

Table 8.5: Prevalence of non-insulin dependent diabetes mellitus (NIDDM) and impaired glucose tolerance in men aged 59 to 70 years

Birthweight Pounds*	Number of men	% with impaired glucose tolerance or NIDDM (plasma glucose <7.8 mmol/l)	Odds ratio adjusted for BMI (95% confidence interval)
≤ 5.5 (2.50)	20	40	6.6 (1.5 to 28)
- 6.5 (2.95)	47	34	4.8 (1.3 to 17)
-7.5 (3.41)	104	31	4.6 (1.4 to 16)
- 8.5 (3.86)	117	22	2.6 (0.8 to 8.9)
- 9.5 (4.31)	54	13	1.4 (0.3 to 5.6)
> 9.5 (4.31)	28	14	1.0
Total	**370**	**25**	

*Figures in parentheses are kilograms.

Source: Hales CN, Barker DJP, Clark PMS et al (1991) Fetal and infant growth and impaired glucose tolerance at age 64. *British Medical Journal* **303**: 1019-22. Reproduced with the permission of the British Medical Journal.

The associations between small size at birth and hypertension and NIDDM are again independent of social class, cigarette smoking and alcohol consumption. Influences in adult life, however, add to the effects of the intrauterine environment. The prevalence of impaired glucose tolerance, for example, is highest in people who had low birthweight but became obese as adults.

8.5   Hypertension
Hypertension and body size at birth

Associations between low birthweight and raised blood pressure in childhood and adult life, such as those in a sample of the Hertfordshire cohort shown in **Table 8.6**, have been extensively demonstrated around the world.

Table 8.6: Mean systolic pressure in men and women aged 60 to 71 years according to birthweight

Birthweight pounds*	Systolic blood pressure mm Hg (adjusted for sex)**
- 5.5 (2.50)	168 (54)
- 6.5 (2.95)	165 (174)
- 7.5 (3.41)	165 (403)
- 8.5 (3.86)	164 (342)
- 9.5 (4.31)	160 (183)
>9.5 (4.31)	163 (72)
All	**164 (1228)**
Standard deviation	25

*Figures in parentheses are kilograms.

**Figures in parentheses are numbers of subjects.

Source: Law CM, de Swiet M, Osmond C et al (1993) Initiation of hypertension in utero and its amplification throughout life. *British Medical Journal* **306**: 24-7. Reproduced with the permission of the British Medical Journal.

Figure 8.1 shows the results of a systematic review of published papers describing the association between birthweight and blood pressure. The review was based on 34 studies of more than 66,000 people of all ages in many countries.[33] Each point on the figure, with its confidence interval, represents a study population and the populations are ordered by their ages. The horizontal position of each population describes the change in blood pressure that was associated with a 1kg increase in birthweight. In almost all the studies, an increase in birthweight was associated with a fall in blood pressure. The associations are less consistent in adolescence, presumably because the tracking of blood pressure from childhood through adult life is perturbed by the adolescent growth spurt. The associations between birthweight and blood pressure are not confounded by socioeconomic conditions at the time of birth or in adult life.[35] Although the differences in mean systolic pressure are small by clinical standards, their public health implications are significant. Available data suggest that lowering the mean systolic pressure in a population by 10mmHg would correspond to a 30 per cent reduction in total attributable mortality.[36] Similarly to CHD and stroke, the association between low birthweight and raised blood pressure depends on babies who were small for dates, after reduced fetal growth, rather than on babies who were born pre-term.[23]

Figure 8.1: Difference in systolic pressure (mmHg) per kg increase in birthweight (adjusted for weight in children and BMI in adults)

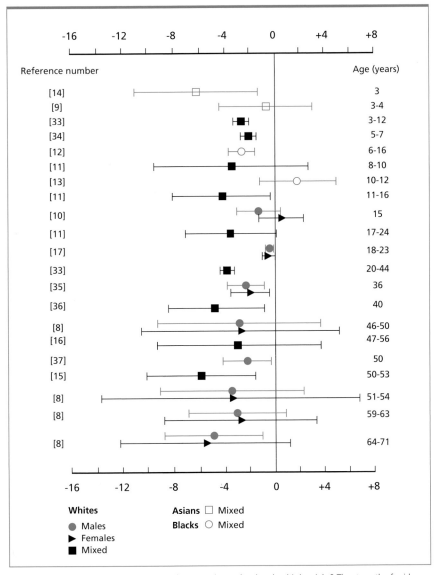

Source: Law CM & Shield AW (1996) Is blood pressure inversely related to birthweight? The strength of evidence from a systematic review of the literature. *Journal of Hypertension* **14**: 935-41. Reproduced with the permission of the Journal of Hypertension.

Although in the various studies of adults alcohol consumption and higher body mass have also been associated with raised blood pressure, the associations between birthweight and blood pressure were independent of them. Nevertheless, body mass remains an important influence on blood pressure and, in humans and animals, the highest pressures are found in people who were small at birth but become overweight as adults. The BMA's 2007 report on *Fetal alcohol spectrum disorders – a guide for healthcare professionals* also highlighted the adverse effects of prenatal alcohol exposure on the developing fetus and the spectrum of structural anomalies, and behavioural and neurocognitive impairments, that can result.[37]

Hypertension and placental size

Table 8.7 shows the systolic pressure of a group of men and women who were born, at term, in Sharoe Green Hospital in Preston, 50 years ago.

Table 8.7: Mean systolic blood pressure (mmHg) of men and women aged 50, born after 38 completed weeks of gestation, according to placental weight and birthweight

Birthweight pounds*	Placental weight**				
	≤ 1.0 (454)	- 1.25 (568)	- 1.5 (681)	>1.5 (681)	All
- 6.5 (2.9)	149 (24)	152 (46)	151 (18)	167 (6)	152 (94)
- 7.5 (3.4)	139 (16)	148 (63)	146 (35)	159 (23)	148 (137)
> 7.5 (3.4)	131 (3)	143 (23)	148 (30)	153 (40)	149 (96)
Total	**144 (43)**	**148 (132)**	**148 (83)**	**156 (69)**	**149≠ (327)**

*Figures in parentheses are kilograms.

**Figures in parentheses are number of subjects.

≠SD = 20.4 at term

Source: Barker DJP, Bull AR, Osmond C et al (1990) Fetal and placental size and risk of hypertension in adult life. *British Medical Journal* **301**: 259-262. Reproduced with the permission of the British Medical Journal.

The subjects are grouped according to their birthweights and placental weights. Consistent with findings in other studies systolic pressure falls between subjects with low and high birthweight. In addition, however, there is an increase in blood pressure with increasing placental weight. Subjects with a mean systolic pressure of 150mmHg or more, a level sometimes used to define hypertension in clinical practice, comprise a group who, as newborn babies, were relatively small in relation to the size of their placentas.

Hypertension and fetal undernutrition

Several lines of evidence support the thesis that it is poor delivery of nutrients and oxygen that programmes raised blood pressure in humans. First, experimental undernutrition of pregnant animals is known to cause lifelong elevation in the blood pressure of the offspring.[38,39] In humans, a mother's fatness, weight gain in pregnancy, and diet are all related to the offspring's blood pressure, whereas other influences on fetal growth, including maternal height, parity (the number of times the mother has given birth) and cigarette smoking are unrelated to the offspring's blood pressure, other than in small pre-term babies.[40,41] In Jamaica, children whose mothers had thin triceps skinfolds in early pregnancy and low weight gain during pregnancy had raised blood pressure.[40] In the Gambia, low pregnancy weight gain was associated with higher blood pressure in childhood.[42] In Aberdeen, the blood pressures of middle-aged men and women were found to be related to their mother's intakes of carbohydrate and protein during pregnancy.[43] Both low ratios of protein to carbohydrate and high ratios were associated with raised blood pressure. A number of possible mechanisms linking reduced fetal growth and raised blood pressure are currently being investigated.[17,44]

8.6   Non-insulin dependent diabetes mellitus

Insulin has a central role in fetal growth, and disorders of glucose and insulin metabolism are an obvious possible link between early growth and cardiovascular disease. Although obesity and a sedentary lifestyle are known to be important in the development of NIDDM, they seem to lead to the disease only in predisposed individuals.

8.7   Non-insulin dependent diabetes mellitus and body size at birth

A number of studies have confirmed the association between birthweight, impaired glucose tolerance and NIDDM, first reported in Hertfordshire.[45-50] Studies in Preston, UK and Uppsala, Sweden, where detailed birth measurements were available, found that thinness at birth was more strongly related than birthweight to impaired glucose tolerance and NIDDM.[47] **Table 8.8** shows that in Uppsala the prevalence of diabetes was three times higher among men in the lowest fifth of ponderal index at birth.

Table 8.8: Prevalence of non-insulin dependent diabetes by ponderal index at birth among 60 year old men in Uppsala, Sweden

Ponderal index at birth (kg/m³)	Number of men	Prevalence (%) of diabetes
< 24.2	193	11.9
24.2 -	193	5.2
25.9 -	196	3.6
27.4 -	188	4.3
≥29.4	201	3.5
Total	**971**	**5.7**
P value for trend 0.001		

Source: Lithell HO, McKeigue PM, Berglund L et al (1996) Relation of size at birth to non-insulin dependent diabetes and insulin concentrations in men aged 50-60 years. *British Medical Journal* **312**: 406-10. Reproduced with the permission of the British Medical Journal.

Among the Pima Indians in the USA, a raised prevalence of NIDDM was associated with both low birthweight and with birthweights over 4.5kg.[50] The increased risk of NIDDM among babies with high birthweights was associated with maternal diabetes in pregnancy, which is unusually common in this community.

The adverse effects of low birthweight and thinness at birth on glucose/insulin metabolism are already evident in childhood. Seven-year-old children in Salisbury who were thin at birth had raised plasma glucose concentrations after an oral load.[51] In a group of older British children, those who had lower birthweight had raised plasma insulin concentrations, both fasting and after oral glucose.[52] This is consistent with the association between low birthweight and insulin resistance. Low birthweight or stunting at birth have been found to be associated with reduced glucose tolerance among children in India and Jamaica. These findings in children provide further support for the hypothesis that NIDDM originates from impaired development in utero and that the seeds of the disease in the next generation have not only been sown but are already apparent in today's children.

Mechanisms
The processes that link thinness at birth with insulin resistance in adult life are not known. Babies born at term with a low ponderal index have a reduced mid-arm circumference, which implies that they have a low muscle bulk as well as less subcutaneous fat. One possibility is that thinness at birth is associated with abnormalities in muscle structure and function which persist into adult life, interfering with insulin's ability to promote glucose uptake.[53] Another possibility is that insulin resistance represents persistence of a glucose-sparing metabolism adopted in fetal life in response to undernutrition. The

undernourished fetus reduces its metabolic dependence on glucose and increases
oxidation of other substrates, including amino acids and lactate. A third possibility
is that persisting hormonal changes underlie the development of insulin resistance.
Glucocorticoids, growth hormone and sex steroids are thought to play a major role
in the evolution of the insulin resistance syndrome.[54]

8.8   Serum cholesterol and blood clotting

Studies in Sheffield show that the neonate that has a reduced abdominal circumference
at birth, although within the normal range of birthweight, has persisting disturbances
of cholesterol metabolism and blood coagulation which predispose to CHD.[55,56] This is
thought to reflect impaired growth of the liver, two of whose functions are regulation
of cholesterol and blood clotting. The differences in serum total and low density
lipoprotein cholesterol concentrations across the range of abdominal circumference
are large, statistically equivalent to 30 per cent differences in mortality caused by CHD
(**see Table 8.9**).

Table 8.9: Mean serum cholesterol concentrations according to abdominal
circumference at birth in men and women aged 50-53 years

Abdominal circumference inches*	Number of people	Total cholesterol (mmol/l)	Low density lipoprotein cholesterol (mmol/l)
≤11.5 (29.2)	53	6.7	4.5
- 12.0 (30.5)	43	6.9	4.6
- 12.5 (31.8)	31	6.8	4.4
- 13.0 (33.0)	45	6.2	4.0
> 13.0 (33.0)	45	6.1	4.0
Total	**217**	**6.5**	**4.3**

*Figures in parentheses are centimetres.

Source: Barker DJP, Martyn CN, Osmond C et al (1993) Growth in utero and serum cholesterol concentrations in
adult life. *British Medical Journal* **307**: 1524-7. Reproduced with the permission of the British Medical Journal.

8.9   Chronic bronchitis and fetal growth

Much of the socioeconomic and geographical inequality in death rates in the UK is
the result of differences in the occurrence of cardiovascular disease and chronic airflow
obstruction. Death rates from 'chronic bronchitis' are highest in the cities and large towns;
and people born in cities and large towns in the UK have an increased risk of death
from chronic bronchitis irrespective of where they move to in later life, either within or
outside the country.[57,58] This suggests that the disease originates in early life.

In Hertfordshire, standardised mortality ratios for chronic bronchitis among men with birthweights of 2.5kg or less were twice those among men with birthweights of more than 4.3kg.[59]

For many years there has been interest in the hypothesis that lower respiratory tract infection during infancy and early childhood predisposes to chronic airflow obstructions in later life.[60-64] The large geographical differences in death rates from chronic bronchitis in England and Wales are closely similar to the differences in infant deaths from respiratory infection earlier in the twentieth century.[65] Follow-up studies of individuals provide direct evidence that respiratory infection in early life has long-term effects. When the national sample of 3,899 British children born in 1946 were studied as young adults, those who had had one or more lower respiratory infections before two years of age had a higher prevalence of chronic cough.[66] A link between lower respiratory tract infection in early childhood and reduced lung function and death from chronic bronchitis in adult life has been shown in follow-up studies in Hertfordshire (see **Table 8.10**) and Derbyshire.[59,67,68]

Table 8.10: Mean forced expiratory volume in one second (FEV1) litres, adjusted for height and age among men aged 59-67 years according to birthweight and the occurrence of bronchitis or pneumonia in infancy

Birthweight pounds*	Bronchitis or pneumonia in infancy**	
	Absent	**Present**
≤ 5.5 (2.5)	2.39 (22)	1.81 (4)
- 6.5 (2.9)	2.40 (70)	2.23 (10)
- 7.5 (3.4)	2.47 (163)	2.38 (25)
- 8.5 (3.9)	2.53 (179)	2.33 (12)
- 9.5 (4.3)	2.54 (103)	2.36 (5)
> 9.5 (4.3)	2.57 (43)	2.36 (3)
Total	**2.50 (580)**	**2.30 (59)**

*Figures in parentheses are kilograms.

** Figures in parentheses are numbers of men.

Source: Barker DJP, Godfrey KM, Fall C et al (1991) Relation of birthweight and childhood respiratory infection to adult lung function and death from chronic obstructive airways disease. *British Medical Journal* **303**: 671-5. Reproduced with the permission of the British Medical Journal.

This suggests that infancy may be a critical period in which infection may change lung function. Further evidence of the long-term effects of respiratory infection in early life came from a study of 70-year-old men in Derbyshire, England, which also made use of health visitors' records.[68] The FEV1 of men who had had pneumonia before the age of two years was 0.65 litres less than that of other men, a reduction in FEV1 of approximately twice that associated with lifelong smoking.

The simplest explanation of these observations is that the infection of the lower respiratory tract during infancy has persisting deleterious effects that, when added to the effects of poor airway growth in utero, predispose to the development of chronic bronchitis in later life. Factors implicated in 'programming' of the respiratory system include exposure to viral respiratory infections during infancy.[69]

8.10   Preventing chronic disease in the UK

The findings outlined here suggest that CHD, stroke, NIDDM, hypertension and chronic airflow obstruction originate in utero. Emerging evidence suggests that prenatal development may also contribute to other chronic diseases, including osteoporosis,[70] cancers of the reproductive system,[71,72,73] other cancers[74] and schizophrenia.[75] The emergence of epigenetics is giving insights into the molecular mechanisms that underlly this. Protecting the nutrition and health of girls and young women and their babies must be a public health priority. The history of the UK gives an insight into social conditions that have been harmful to mothers and babies in the past. Poverty, inadequate food, poor housing, and overcrowding led to the deaths of many infants, reduced the life expectancy of those who survived, and laid the foundations for today's inequalities in health.[76,77]

The daily exposure to weight-related articles in newspapers, magazines and on television, and the thinness of role models in the fashion industry contributes to feelings of insecurity and self-doubt about acceptable body image and puts pressure on women to become unduly thin.[78,79] The babies of thin women may be at increased risk of CHD, NIDDM and raised blood pressure.[4,26,42,80-82] Encouraged by an obesogenic environment, other young women today are unduly fat. The babies of women who are overweight may also be at increased risk of CHD and NIDDM.[28,83] The effects of a mother's body size are largely independent of its effects on the size of the baby. So too, it seems, are the effects of what she eats in pregnancy. Even famine has unexpectedly small effects on growth but the baby's physiology and metabolism are permanently altered.[84]

The new developmental model for chronic disease

Under the new developmental model for the origins of chronic disease, the causes to be identified are linked to normal variations in the processes of development that lead to variations in the supply of nutrients to the baby.[85] These variations programme the function of a few key systems that are linked to chronic disease, including the immune system, anti-oxidant defences, inflammatory responses, the number and quality of stem cells and the balance of the autonomic system. There is not a separate cause for each different disease. Rather, as cigarette smoking has shown, one cause can have many different disease manifestations. Which chronic disease originates during development may depend more on timing during development than on qualitative differences in experience.

Exploration of the developmental model will illuminate people's differing responses to the environment through their lives. As René Dubos wrote long ago, 'The effects of the physical and social environments cannot be understood without knowledge of individual history'.[86] The model will also illuminate geographical and secular trends in disease. Because the human body has changed over the past 200 years, different chronic diseases have risen and then fallen, to be replaced by other diseases.[87,88]

Coronary heart disease, NIDDM, breast cancer and other chronic diseases are unnecessary. Their occurrence is not mandated by genes passed down to us through thousands of years of evolution. Chronic diseases are not the inevitable lot of humankind. They are the result of the changing pattern of human development. We could readily prevent them, had we the will to do so. Prevention of chronic disease, and an increase in healthy aging, require improvement in the nutrition of girls and young women. Many babies in the womb in the western world today are receiving unbalanced and inadequate diets. Many babies in the developing world are malnourished because their mothers are chronically malnourished. Protecting the nutrition and health of girls and young women should be the cornerstone of public health. Not only will it prevent chronic disease but it will produce new generations who have better health and wellbeing through their lives.

The Southampton Initiative for Health

The Southampton Initiative for Health may point to a way forward in the UK.[89-91] This is a programme of public health interventions in collaboration with the Sure Start Children's Centres that aims to optimise the nutritional status and health of women of childbearing age and their families. The Southampton Women's Survey has shown that women from disadvantaged backgrounds eat a less varied and balanced diet and are less physically active than women from more advantaged circumstances. Further work with disadvantaged women in Southampton has demonstrated that the barriers to healthy eating are often related to a lack of self-efficacy and a low sense of control. The Southampton Initiative aims to improve the health behaviours of disadvantaged women and their children in Southampton. This is being achieved by training health and social care staff in behaviour change skills that enable them to help women address barriers to behaviour change and set goals for themselves.

8.11   Recommendations

Interventions to improve maternal nutrition
• Young women should receive consistent dietary messages to encourage consumption of fruit and vegetables, starchy foods and oily fish, and to limit consumption of dietary fat, salt and added sugar. This should be accompanied by the message that poor diet

and nutritional status could impact on their ability to meet the nutrient needs of future pregnancies.

- Targeted environmental changes can have an impact and should be tried. Interventions to change aspects of the food environment, so that consumers are encouraged to choose healthier foods, may offer important opportunities to achieve change in eating habits. For example, changing the location of fruit and vegetables in supermarkets may have an effect.
- Work should be undertaken to improve the knowledge base of young women. Interventions that include elements of education or counselling, support and empowerment can improve nutrition knowledge and behaviour among young women.
- A multifaceted approach should be used to improve diet during pregnancy. Interventions that combine food supplementation, nutrition counselling and referral to health and social services, can lead to improvements in maternal diet during pregnancy, increased maternal weight gain and increased breastfeeding rates.
- Cooking and food preparation skills are key to a good diet; help with these should be offered. Practical cooking/food sessions should be delivered by peers, which aim to give low-income families food knowledge and skills to bring about dietary change and improve food practices among recipients.
- The efficacy of health visitors and others at increasing breastfeeding rates should be recognised and resourced. Interventions that educate women about the benefits and practice of breastfeeding are effective at increasing breastfeeding initiation. Appropriate support for breastfeeding mothers can prolong the duration of breastfeeding.

Chapter 9: Conclusions and summary

> *Improving the prospects for disadvantaged children is not an expense but an excellent investment, one that can be postponed only at much greater cost to society.*
> Committee for Economic Development, 1987[1]

The health of our children is of crucial importance for their own future and that of the nation. It is an essential basis for continuing stability of society within a robust economic framework. Every child born in the UK has an equal right to develop a sense of physical, emotional, intellectual, psychological and spiritual wellbeing, and ensuring child health should be a central objective of public health policy.

The 1999 BMA report, *Growing up in Britain*, recognised the multifactorial nature of child health and identified several areas of inequality in the attainment of health in 0 to five year olds in the UK. These are largely attributable to social determinants; children share the same gradients in health expectation as adults. High-profile reports and policies since that time have recognised, and tried to address, the nature and prevalence of social determinants in the UK and their effect on health. There have been some successes, but the reality is that most of the inequalities identified in 1999 persist, and in many cases the gap between the most privileged and least privileged in our society has widened. This has consequences for the health of our youngest children and their reasonable expectation of leading healthy adult lives.

This report re-examines the factors identified in 1999 and looks at the changes in our society since then, in the context of their effect on the health of our youngest children. It is disappointing to note that much of the evidence presented in this updated report echoes the conclusion of the 1999 report that 'inequity within the UK is increasing rather than decreasing'.

A specific list of key recommendations for future policy and research is presented at the end of each chapter and these have been collated and presented together in Chapter 10. The aim of this chapter is to present an overview of the present state of children's health and children's services in the UK, with general observations on improvements to research, policy and practice that are urgently needed, as well as a vision for children's health services for the next 10 years.

9.1　　Continuing need to reduce health inequalities

As already noted, a combination of social, economic and personal factors influence child health, and a multidisciplinary approach that takes account of the interactions of all these factors is required to reduce the detrimental effects of disadvantage. As Marmot and his team concluded in *Fair Society, Healthy Lives* 'every child should have the best start in life'. Many of the factors involved have an influence before conception and birth and their effect is likely to persist for the whole of an individual's life.

Chapter 3 of this report has identified the main factors that adversely affect child health: broadly, the socioeconomic factors involved are poor housing, low income or lack of a job, family composition and belonging to a black or minority ethnic group. These are likely to be accompanied by a poor environment for making lasting emotional attachments, poor-quality child care, low educational attainment, poor nutrition and lack of exercise. Without intervention, disadvantages persist and poor health and low levels of wellbeing are likely to be lifelong. The effect of poverty underpins almost all disadvantage – it is a factor that contributes to or exacerbates almost all other risk factors. It is also apparent that the effects of socioeconomic disadvantage on child health are not just additive but multiplicative (see **Chapters 3** and **7**).[2]

In 2003, the DH published ECM, and identified a framework with five important outcomes: being healthy, staying safe, enjoying and achieving, making a positive contribution and economic wellbeing.[3] A series of reports since then, from UNICEF, and the OECD amongst others, have shown that the UK is failing to provide these underpinning elements (see **Chapter 2**).[4] It seems we are failing in every aspect of the ECM framework – children's health and safety; material wellbeing; educational wellbeing; family and peer relationships; behaviour and risks; and subjective wellbeing.

In 2010 the Marmot Review emphasised the importance of investment in children to reduce health inequalities at all ages.[5] The report unequivocally states that 'Britain is failing its young children on a grand scale'. It stresses that the close links between early disadvantage and poor outcomes over time can only be broken by taking action to reduce health inequalities before birth, and continuing these throughout the life of the child.[5]

As discussed in **Chapter 2**, political solutions to the structural causes of ill health are required, even though the manifestations are seen and measured in the health sector. Early intervention is key to reducing costs further down the line, and the importance of adopting a multidisciplinary approach to child health cannot be overemphasised. As noted in the 1999 BMA report, 'tackling particular factors in isolation will not achieve the desired outcome of reversing the trend in the UK towards an increasingly inequitable society'. Consistent and reliable funding underpins evidence-based and multidisciplinary interventions. Policy makers must produce evidence-based guidance and policies that reduce the inequalities in health for our youngest children, thereby ensuring the health and wellbeing of the whole population.

9.2   The current situation and changes since 1999

As highlighted in **Chapter 3**, the overall health and mortality of children in the UK is improving but health inequalities appear to be widening and the gradient of mortality has become steeper.[6-8]

The family

The UK ranks twenty-fourth out of 27 European countries in a composite measure of pressure on families and has the highest proportion of children living in a household where no one is employed.[9] Twelve per cent of British children (aged 11 to 15 years) live in step-families and 16 per cent in single-parent families.[10] These figures are higher than other western European countries, though lower than the USA.

In 2011/12, the highest number of children ever recorded in the UK was referred for out-of-home care.[11] Most referrals were because of abuse or neglect and this was an increase of over 10 per cent in one year.[12] More than 64,000 children in the UK live in the care of local authorities rather than with their parents.[12] The evidence presented in **Chapters 2** and **7** shows that cared for children fare poorly in later life so their outlook is poor.[13] The cost to the state is also enormous: for 2009/10 the average cost per 'looked after' child was estimated to be £37,669 per year.[14]

Educational achievement

Pressure on the family and a poor social-emotional environment translate into low achievement for children of disadvantaged families: fewer than two-thirds of five year olds had achieved a good level of development in 2011, measured in terms of ability to concentrate, speak, recognise words and dress themselves. One-third of children in Britain aged between 11 and 16 years do not own a book.

Changes in health conditions

Currently the major cause of child morbidity is no longer infectious diseases. Three-quarters of childhood diseases are attributable to long-term conditions.[15] Many can be linked to socioeconomic disadvantage.

The largest category of non-communicable disease is mental health; unipolar depression is the single most common cause. The majority of young people who die following suicide or substance misuse have not been in contact with mental health service, due in part to the stigma of referral to CAMHS. The DH has recognised the importance of these problems and in 2011 issued a strategy for preventing mental illness and intervening early in childhood.[16]

Nutrition, exercise and obesity

While there are still some instances of undernutrition and some vitamin deficiencies are of concern, overnutrition is a more important risk factor for child health. More than 20 per cent of children entering school (age 4+ years) are overweight or obese and are therefore at increased risk of ongoing overweight and obesity and of incurring the physical health problems such as diabetes, CHD, and osteoarthritis in later life.[17] Fewer than half of children aged 11 to 15 years engage in at least one hour per day of moderate to vigorous physical activity, and the rate decreases with age. Tobacco, alcohol, physical inactivity, overweight and lack of fruits and vegetables in the diet are all important risk factors for child health. As discussed in **Chapter 2**, all these risk factors appear to be linked to socioeconomic disadvantage and are amenable to intervention.

Modification of risk factors

Many childhood diseases and deaths are preventable, and it is clear that socioeconomic disadvantage, especially poverty, underpins almost all risk factors for child health in the UK. Many of the risk factors are modifiable. There is a moral obligation on Government to direct policies and resources to addressing the underlying causes of preventable ill health.

In 1999, the BMA report stated that 'The United Nations Development Programme considers that the UK is now one of the most unequal industrialised countries in the world. The relationship between inequality and ill health is therefore more relevant than ever before'. If anything this situation has worsened since then.

9.3   Policies and interventions for prevention of health risk

Effective policies are evidenced-based; the evidence on risk factors and on what works is increasingly available and must form the basis of policies. Health agencies should engage with others to introduce policies that cross health and social divides, are evidence based and intervene as early as possible in the cycle of deprivation and disease.

The country's resources are finite, and choices have to be made about where to direct them. It is imperative to research the evidence about which interventions are most likely to have a lasting impact, and also which are the most cost-effective. Early intervention is always going to be cheaper than interventions to deal with the consequences of deprivation and ill health.

A life-course approach

The future health and wellbeing of the UK is linked to how successfully we manage the health and wellbeing of today's children. The life-course approach suggests that many of the risk and protective factors that influence health and wellbeing across the lifespan also play an important role in birth outcomes and in health and quality of life beyond the initial years.[18] The Marmot Review in 2010 identified the need for a 'life-course approach'. Such an approach should combine risk reduction with promotion of health with the aim to influence the whole life-course trajectory.[5] It requires a variety of interventions across different sectors and involves preconception and pregnancy care, as well as social support and healthcare for the whole of the child's family.

The need for health professionals to work closely together in integrated services to serve the best interests of children and young people has been recognised for more than 30 years. The Court Report in 1976, the NSF for Children in 2004, and the Marmot Review and Kennedy Report in 2010 all emphasise this view.[5,19-21] It is also recognised that the two most effective types of intervention are educational and family support, which may be interpersonal, emotional, practical or financial.[22,23]

Family support

Families under stress are ill equipped to provide the social and emotional environment necessary for children to develop in a healthy way. Poverty lies at the root of most inequalities. Support for families should be high priority – to optimise the health and wellbeing of our children. This requires all agencies involved in supporting children and families to work together and communicate with each other. Policies on pay and childcare must provide a living income for all families and high-quality support for their children.

Sure Start Children's Centres are a success story in troubled families as well as an excellent example of multidisciplinary care in action. They can have an enormous positive impact bringing together support agencies from the NHS, social services, education and the voluntary sector. Aimed at pregnant women, they continue supporting them and their children until they reach primary school age. Discussed in more detail in **Chapter 3** – evidence has shown beneficial effects in children and their families in Sure Start areas.

Sure Start Children's Centres are easy to access, usually based in familiar community venues, and serious efforts including home visits are made to reach families that might not otherwise engage with health and social services.[24] The services are under one roof and a trusting relationship is built up within the community. The UK coalition agreement 2010 pledged to 'take Sure Start back to its original purpose of early intervention [and] increase its focus on the neediest families',[25] and the 2010 Comprehensive Spending Review protected Children's Centre funding in cash terms. Since then local authority budgets have been reduced and services are no longer ring-fenced; some centres have closed or are providing a reduced number of services. Some service users may be referred from a local 'satellite' centre that provide limited services to a larger Children's Centre that may be some distance away. This is no longer a true community service and there may be a reduction in the effectiveness of the centres if access to services becomes more difficult.

Poverty

One of the Marmot Review's key recommendations was 'to develop and implement standards for minimum income for healthy living'.[5] This should reduce the numbers in persistent and reoccurring (child) poverty, while reducing 'adverse health outcomes attributable to living on low incomes'.[5] The current economic climate threatens progress in this area.

The Labour Government pledged in 1997 to halve child poverty by 2010, to eradicate it within 20 years, and to reduce health inequalities. A three-strand approach was proposed: universal child care provision, increased financial support for families, and initiatives to make work pay. Child poverty fell steeply in absolute terms between 1999 and 2010 (with a plateau between 2004/5 and 2008),[26,27] (see **Chapter 5**) but the 2010 target was not met.[28] Forecasts produced by the Institute of Fiscal Studies indicate that child poverty will remain broadly constant between 2009/10 and 2012/13, before rising slightly in 2013/14.

In its 2007 study,[29] UNICEF ranked the UK as the worst performing of the 21 countries it assessed against various dimensions of children's wellbeing. At the time David Cameron, then in opposition stated 'If today, Britain is the least family-friendly country in the developed world, the aim of the next Conservative Government is to make it the most family-friendly'. To date (see **Chapter 2**) the current administration's policies are unlikely to be described by health policy analysts as family-friendly. Cuts to child benefit, Sure Start centres closures, and regressive tax policies have differentially affected women and children (see **Chapter 7**). The Welfare Reform Act and Health and Social Care Act arguably will have profoundly deleterious effects on the most vulnerable patients.[30-32] While UNICEF's update to its 2007 study (published in April 2013)[33] found that the UK had seen a modest improvement, this only relates to data up to 2009/10, and does not therefore reflect the Coalition government policies. It is unlikely, given the current economic situation and policy environment, that the trend in improving child wellbeing will continue for the next few years.

Poverty underlies almost all child health inequalities and alleviation of poverty should be a Government priority. As discussed in **Chapter 3**, it is essential that all families have a minimum living income, set at a realistic level and constantly updated. A recent report from KPMG (2012), claiming that one in five workers in the UK earns less than a living wage, is not encouraging.[34] A 2012 research report from Action for Children, The Children's Society and the NSPCC has estimated that between 2008 and 2015 there will be an increase of just over 14 per cent in the number of families living with five or more vulnerabilities and that 'changes to the tax and benefits system will, on average, have a negative impact on every type of vulnerable household [they] analysed. Tax and benefit changes will disproportionately hit the most vulnerable and their negative effect on family income will increase, the more vulnerable you are'.[35]

Child care

While material wealth is important, so is the quality of a child's social and emotional environment. Policies that ensure optimal child care are essential, recognising that factors such as poverty, mental health problems, unemployment or homelessness can affect the child by the overall reduction in parental capacity to meet their own, and their children's, emotional needs. The 2012 *Social Justice: transforming lives* strategy allocates the extension of free nursery places for all children and to targeted interventions to help families identified as vulnerable. Although this is encouraging, optimal child care also requires support of families where most children spend most of their time, so this needs to be understood within the context of other cuts and changes to tax and benefits and the forecasts of net disadvantage to families.[27]

Healthy foods and exercise

The rapid increase in the number of obese people in the UK represents a major public health challenge that requires urgent action. The DH Change4Life campaign introduced in 2009 aims to inspire a societal movement in which everyone who has an interest in preventing obesity, including government, business, healthcare professionals, schools, families, and individuals can play a part.[36] Free child care in the early years setting also offers an opportunity to develop good nutrition habits.

Advice and education have limited effectiveness and it is likely that legislation and tax changes will be needed to make any major change to people's habits. The food industry has a powerful voice and a conflict of interest with Government attempts to reduce overconsumption. Sponsorship of schools and sporting events by companies that sell unhealthy foods or drinks is not helpful alongside attempts to encourage healthy eating. Rules on television advertising to children have limited effectiveness, as many children watch programmes outside the times when advertising is not allowed.

As discussed in **Chapter 4**, it is essential that Government moves away from partnership with industry and looks at effective alternatives to self-regulation to ensure that there is a transparent and effective policy development process.

The poor level of exercise in children is another area that should be amenable to intervention and education. If facilities for exercise or sport are difficult to access or too expensive they will not be used. Investment in open spaces, leisure centres, sports facilities and exercise equipment in parks would help to increase engagement in activity and reduce health problems resulting from a sedentary life. Selling off school playing fields may raise money for local authorities in the short term, but the loss of open space is likely to have a long-term effect on children's health. One example of an initiative that works to increase exercise is the charity Living Streets' Walk to School campaign, which reaches more than 1.9 million children each year.[37]

Health services

As discussed in **Chapter 1**, although the past decade has seen some improvements in children, young people and families' health services, the care provided by UK child health services is inferior in many regards to that in comparable European countries.

As stated in **Chapter 2**, prevention of chronic disease, addressing risk factors for ill health and improving life chances are priorities for the entire health system, and the greatest gains will accrue from starting at the earliest stage of life. Despite the shift from acute to chronic and long-term illnesses in children, child health care in the UK is still delivered in a hospital-centric manner. A different model of care that focuses on prevention and integrated services is required.[38] This requires a re-examination of curricula for training health professionals and those in other integrated professions.[39]

Whole-population approaches

Whole-population approaches in the form of education or advertising campaigns can have a significant effect on public awareness and behaviour. Examples are education about nutrition (eg the five-a-day message) or exercise. As discussed in **Chapter 5**, these can have the effect of 'shifting the risk curve' so that individuals who might otherwise have been at risk are moved out of a risk group, and those at high risk are moved to lower risk.

9.4   Funding and the focus of services

Under coalition policy, there has been a move to focus services on the sharper end of social welfare need and there have been cuts to resources needed to offer preventive services (see **Chapter 5**).[40] It is shortsighted to remove funding from prevention; early intervention costs much less than dealing with the consequences later in a child's life.[41] As the Rt Hon Eric Pickles MP, Secretary of State for Communities and Local Government, said in his 2010 speech to the Conservative Party conference: 'council spending on early intervention for children and families can deliver £10 of savings for every pound spent. Investing money to address the causes of social breakdown is far more effective than subsidising the symptoms'.[41]

Current spending on early intervention is low: national estimates have put prevention spending at 4 per cent of total health spending.[42] The OECD reports that for every £100 spent on early childhood (0 to five years) in the UK, £135 is spent on middle childhood (6 to 11 years) and £148 is spent on late childhood (12 to 17 years).[43]

It is not easy to measure the cost savings of any intervention, because early intervention is multidisciplinary and good outcomes are reflected in the absence of problems, and reduction in costs to society, in later life.[44] A common calculation is the 'social return on investment'. Calculations invariably show impressive ratios between initial outlay and later savings. For example, a study of family support interventions in children's centres by Barnardo's showed that family support workers generated £4.50 social return on investment for every £1 spent.[44]

Identification of children in need of intervention

Early intervention requires early identification of children at risk and that information from professionals who identify early problems is acted on promptly. Evidence presented in this report suggests that this does not always run as smoothly as it should (see **Chapter 5**).

Primary care is well placed to spot signs, recent high-profile cases of child maltreatment have reinforced the forensic role of paediatricians and their part in judicial proceedings, with much less attention to preventive roles. As discussed in **Chapter 5**, there are numerous reports of lack of feedback from social services to GPs or schools, so that families have to tell the same story to different agencies, which do not communicate with each other. Schools are also well placed to intervene before small problems become larger. In many situations scope for early intervention is largely limited to referral to social services, which has a very high threshold for acceptance of cases. A similar scenario is reported for referrals to CAMHS (see **Chapter 5**).

The Munro review of child protection in 2011 reiterated the importance of a preventive, proactive approach, targeted at vulnerable families and recognised the importance of other public services, schools, primary care and adult mental health services to aid social care in their proactive, preventive approach. Other public services could also intervene early in response to concerns about child maltreatment. Specific policies and guidelines are urgently needed to address this matter.

9.5 The importance of research to improve the evidence base for interventions

Money spent on interventions must achieve maximum benefits; outcomes should be measured preferably in longitudinal and randomised controlled population-based trials.

A comprehensive childhood disease incidence and prevalence databases – with indicators of wellbeing, development, and risk profiles, all linked to demographic information – is essential for health planning but does not currently exist (see **Chapter 2**). The Child and Maternal Health Observatory is helpful but will only ever be as good as the data available, which remain insufficient.[45]

Many interventions to reduce ill health and reduce inequity are short term and do not allow sufficient time for gathering of robust evidence from longitudinal studies, and less than 10 per cent of over 150 known approaches currently used in England have good evidence of effectiveness.[46] Future policy should concentrate on this area in order that limited resources can be focused on interventions with proven effectiveness. The use of HPSR must allow for recommendations on the basis of 'best available knowledge rather than the most desirable evidence' in order to help us understand how well systems work, and what should be done differently to strengthen child health system performance.

Research on effectiveness requires documentation of measurable outcomes. It is easy to measure levels of income, joblessness or inadequate housing, but outcomes should also include subjective measures of wellbeing or the absence of difficulties years or decades later. Outcomes will also be reflected in reduced costs for health and social care; these are hard to measure and may not be apparent for many years. Government terms of five years or less, lead to a temptation to record and publish only short-term outcomes. It is essential in the context of child health that the whole life-course trajectory is examined and long-term studies must be conducted.

All the reviews into child protection and welfare services conducted by the government, except the Munro review, have been in response to a child death.[40] Government reports and policy place too much emphasis on media reports and high-profile cases. As evidenced in **Chapter 5**, inquiries into individual deaths and national reviews of the 100 or so serious case reviews each year (death or serious injury where maltreatment was a factor) have had a significant impact on policy, while scant attention has been paid to population-based research.[45]

Examples of effective evidence-based interventions
There is strong evidence that intervention during a child's early years improve the health and cognitive development of the child.[48] The HCP[49] and FNP Programme focus on at-risk families; early evaluation of the FNP programme has been positive[50] with a full report due in 2013 and plans to increase capacity from 6,000 to 13,000 by 2015.

Sure Start has reported success.[51,52] No longitudinal evaluation has yet been possible but it may be more effective for moderately disadvantaged than severely disadvantaged families.[51,52] A similar programme in the USA running since 1962 has been shown to be very successful in improving social outcomes.[53]

A good example of evidence-based interventions to improve nutrition and prevent obesity in young children is HENRY, a national organisation that works with health trusts, local authorities and voluntary organisations to provide tailored packages according to local need, using evidence-based methods to provide early interventions. There is evidence that its interventions produce positive and lasting lifestyle effects.[54]

9.6 Vision for the future

'Britain is failing its young children on a grand scale' and compares poorly to other western countries.[5] This is not acceptable. It is time to reverse the trend and move towards a more equitable society.

The complex social and economic determinants of chronic ill health and of unfulfilled lives cannot be tackled by focusing, in isolation, on the duties of individual professional bodies or on short-term programmes with little evidence for their effectiveness. A multidimensional policy response is required to tackle the multiple factors involved, from preconception onwards.

There will never be enough money to address all the needs of society. It is essential to focus resources on where they have most effect, and where they are most needed. Without presenting specific recommendations, as these are given in the next chapter, the following summarises our view of the revised thinking needed to generate the best policy approaches to reducing inequalities and improving child health.

- Policies aimed at single issues have their place but a joined-up approach is essential, and a whole environment that values and supports family life is the single most important issue.
- The effect of poverty underscores almost all socioeconomic disadvantage and the burden of the financial crisis appears to be falling disproportionately on the poor. Urgent Government intervention is needed to ensure a realistic minimum wage and threshold for payment of income tax.
- Many interventions are short term and not based on evidence of what works. There is no place for short-term and 'knee-jerk' responses, such as those generated by high-profile child protection cases. All policies and interventions should be based on the best evidence available and outcome indicators should be built into the design of all new interventions.
- Gathering evidence requires that the views of parents and children are listened to and acted on. Specific projects can be run with specific groups in mind. Assessments should carefully monitor whether services offered are actually reaching the intended groups. Evidence of the effectiveness of interventions should be gathered in long-term, population-based studies that also document the response of the parents and children involved.
- Whether or not they are directly concerned with the needs of children, all Government polices and programmes should consider their effect on children. As noted in the 1999 BMA report, policies, such as those relevant to transport, housing, environment, employment, and fiscal/welfare, will have effects on children, but these are often overlooked.
- There has been a trend in recent years towards PbR. It should be recognised that, while this can be helpful in some settings, such as acute or preventive medicine, not

all of the desired results are readily measurable. Reducing interventions to results that can be recorded by ticking a box is not helpful in addressing the complexity of general child health and wellbeing, not least because many outcomes are not short-term ones and are only realised by an absence of problems later in life. There is no escape from the need for long-term population based studies to gain real evidence of effectiveness.

- While the introduction of PbR for CAMHS planned for 2014 may help to encourage clarity about the focus of mental health interventions for young people, it is important that the requirement to fill in forms and tick boxes does not interfere with the development of relationships between families and professionals.
- There is little doubt that early intervention and family support are effective, but involvement has to be voluntary; in order to engage those who are most at risk, services need to be easily accessible and provided in an advisory and non-stigmatising, non-threatening way. Sure Start is a good model for this and this approach could be extended to other situations and age groups, such as schools and workplaces.
- Those most in need of support are likely to be those that are hardest to reach – for example, no one can be forced to attend a Sure Start Children's Centre. Seemingly unrelated community activities such as a special interest group, a mother and toddler group or a family fun day may enable professionals to reach stressed families they would not otherwise make contact with.
- Since it is impossible to measure the cost-effectiveness of such support, in the current financial climate these types of activities are in the front line for cuts. In our view, this is short-sighted.
- Building communities in this way is also likely to develop support within the community and eventually reduce the need for costly professional input. Investing in, and supporting, community groups to help them get started is likely to pay off in the long term.
- When money is short, there is a tendency to remove funding from prevention and deal only with more major problems, which are often the outcome of failure to intervene early. Given the very favourable ratios of money saved to money invested in early intervention, this is also rather short sighted.
- Not all those children at risk will be discovered by Sure Start. If more serious problems develop, perhaps at school, the threshold for referral to Social Services or CAMHS is currently very high. Integrated systems to involve a range of professions to avert serious problems are not in place and individuals experience many problems navigating the system. One way to alleviate this is to assign a key support worker to individuals identified to support their needs and help them access all the services required. Development of effective integrated multiprofessional systems would be a major improvement to the current situation.
- Long-term and chronic medical conditions, which are increasing in prevalence, have an effect on many aspects of an individual's life and require a different approach to medical care. A reduced requirement for acute care should allow an increased emphasis

on preventive and social care. The need to deal with acute social problems reflects a failure to intervene early in a multidisciplinary and holistic way. Both situations point to a need to rethink the way services are run.

- One of the successes of Sure Start has been the result of a common funding source for health and social care services under one roof and this is a model that could be examined for all health and social care in the future.
- Finally, and very importantly, a vision for radical change to the way health and social care is delivered as the 21st century progresses will require a re-examination of the way in which professionals involved in multidisciplinary and cross-professional care are trained. It is essential that all professions involved develop the skills necessary for collaborative teamwork and communication across disciplines and to assimilate the complex needs of individual service users.[39]

Summary: four key messages

1. Poverty lies at the root of most health disadvantages and must be reduced.
2 Early intervention, with family support and education is cost effective and essential to optimise the life chances for those experiencing socioeconomic disadvantage.
3. Interventions should be evidence based.
4. Integrated and coordinated multiprofessional care is essential for optimal health and social care.

Chapter 10: Recommendations for childhood health: a life-course approach

> *Successful improvement of health at key life stages requires a continuum of interventions across the life-course, combined with efforts to strengthen health delivery systems and address the broader social and economic determinants of health.*
> Zsuzsanna Jakab, WHO Regional Director for Europe[1]

The future health and wellbeing of the UK is linked to how successfully we manage the health and wellbeing of today's children. We must value children for who they are at the moment, as well as who they will become. Children's services, and the processes and structures that enable them, should be coordinated in the interests of children and families. This will require financial and organisational coordination, supportive local and national policy, and adequate resources invested for sufficient time to enable improvement. The life-course approach suggests that many of the risk and protective factors that influence health and wellbeing across the lifespan also play an important role in birth outcomes and in health and quality of life beyond the initial years.[2] It is clear that conditions early in life have long-term effects on adult health. Because of this, inequalities in children's socioeconomic circumstances contribute to inequalities in health in adulthood.

A life course perspective offers a more joined up approach with implications for long-term health gain and places emphasis on education and early intervention. It approaches health as an integrated continuum rather than as disconnected and unrelated stages. It puts forward a complex interplay of social and environmental factors mixed with biological, behavioural, and psychological issues that help to define health outcomes across the course of a person's life. In this perspective, each life stage exerts influence on the next stage; social, economic, and physical environments also have influence throughout the life course.

The following sets out the recommendations put forward in this report and incorporated into a life-course approach.

PRE-CONCEPTION AND PREGNANCY

Helping parents with their plans for a healthy family. Early support for a healthy pregnancy.

- Parenting begins before birth and the developing fetus can be affected by smoking, drugs (including alcohol), poor nutrition and excessive maternal stress or anxiety.
- Intervention for care in pre-conception and during pregnancy, involving both parents, is important.
- By identifying those families at higher risk and with lower protective factors early in the pregnancy, it is possible to build resilience and achieve healthier outcomes.
- Parenting is the single largest variable implicated in childhood illnesses and accidents; teenage pregnancy and substance misuse; truancy, school disruption, and underachievement; child abuse; unemployability; juvenile crime; and mental illness.
- A growing body of research suggests that good parenting skills and a supportive home learning environment are positively associated with children's early achievements and wellbeing. Easily accessible and tailored approaches for preparation for parenting and parenting support have been shown to improve outcomes for the child and family, especially for those more at risk.
- A healthy pregnancy is important for the neurological development of the child, and the potential impact on child development of maternal anxiety and depression in pregnancy.
- Young women should receive consistent dietary messages to encourage consumption of fruit and vegetables, starchy foods and oily fish, and to limit consumption of dietary fat, salt and added sugar. This should be accompanied by the message that poor diet and nutritional status could impact on their ability to meet the nutrient needs of future pregnancies.
- Targeted environmental changes can have an impact and should be tried. Interventions to change aspects of the food environment, so that consumers are encouraged to choose healthier foods, may offer important opportunities to achieve change in eating habits. For example, changing the location of fruit and vegetables in supermarkets may have an effect.
- Work should be undertaken to improve the knowledge base of young women. Interventions that include elements of education or counselling, support and empowerment can improve nutrition knowledge and behaviour among young women.
- A multifaceted approach should be used to improve diet during pregnancy. Interventions that combine food supplementation, nutrition counselling and referral to health and social services, can lead to improvements in maternal diet during pregnancy, increased maternal weight gain and increased breastfeeding rates.

- Cooking and food preparation skills are key to a good diet; help with these should be offered. Practical cooking/food sessions should be delivered by peers, which aim to give low-income families food knowledge and skills to bring about dietary change and improve food practices among recipients.
- The efficacy of health visitors and others at increasing breastfeeding rates should be recognised and resourced. Interventions that educate women about the benefits and practice of breastfeeding are effective at increasing breastfeeding initiation. Appropriate support for breastfeeding mothers can prolong the duration of breastfeeding.

BIRTH AND INFANCY

Working with families to protect the new born child. Supporting an environment that supports 'attachment', encourages breast feeding and recognises the early signs of postnatal depression.

- Good service provision should include an understanding of the needs of the local population, which inform a flexible and responsive service.
- A range of maternity services should be provided in a networked manner, so that women have access to a full range of choices, such as screening, birth centre care and homebirth.
- Good service provision should include activity to reduce premature births by increasing early antenatal booking (especially for the more at-risk mothers).
- An annual report on the health of children, similar to the Chief Medical Officer's report on the State of the Public Health, should be published, with a view to monitoring health trends in children so that remedial action can be taken where needed and progress monitored.
- Comprehensive, reliable, regularly collected data on child health and health care needs is required to inform health services planning and evaluation.
- The planning, commissioning and evaluation of children's health services should be informed by child public health professionals.
- First contact care for children should be improved by ensuring that all staff are appropriately trained and supervised.
- Chronic care for children should be improved by developing chronic care health service models, appropriate for children's needs, and effectively managing transition to adults' services.

- Parents and families, particularly in areas of high need, should be supported.
- Investment in UNICEF 'Baby Friendly' accreditation of acute Trusts and community providers needs to be maintained in order to ensure that the recent progress made, in increasing breastfeeding initiation, is not lost.
- There is a clear need to re-examine the extension of statutory maternity leave and to improve the availability and quality of childcare close to the mother's workplace.
- Thirty years after the publication of the International Code on Marketing of Breastmilk Substitutes, there remain gaps in the legal framework controlling the marketing and promotion of breast milk substitutes in the UK. The attachment of health claims to products such as infant formula and follow-on formula may exploit these and there is a need to monitor the impact of this development.
- It is beyond doubt that breastfeeding improves the health of babies and their mothers even in an industrialised country like the UK. Breast milk provides all the nutrients required at this age, in a form that is hygienic and easy to digest.
- The promotion, protection and support of breastfeeding, coupled with appropriately paced diversification of the diet to encourage acceptance of a wide range of healthy foods, is fundamental to the prevention of obesity in later life.

EARLY YEARS
Laying the foundations for a bright, healthy future and providing children with the best start in life.

- There is now strong evidence that intervention during a child's early years, particularly through the provision of skilled home visitors, can provide the type of support necessary to improve the health of the child, as well as their cognitive development.
- Severe adversities and maltreatment in infancy and the early years can have a lifelong impact on a child's brain development, physiological reactions to stress and later mental and physical health. Devoting resources to supporting families with young children can potentially prevent a proportion of these adverse outcomes, with benefits both for the individual child and in avoiding later financial and other costs for society.
- There is good evidence that providing structured parenting programmes based on social learning principles for parents whose children aged three to eight years

have severe behaviour problems, is an effective intervention with the potential to divert children from negative developmental trajectories that are distressing to them, their families and their neighbourhoods and expensive to society.

- There is emerging evidence that promoting parents' attunement to their child's communications, using video-based techniques, can develop parental skills and help troubled parent-child relationships get back on track.
- Good service provision should include plans for improved access to immunisation services for those who are at risk of not being fully immunised. It should also include accurate and up-to-date information provided in a variety of formats for parents and carers about the purpose and safety of immunisation programmes, to enable informed decisions to be made.
- There is a need to invest in practical help from trained supporters – health professional or from the mother's peer group. The importance of this has been highlighted in several position statements and policy documents but implementation is still very poor.
- The foods that parents introduce to their children reflect their own dietary preferences and lifestyle, implying that changing behaviour necessitates engagement with whole families rather than merely offering advice on children's diets. This means engaging with families in a range of environments including retail outlets, early year's settings, children's centres and Sure Starts.
- Competencies at an appropriate level related to infant and young child nutrition should be clearly defined core components of training for all professionals who care for young children and work with their parents. There is a need to ensure that the workforce has more access to specialised and contextualised advice, and that it can access suitable training.
- Positive action should be taken to reduce the consumption of sweetened drinks and high-sugar foods through healthy diet advice from conception and into early years.
- Uptake of the Healthy Start scheme, use of the vouchers and availability and consumption of the vitamin supplements need to be monitored and reviewed.
- Diversifying the number, and improving the quality of 'drop-in' services available through Sure Start and Children's Centres may also improve access to services capable of fulfilling the range of functions required to support breastfeeding, complementary and young child feeding.

CHILDHOOD
Encouraging healthy behaviours, empowering the next generation.

- The social and physical (built) environment should be adapted to prevent child obesity and promote a culture of playing outside.
- The health knowledge and behaviours of school-age children should be improved.
- The built environment should be improved to support healthy lives for children and families and to reduce accidents and injuries.
- Promotion of activity and identification of safe play space is also an important objective.
- A variety of policy and regulatory steps should be taken to reduce alcohol and tobacco use.
- Interventions, for example, to ensure a higher percentage of children are ready for school at school starting age, should be undertaken. Where positive results are seen, the activity or intervention should be widely promulgated and implemented in areas with the same problem. All research-implementation cycles should be subjected to surveillance to measure efficacy.
- Children's services should implement programmes which will increase the availability of fluoride, improve the diet by reducing sugar intake and encourage preventive dental care.
- Policies should be developed to support healthy eating through early years or schools' healthy eating policies.
- A family-based approach to childhood weight management to change attitudes and behaviours, with programmes that include physical activity, diet and emotional wellbeing should be encouraged. There should be an emphasis on encouraging positive changes in behaviour that can be maintained over the long term.
- Health service should include the use of brief interventions and opportunities such as smoking cessation support to encourage children to make changes to help them achieve a healthy weight.
- All public sector and voluntary providers should promote opportunities for active travel, healthy food and drink.

ADOLESCENCE
Enjoying adolescence safely and preparing well for adulthood.

- Unhealthy risk-taking behaviours by young people are often a consequence of wider issues such as deprivation, inequalities and social exclusion. They can also be linked to lower educational attainment and involvement in either the care or criminal justice system. Increased risk behaviours are associated with factors such as alcohol and drug misuse.
- Strong social and family networks, healthy standards provided by significant adults, and involvement in family, schools and community can reduce risk taking.
- A variety of policy and regulatory steps should be taken to reduce alcohol and tobacco use.
- There should be a joined-up services between CCGs, community and acute young people's services, and local authority children's services that have young people at the centre of commissioning plans.
- Partnerships between community, family and educational support schemes should be encouraged.

THREADS ACROSS THE LIFE COURSE
Ensuring a healthy future for our children.

- Accountability for children's health and wellbeing is key to ensuring progress is made. This should be at Ministerial level within the Cabinet, and should incorporate a framework of monitoring, reviewing, and remedying processes. A national oversight mechanism, with responsibility for child health services, should be set up, and report at Ministerial level so that there is sufficient influence to implement remedying action when problems are detected.
- Funding for health and welfare of children – including for health (primary, secondary and community), education, social care – should be consolidated in one fund, to enable the joined-up planning and delivery of care.
- Investment in improving the quality of social and other housing is essential to improving health and wellbeing of children and adults.

- Local Government must make health and wellbeing a priority within its housing policy, and report annually on progress to achieving a housing stock that is conducive to the health of housing occupants.
- Community and family support schemes require ongoing investment to reduce adverse impacts on child health and wellbeing. Local and national governments must be helped to understand that interventions may take time to have an effect, and that consistent and reliable funding must underpin evidence-based interventions.
- The high levels of all types of poverty experienced in the UK, including by children, are unacceptable. Society in the UK should expect its Governments to take more effective action to reduce the social, and therefore the health inequalities, currently experienced. Work on the MIHL should inform Government's policy on benefit reform. Health professionals should lobby actively on ensuring a healthy living basis to minimum income protection.
- The universal services provided by health visitors working closely with GPs in strong primary care teams should be strengthened.
- Policy should serve to improve the 'match' between healthcare needs and services.
- National and local policy on matters affecting the social and economic determinants of health should be devised and evaluated according to the ECM outcomes, and with reference to the needs and interests of children.

Child maltreatment
- Future polices to tackle child maltreatment should take a public health approach and focus on preventive and family welfare services to improve support for parenting. Research evidence suggests that this approach, rather than a forensic approach of diagnosis and establishing culpability, is likely to make most impact on child maltreatment and child welfare.
- Robust population health research should be used to inform policy, rather than enquiries into individual child deaths.
- In the area of child protection, use of routine data and linkage of data from health, social care, the judicial system and education is essential for understanding which professionals are coming into contact with children and patterns of this contact, which children might not have any early or preventive services, where services might be duplicated and which outcomes are linked to input from which services.
- There is an urgent need for randomised controlled trials to evaluate which interventions work and for whom. These studies are needed both for preventive social welfare interventions and for the coercive interventions such as out-of-home care.

- Healthcare should play a more clearly recognisable role in addressing the health determinants and consequences of child maltreatment.
- Healthcare practitioners should focus on targeting families who stand to benefit from effective interventions to improve parent-child interaction and thereby reduce the risk of child maltreatment and its consequences. Clear guidance is needed on how healthcare professionals can access therapeutic interventions directly, without always going through social care services.
- GPs should be given a more proactive role in the ongoing support, monitoring and management of parents whose health needs increase the risk of harmful parent-child interaction.

The child with a disability

- People with disabilities have poorer health than the rest of the population. Early intervention and a community approach have been shown to prevent deterioration of disabled young people's health.
- Government should revisit the Kennedy report in the light of the changes planned in the Health and Social Care Act and consider Local Service Partnerships as a vehicle for change, supported by local children's budgets and simplified outcome measures.
- The benefits of the new systems envisaged for the Children and Families Bill should be shared by all children with disability.
- There should be implementation of PbR, bearing in mind the chronic nature of difficulties and the benefits of a consultation model.
- Child development should be put on the curricula of teaching training courses.
- Professional bodies should campaign for awareness regarding the impact of benefit cuts on families of disabled children. They should also collaborate to produce professional guidance and standards on pre-diagnosis assessment and generic problems, in order to inform the development of local offers.
- Clinicians in leadership roles should collaborate with local partners to produce care pathways and 'offers' for local disability services. They should also get involved with local CCGs to ensure appropriate commissioning.
- All clinicians should ensure that the families they work with understand what services are available, and feel empowered to make their voices heard. They should also ensure that the families they work with are in receipt of all relevant benefits.

Emotional and behavioural problems

- Many of the risk factors for mental health problems in children are often found in association with each other. Poverty, poor housing, domestic violence, parental mental ill health and drug abuse may cluster together in families, and have a negative effect on children that is multiplicative rather than additive. As less money is spent on social services, family support and health care, it is important that it is targeted towards effective services that are accessible to those most in need.

- Inequalities in access to mental health services need to be addressed. Interpreters need to be available, staff need to be trained to be culturally aware, staff need to be flexible in how and where services are offered.
- As the coordinating role of social services and the local education authority is reduced, with more emphasis on services provided by a range of voluntary and statutory providers seeking funding in competition with each other, maintaining interagency networks remains important if holistic and integrated care is to be provided to families with complex needs.
- The current focus on outcomes-based evaluation of services is an opportunity to learn more about what works to improve children's emotional wellbeing and mental health. Similarly, the introduction of CAMHS PbR planned for 2014 will help to encourage clarity about the focus of CAMHS interventions. It is important that both these changes to practice do not become bureaucratic exercises where form-filling and data collection interfere with the development of creative relationships between families and professionals.
- Parents and staff working with young children need to be able to distinguish between normal and abnormal developmental trajectories so that, when necessary, appropriate referrals can be made for specialist assessments and interventions.
- Sufficient specialist CAMHS staff should be available in each locality for assessments and interventions to be offered in a timely manner.

Appendix 1: Author's biographies and declarations of interest

The authors comprise BMA staff and senior members of affected professions who have demonstrated experience and interest in relation to the issue of child health.

Dr Jim Appleyard

Former Consultant Paediatrician at the Kent and Canterbury Hospital (1971 to 1998), Professor of Paediatrics St George's University, Greneda (1985 to 1997)

Dr Appleyard founded the first Child Developmental Centre, named after Dr Mary Sheridan in 1972 and the Neonatal Special Care Unit in 1973. He has been a patron of the Dyspraxia Trust since its foundation 25 years ago. Dr Appleyard was the first Chairman of the Manpower Committee of the British Paediatric Association (now the Royal College of Paediatrics and Child Health) and, through the British Medical Association, worked towards the integration of the Child Health Services. He was Chairman of the Representative Body of the British Medical Association (1992 to 1995) and is currently the Vice President of the International Association of Medical Colleges.

Declaration of interests:
Jim Appleyard declares that he has no conflicts of interest.

Professor David J P Barker

Director, Medical Research Council Environmental Epidemiology Unit, University of Southampton

David Barker MD PhD FRS is a physician. He is Professor of Clinical Epidemiology at the University of Southampton, UK, and Professor in Cardiovascular Medicine at Oregon Health and Science University, USA. Twenty-five years ago he showed, for the first time, that people who had low birth weight are at greater risk of developing coronary heart disease and diabetes. This is now widely accepted. It has led to a new understanding that chronic adult diseases are 'programmed' by malnutrition in the womb. Dr. Barker's work is relevant around the world. In the Western world, many babies are malnourished because their mothers eat diets that are unbalanced and monotonous, or because their mothers are either overweight or excessively thin. In low-and middle-income countries, many babies are malnourished because their mothers were chronically undernourished when they were young. Dr Barker has lectured and written extensively on nutrition in the womb and its lifelong consequences. He has received a number of international awards, including the Danone Nutrition Award, the Prince Mahidol Prize and the Richard Doll Prize.

Declaration of interests:
David Barker declares that he has no conflicts of interest.

Dr Max Davie
Consultant Paediatrician, Mary Sheridan Child Development Centre, Lambeth.
Dr Davie is a consultant community paediatrician, working in Lambeth as part of Guy's and St Thomas' Hospital NHS Trust Community services. He has a special interest in the assessment and diagnosis of neurodevelopmental conditions in school-age children and in the mental health of paediatric patients more generally. He is academic convenor of the British Paediatric Mental Health Group and co-opted member of the mental health College Specialist Advisory Committee at the Royal College of Paediatrics and Child Health. He is a member of the Expert Reference Group for Child and Adolescent Mental Health Services Payment by Results and commissioning at the DH. He has a strong interest in medical education at all levels, and both teaches and leads educational programmes locally. He has three young children, and consequently has no spare time!

Declaration of interests:
Max Davie declares that he has no conflicts of interest.

Dr Jessie Earle
Consultant Child & Adolescent Psychiatrist, Haringey Child and Adolescent Mental Health Services Clinic
Dr Earle is a child and adolescent psychiatrist working in a multidisciplinary community Child and Adolescent Mental Health Services in Haringey, North London, which is an area of great cultural and socioeconomic diversity. Before training as a doctor at University College London, she studied social anthropology at Cambridge University. Her interest in young children's emotional and behaviour problems developed over many years while writing and delivering a distance-learning postgraduate diploma for health visitors at St George's Hospital Medical School, focused on promoting young children's mental health. Her current interests include early intervention, developing effective inter-agency networks, and working with parents who struggle to parent successfully. In her spare time, she enjoys spending time with her teenage children, reading and walking.

Declaration of interests:
Jessie Earle declares that she has no conflicts of interest.

Ms Grace Foyle

Senior Policy Executive, British Medical Association

Grace Foyle is a senior policy executive in the Science and Education Department at the British Medical Association. She leads the work of the Association's Patient Liaison Group and undertakes research and policy projects for the Patient Liaison Group, the Equality and Diversity Committee, and the Board of Science. Grace has a bachelor of honours degree in Public Health Nutrition and a Diploma in Food Technology. Prior to joining the British Medical Association, Grace worked as a food policy executive at the Food and Drink Federation and also volunteered as a community nutritionist at Shoreditch Spa, providing nutritional advice to low socioeconomic groups in East London.

Declaration of interests:
Grace Foyle declares that she has no conflicts of interest.

Professor Ruth Gilbert

Professor of Clinical Epidemiology, the Centre for Paediatric Epidemiology and Biostatistics, University College London Institute of Child Health

Professor Ruth Gilbert is a clinically qualified and accredited paediatrician trained in epidemiology. Her research includes a focus on the contribution of healthcare services to the detection of, and response to, child maltreatment. She has evaluated screening for child maltreatment in accident and emergency departments, patterns of maltreatment and other forms of victimisation in injured children admitted to hospital, and how general practitioners recognise and respond to child maltreatment. Most recently, she led an international comparison of trends in child maltreatment in six countries, based on multiple sources of routine data. She is currently involved in research that examines the trajectory of maltreated or victimised children and their risk of death in adolescence and early adulthood.

Declaration of interests:
Ruth Gilbert declares that she has no conflicts of interest.

Dr Elizabeth Rough (PhD)
Research and Policy Executive, British Medical Association
Elizabeth Rough PhD is a research and policy executive in the Science and Education Department at the British Medical Association. She supports the work of the Association's Board of Science and undertakes research and policy projects for the Patient Liaison Group, the Equality and Diversity Committee, and the Board of Science. In 2011, she completed a PhD in science policy at the University of Cambridge, with a particular focus on the development of UK nuclear energy policy since the 1950s. Prior to joining the British Medical Association, Elizabeth worked as a researcher on a range of projects related to public health, including newborn screening, substance use, and human trafficking.

Declaration of interests:
Elizabeth Rough declares that she has no conflicts of interest.

Dr Anthony Williams
Reader in Child Nutrition & Consultant in Neonatal Paediatrics, Clinical Sciences St George's, University of London
Dr Williams MBBS DPhil studied medicine at University College London and the Westminster Hospital, qualifying in 1975. He was appointed a consultant in neonatal paediatrics at St George's Hospital in 1987 after further training in London, Leicester, Liverpool and Bristol. His interest in child nutrition developed while he was undertaking research in Oxford during the early 1980s. He is currently an adviser to UK Government departments and in the past has also advised the European Food Safety Authority and World Health Organization. Tony is an honorary Fellow of the United Nations Children's Fund, a trustee of Women and Children First and professional adviser to a number of UK charities supporting parenting and early child nutrition.

Declaration of interests:
Anthony Williams declares that he has no conflicts of interest.

Dr Ingrid Wolfe

Consultant Child Public Health, Guy's and St Thomas's Hospital; Programme Director Evelina London Child Health Project; Honorary Senior Lecturer, King's College London.

Ingrid Wolfe is qualified in public health and paediatrics, and divides her time between child health services, systems, and policy research with the European Observatory on Health Systems and Policies, and the NHS where she is developing an integrated health service model for children in Lambeth and Southwark. Ingrid's main academic interests are in child health services research and policy in the UK and Europe. Ingrid is a child public health policy advisor for the European Pediatric Association and Strategic Pediatric Alliance, and Chair of the Faculty of Public Health's Child Public Health Interest Group.

Declaration of interests:
Ingrid Wolfe declares that she has no conflicts of interest.

Dr Jenny Woodman (PhD)

Medical Research Council Centre of Epidemiology for Child Health, Institute of Child Health

Jenny Woodman is a public health researcher trained in epidemiology and qualitative methods. She is nearing the end of a Medical Research Council/ Economic and Social Research Council funded interdisciplinary PhD studentship that uses mixed methods to investigate different dimensions of GP responses to concerns about possible child abuse and neglect by GPs in England. Her research combines qualitative interviews with GPs and health visitors and observations of team meetings, with analyses of a cohort of 1.5 million children registered at GP practices in the UK (from The Health Improvement Network (THIN) database) to estimate the frequency and type of recorded concerns in children's health records. She has previously undertaken systematic reviews on the recognition of child maltreatment in accident and emergency departments and in primary care. Findings will inform future projects to develop and test a complex intervention to improve outcomes for children who prompt concerns about possible abuse and neglect in primary healthcare settings.

Declaration of interests:
Jenny Woodman declares that she has no conflicts of interest.

Appendix 2:
BMA policy on child health

The BMA has produced several evidence-based reports which specifically focus on children's health, including:

- Early life nutrition and lifelong health (2009)
- Under the influence: the damaging effect of alcohol marketing on young people (2009)
- Forever cool: the influence of smoking imagery on young people (2008)
- Breaking the cycle of children's exposure to tobacco smoke (2007)
- Domestic abuse (2007)
- Fetal alcohol spectrum disorders – a guide for healthcare professionals (2007)
- Child and adolescent mental health (2006)
- Preventing childhood obesity (2005)
- Smoking and reproductive life (2004)
- Adolescent health (2003)
- Childhood immunisation: a guide for healthcare professionals (2003)
- Injury prevention (2001)
- Eating disorders, body image and the media (2000).

It is worth noting that as part of the wider remit, much of the Board of Science's other work also considers children and young people. This includes the Board's work on:

- alcohol misuse
- smoke-free public places
- gambling addiction
- risk.

The BMA's Ethics Committee have also produced a toolkit for doctors on children and young people. Their work also includes information on:

- child protection
- parental responsibility.

BMA ARM policy on child health
2012

That this Meeting asks the BMA to highlight the under-investment in transition care for disabled children (from the paediatricians to adult physicians) and actively promote investment in transition by commissioners.

That this Meeting believes that one of the primary goals of any society is to promote the welfare of children and protect them from harm, and that doctors have a key role in this regard. This Meeting therefore believes:
i)   it is essential that the dissolution of primary care trusts and their replacement by Clinical Commissioning Groups does not damage multi-agency arrangements to safeguard children;
ii) that Clinical Commissioning Groups should be required to fund an appropriate number of sessions for a Designated Doctor for Safeguarding Children, and a Named Public Health Professional for Safeguarding Children, in each area served by a Local Safeguarding Children Board;
iii) that the BMA should work with other relevant stakeholders to ensure that doctors undertaking child protection work have comprehensive access to appropriate training and mentoring programmes.

That this Meeting calls on the UK governments:i) to promote the culture of children playing outside in view of the health benefits associated with outdoor play; ii) to instruct local authorities to stop selling off outdoor play spaces for development purposes and instead invest in the development and maintenance of these spaces to ensure they are safe, stimulating and easily accessible to all children in the UK.

That this Meeting notes:
i)   the findings of the Marmot review on health inequalities which found that those living in poorest areas live an average seven years less than those in the richest ones;
ii) that the Marmot report believes the provision of a good start for children, free from poverty, is the single most important recommendation it can make. This Meeting believes that child poverty is unacceptable at any level in one of the world's richest countries and resolves to ask the governments across the UK to take action on this issue to ensure that it is addressed both in terms of policy and resources by the administrations in London, Edinburgh, Belfast and Cardiff.

That this Meeting urges:
i)   the BMA to adopt a policy of supporting mandatory fortification of flour with folic acid to prevent neural tube defects in line with the recommendations of the Food Standards Agency and the Scientific Advisory Committee on Nutrition;
ii) the UK nations to form legislation to make it a requirement for folic acid supplements to be in flour and flour based products.

2011

That this Meeting notes that the judgement in the "XYZ" case (High Court 11 May 2011) effectively abolishes the anonymity of expert witnesses in child protection proceedings, and calls on BMA Council and the Medico-Legal Committee to consider what subsequent actions need to be taken to protect both children and doctors.

That this Meeting views the primary medical care of children as an essential part of core general practice and would oppose any attempt to replace that function with specialist children's GPs.

686 (a) Motion by the Conference of LMCs: That this Meeting views the paediatrics as an essential part of core general practice and would oppose any attempt to create a specialist 'children's GP'.

That this Meeting believes that only by addressing proper movement skills and nutritional adequacy can we tackle the growing issues of low basic fitness levels, postural and movement inefficiency and childhood obesity. This Meeting therefore:
i)   calls on the UK departments of education to ensure that all schools deliver an appropriate physical education curriculum that ensures our children have achieved basic movement skills on which to build regular exercise;
ii) calls on the Westminster and devolved governments to have a commitment to promoting the health of our children by prioritising the importance of health, diet and nutrition in schools.

That this Meeting believes that the abolition of practice boundaries will lead to a deterioration of patient care and fundamentally compromise patient safety especially in areas of mental health care and the safeguarding of vulnerably children and adults and calls on the Department of Health to abandon this flawed policy.

2010

That this Meeting expresses grave concern about the ongoing high levels of alcohol related health and social damage in this country, and:
(i)   exhorts the BMA and government to consider further measures to educate the population and encourage sensible and appropriate drinking;
(ii)   supports a rise in the cost of alcohol as a method of reducing alcohol consumption in the home, in public places, and by children;
(iii) supports a rise in the cost of alcohol as a method of supporting traditional pubs which can, at their best, be a vital part of our social fabric;(as a reference)
(iv)   insists that, as well as supporting a minimum price for a unit of alcohol, alcohol purchases should not be eligible for 'customer loyalty points';
(v)   demands a complete ban on alcohol advertising;
(vi)   calls for a properly enforced ban on drunkenness on public transport

That this Meeting recognises the positive health benefits of physical activity, and recommends that increasing walking and cycling in daily activity should be a public health priority for children and adults.

That this Meeting notes the recommendations of the Care Quality Commission report 2009, which highlights the need for NHS bodies to assure the training of their staff in child safeguarding, and calls on the UK Health Departments to confirm:
(i)   that all commissioning bodies have responsibility for providing protected funding for child protection training;
(ii) that named and designated doctors' job descriptions should include protected time for training staff within their organisation;
(iii) that competence levels and training needs are not always the same across different medical specialties.
(iv) that Local Safeguarding Children Boards (or equivalent) must make engagement with paediatricians, general practitioners and patients a high priority for 2010-2011.

2009
That this Meeting believes that in the interests of promoting optimal healthcare for all children:
(i)   individual health visitors should be linked to GP surgeries
(ii) health visitors should have mandatory training in the prevention, recognition and management of childhood obesity.

That this Meeting believes that, in order to improve public health and fitness and tackle obesity in adults and children, there should be:
(i)   no further reduction in the number of public swimming pools in the UK;
(ii) expansion of safe cycle paths and networks;
(iii) action at local level to ensure that recreational facilities are available to all regardless of their socioeconomic status and level of physical and psychological ability;
(iv) no discouragement for children who wish to play active games such as football and skipping etc in the playground;
(v) more extensive use of the media, including children's programming, to promote healthy lifestyle messages.

That this Meeting notes with great concern the report by Lord Laming into the death of Baby P in Haringey, and calls on Council to:
(i)   lobby Health Departments for improved funding for training for health professionals in safeguarding children;
(ii) press governments to introduce independent chairs for statutory safeguarding bodies at local level [such as Local Safeguarding Children Boards];
(iii) press governments to review their guidance such that statutory safeguarding bodies at local level have voting representation from paediatricians, child psychiatrists and general practitioners.

That this Meeting recognises the increased prevalence of obesity in children and the contribution that poor diet plays in this. We call upon the BMA Board of Science to research into easy to understand, child friendly food labelling and, in particular, to consider the recent research by the Food Standards Agency which confirms preference for a "traffic light" system.

That this Meeting:
(i) reaffirms the Association's 1999 condemnation of the advertising of tobacco at the point of sale;
(ii) calls on the BMA to lobby for legislative change to make illegal all tobacco advertising throughout the UK;
(iii) calls for restrictions on vending machines, where children can currently purchase cigarettes out of sight of adult supervision.

That this Meeting overwhelmingly supports Lord Laming's Inquiry into the death of Baby P and welcomes the resulting drive to increase the number of health visitors in primary care.

That this Meeting would strongly support moves by the BMJ Publishing Group to introduce a standard patient consent for publication form which would be acceptable to the majority of journals, therefore avoiding the need for repeated consent forms, if an article is submitted to and refused by consecutive journals.

2008
That this Meeting:
(i) recognises that the welfare of vulnerable children is served by doctors prepared to work in child protection including expert witness work;
(ii) expresses support for any doctor who fulfils their duty in safeguarding children;
(iii) believes that the recent handling by the GMC of doctors undertaking their duty in safeguarding children will deter health professionals from engagement in child protection work (Carried as Reference);
(iv) believes that the GMC must reconsider how it handles cases involving safeguarding children (Carried as Reference);
(v) reiterates the 2006 ARM call for an enquiry into miscarriages of justice regarding cot death;
(vi) regrets that the government has not done enough to protect the interests of children and of doctors involved in safeguarding children.

2007

That this Meeting believes that the United Kingdom is suffering from an obesity epidemic and that voluntary measures by food industry and media are unlikely to address the problem and:

(i) calls for legislation to ban advertising of unhealthy food to children and a reduction of salt, sugar and hydrogenated fats added to pre-prepared food;

(ii) calls for a halt to the sale of assets such as school playgrounds and sports fields;

(iii AS REFERENCE) calls on government to mandate schools to provide exercise facilities;

(iv) deplores the promotion by sections of the Food and Drinks Industry of GDA (Guideline Daily Amounts) labelling to the exclusion of the "traffic light" system;

That the BMA calls on government to ban the sale of tobacco products in vending machines as an essential measure to prevent the sale of tobacco to children.

That this Meeting is deeply concerned at conditions in which surgical instruments (of a high quality) are manufactured in Pakistan, which involves the employment of children, deficient health and safety measures and low wages. The NHS is a major purchaser of these instruments, at prices very much higher than the producers earn. We call upon the government to institute a fair trade policy for the purchase of these instruments which would be to the health and socio-economic benefit of the workers and their families.

That this Meeting calls on Parliament to debate the merits of more extensive use of 20 mph speed limits on roads, to cover all "walk to school" routes, as a measure that will reduce risk of injury, promote physical activity in school aged children and help shift the balance between motorist and pedestrian.

That this Meeting acknowledges the call by the World Health Organisations to provide hepatitis B vaccines to all children and calls upon the Department of Health to introduce the hepatitis B vaccine into the childhood schedule without further delay.

2006

That this Meeting should call for bans on the advertising of unhealthy food and drink to children.

2005

That this Meeting supports the compulsory wearing of cycle helmets when cycling:

(i) for children;

(ii) for adults.

2003
That this Meeting requests the Board of Science and Education report on the known causes of obesity in school-aged children, the health impact of the increased prevalence of obesity in this group and the measures that need to be taken to halt this trend.

2003
That this Meeting:
(i) believes that the "family friendly" NHS is a myth;
(ii) believes that all doctors have a right to family friendly working hours;
(iii) deplores the lack of readily available childcare in the NHS, and
(iv) believes that if the Department of Health is serious about the family friendly NHS, they should make provision to support doctors taking time off when their children are sick.

2001
That this Meeting strongly believes that all children in the United Kingdom should be protected from tuberculosis by immunisation.

That "looked after children's" medicals require an increase in remuneration and recognition.

2000
That this Meeting, believing that UN sanctions on Iraq are damaging the health of innocent civilians, particularly women and children:
(i) deplores the harmful effects of sanctions on the health care provision for innocent populations in various countries;
(ii) believes that licensed medicines for Iraq should be exempt from scrutiny by bureaucratic sanctions committees;
(iii) asks the BMA to consider asking the World Medical Association to send an official delegation to Iraq to assess the full effect of sanctions on the Iraqi people and make appropriate recommendations to the WHO.

1999
That this Meeting calls for tough action to protect children from the dangers of alcohol.

That this Meeting believes that the target payment system for MMR vaccine is an unfair system. GPs are being forced to bear the consequence of society's reluctance to protect its children. This Meeting recommends a system that excludes the MMR from the target system, and maintains that if the Government truly believes in the benefits of this vaccination, more far reaching measures should be employed to ensure that those at risk are vaccinated as opposed to merely penalising GPs who have no control over the situation.

1997

That this Meeting requests the Government to:

(i)   give the Minister for Public Health responsibility and power to ensure that all Government departments co-operate and collaborate on health issues;

(ii) introduce a new Public Health Act;

(iii) formulate policy to address the undeniable relationship between social inequality and health;

(iv) ensure that the health impact of policies and plans initiated by any government department are assessed;

(v) establish an independent Food Standards Agency to separate the interests of food producers from those of consumers;

(vi) maintain the centrally funded public health laboratory service;

(vii) ensure that the public and especially school children and young people receive education in food hygiene.

1995

That this Meeting calls for a ban on the manufacture, distribution and use of land mines and that a concerted international effort be made to remove outstanding mines as land mines are now one of the biggest killers of children in third world countries.

1994

That the British Medical Association upholds the principle of the sanctity of the life of every human creature, and abhors and condemns the use of the organs of murdered street children in transplantation.

That this Meeting:

(i)   believes that the Department of Education's guidelines on sex education in schools will not promote the health of school children and run counter to the Health of the Nation goals;

(ii) does not believe the Government's stated intention to reduce teenage pregnancy rates when the HEA's excellent work is censored by a Minister for Health and the guidelines on sex education policy for schools show scant respect for young peoples' rights and confidentiality and resource allocations for sexual health are inadequate;

(iii) calls for a public debate on contemporary sex education to take account of the majority of parents' views and appropriate research findings.

1993

That this Meeting welcomes the report of the Joint Working Party on Medical Services for Children, and urges the BMA to press the Department of Health, and NHS Management Executive to require purchasing authorities to commission and fund combined child health services, along the lines recommended in the report, and to provide extra funding to pay for the training and regrading of the doctors concerned.

1991
That this Meeting:
a) urges all health authorities to consider carefully the medical staff implications implicit in the Children Act 1989;
b) believes that the benefits of this legislation will not be fully achieved without the employment of sufficient numbers of suitably trained CMOs, and careful attention to the workload of general practitioners, child psychiatrists and paediatricians;
c) calls upon Government to make available the resources which will permit purchasers adequately to address these issues when contracting for children's services.

1988
That the BMA should ask the DES to include in the national education curriculum at least one hour per year compulsory education in accident and prevention, resuscitation and first aid for all children in full-time education.

That to make more specially trained doctors available for the examination of children suspected of sexual abuse, the police organisation should consider employing doctors trained for this aspect of a police surgeon's work, who would not necessarily undertake all the duties of a police surgeon.

That this Meeting:
(a) welcomes the opportunity provided by the Report of the "Inquiry into Child Abuse in Cleveland 1987" to strengthen services for children and their families in each health district, and
(b) calls on the Government to consult fully with the medical and other professions involved before issuing definitive guidance to inter-agency work in the field of child abuse.

1986
That this Association believes that the correct interpretation of the House of Lords judgement in the case of Gillick v. Wisbech Health Authority is as follows:
(1) That children of under 16 must be entitled to expect that both the existence and the content of a consultation in connection with pregnancy or contraception will normally remain secret.
(2) That in the case of any departure from this rule doctors should be liable to justify their action.

Appendix 3:
UK dietary recommendations for pregnancy

Before pregnancy
A healthy diet is important at any time but particularly when planning a pregnancy. The eatwell plate[a] makes healthy eating easier. Try to eat: • plenty of fruit and vegetables – aim for at least five portions a day • plenty of starchy foods • some milk and dairy foods • some meat, fish, eggs and other non-dairy sources of protein • just a small amount of foods and drinks high in fat and/or sugar.
A 400ug folic acid supplement should be taken daily from the time contraception is stopped until the twelfth week of pregnancy. Women who have previously had a baby with neural tube defects, or who are taking medication for diabetes, epilepsy or coeliac disease should take a 5mg supplement.
Department of Health guidelines on the consumption of alcohol state that women trying to conceive should avoid drinking alcohol, but if they do choose to drink, to minimise the risk to the baby, they should not drink more than one to two units of alcohol once or twice a week and should not get drunk.
During pregnancy
A healthy diet is important in pregnancy. There is no need to eat for two – it's the quality not the quantity of the diet that's important. Try to eat a variety of foods including: • plenty of fruit and vegetables – aim for at least five portions a day • plenty of starchy foods • plenty of iron-rich foods such as pulses, bread, green vegetables, and foods rich in vitamin C that will help the iron to be absorbed • milk and dairy foods – these contain calcium and other nutrients that your baby needs • foods rich in protein such as lean meat*, chicken and fish (aim for at least two portions of fish each week including one of oily fish), eggs and pulses • fibre-rich foods such as wholegrain bread and cereals. Cut down on foods and drinks high in fat and/or sugar such as cakes and biscuits.

a   The eatwell plate is a policy tool that defines the Government's recommendations on healthy diets. It makes healthy eating easier to understand by giving a visual representation of the types and proportions of foods needed for a healthy and well balanced diet. For further information visit the Department of Health website

A 400 g folic acid supplement should be taken daily until the twelfth week of pregnancy. Women who have previously had a baby with neural tube defects, or who are taking medication for diabetes, epilepsy or coeliac disease should take a 5mg supplement.

A 10 g vitamin D supplement should be taken throughout pregnancy.

Do not take dietary supplements that contain vitamin A such as fish liver oils, and avoid liver and liver-containing products.

Caffeine-containing drinks should be consumed in moderation to limit caffeine intake to less than 200mg a day (equivalent to approximately two mugs of instant coffee).

Avoid paté, liver, certain cheeses and raw or partially cooked eggs, shellfish and meats, and unpasteurised milk.

Department of Health guidelines on the consumption of alcohol state that pregnant women should avoid drinking alcohol, but if they do choose to drink, to minimise the risk to the baby, they should not drink more than one to two units of alcohol once or twice a week and should not get drunk.

The BMA believe that the only sensible message for women who are pregnant must be complete abstinence from alcohol.

*Vegetarianism and veganism

It is possible for vegetarians and vegans (people who eat no animal products at all, including dairy products) to be adequately nourished for successful pregnancy and lactation, but they need to be knowledgeable about nutrition and plan their diet carefully. For vegans, there is a high risk of deficient intakes of micronutrients vitamin B12, iodine, calcium, vitamin D and omega-3 fatty acids. There are reports of neurological deficits in children born to vitamin B12 deficient vegan mothers, and the mother should take vitamin B12 supplements, as this micronutrient is found only in foods of animal origin. The high levels of vitamin B12 found in some algae and seaweeds (eg spirulina) are not bioactive. For the other micronutrients listed above, supplements must be taken, or fortified foods (eg many soya milks are fortified with calcium) or specific foods sources included in the diet (eg kelp seaweed for iodine, or flaxseed for omega-3 fatty acids). Good advice can be found on the websites of the Vegetarian Society and Vegan Society.

Appendix 4:
Infant feeding guidelines

World Health Organization	Department of Health
Breastfeeding: Practice exclusive breastfeeding from birth to six months, and introduce complementary foods at six months while continuing to breastfeed on-demand until two years of age or beyond.	**Breastfeeding:** Breastfeeding is best and provides all the nutrients a baby needs for the first six months. Continue exclusive breastfeeding for six months. The longer breastfeeding continues, the greater the benefits.
Formula feeds: Not recommended – all babies should be breastfed. The WHO has developed guidelines for the non-breastfed baby (partly for use by HIV-positive women).[a]	**Formula feeds:** Infant formula is the only alternative to breastfeeding until one year. Cows' milk-based formula is best. Follow-on formula can be used from six months but is not essential. Other types of formula should be used only on medical advice: Hydrolysed protein formula may be useful in cow's milk allergy. Soya formula is an alternative but may also be allergenic. Goats' milk formula is not suitable for babies.
Other drinks: Avoid giving drinks with low nutrient value, such as tea, coffee and sugary drinks such as soda. Limit the amount of juice offered so as to avoid displacing more nutrient-rich foods. Increase fluid intake during illness.	**Other drinks:** Water is the best alternative drink to milk. Breastfed babies don't need any until they start solids. Under six months use tap water, boiled and cooled. Some bottled water has a mineral content too high for babies. Others are OK (labelled accordingly). Bottled water should be boiled too. Fruit juices are a source of vitamin C but reduce the baby's

a   www.who.int/maternal_child_adolescent/documents/9241593431/en/index.html

appetite for milk and can cause tooth decay; avoid before six months. After that use diluted (one in 10 with boiled water) in a feeding cup, at mealtimes only. Squashes, fizzy drinks, flavoured milk, juice drinks, tea and coffee are not suitable for infants.

Starting complementary feeds: Start at six months with small amounts of food and increase as the child gets older while maintaining frequent breastfeeding.

Starting complementary feeds: Solids can be started from six months and gradually increased in amount and variety so that by twelve months, solid foods are the main part of the diet, with breast or formula milk making up the balance.

Progress with complementary feeds: Gradually increase food consistency and variety, adapting to the infant's requirements and abilities. Infants can eat puréed, mashed and semi-solid foods beginning at six months, by eight months 'finger foods', by 12 months the same types of food as the rest of the family, keeping in mind the need for nutrient-dense foods. Avoid foods that may cause choking such as nuts, grapes, raw carrots.

Increase the number of times the child is fed complementary foods as he/she gets older. For the average infant complementary foods should be provided two to three times/day at six to eight months and three to four times/day at nine to 24 months. Additional nutritious snacks (pieces of fruit or bread or chapatti with nut paste) may be offered one to two times/day. If the energy density or amount of food per meal is low, or the child is no longer breastfed, more frequent meals may be required.

Progress with complementary feeds: Start with a teaspoon of smooth vegetable purée (carrot, parsnip, potato, yam) or fruit purée (banana, cooked apple, pear or mango) or cereal (not wheat-based) such as baby rice, sago, maize, corn meal or millet, given with the baby's usual milk (breast or formula) at one feed in the day.

Gradually increase the amount within one feed, and then progress to two and three feeds per day. React to the baby's appetite, giving more if wanted. Solids can include full-fat cows' milk products (yoghurt, fromage frais, cheese sauce). Give cereals once a day. Use home-cooked foods mashed, sieved, or puréed. Introduce puréed red meat, poultry, fish or eggs, or puréed beans or pulses (lentils, hummus) at least once a day. Serve starchy foods (potatoes, yams, rice or bread) two to three times/day, and fruit and vegetables as finger foods at two or more meals/day.

Feed a variety of foods to ensure that nutrient needs are met. Meat, poultry, fish, eggs and vitamin A-rich foods should be eaten daily or as often as possible. Provide diets with adequate fat content.

After illness, encourage the child to eat more than usual.

Vegetarian diets cannot meet nutrient needs at this age unless nutrient supplements or fortified products are used.

As the baby continues to develop, use foods with a thicker and lumpier texture to encourage chewing, even before teeth emerge. Give finger foods (toast, bread, breadsticks, pitta bread or chapatti, peeled apple, banana, carrot sticks, or cubes of cheese). Avoid sweet biscuits and rusks. Later, start minced or chopped meals and fruit between meals. When the baby is mobile (crawling and walking) increase the amount of food. Use full-fat dairy products; low fat is sensible for adults but not babies.

If the family is vegetarian, use pulses (such as red lentils, beans or chickpeas) or tofu as protein sources. Vitamin C in fruit and vegetables helps iron absorption, so include these at mealtimes.

Do not force: Feed slowly and patiently; encourage but do not force. If children refuse foods, experiment with different foods, tastes, textures and methods of encouragement. Minimize distractions during meals. Feeding times are periods of learning and love – talk to children during feeding, with eye to eye contact.

Do not force: Go at the baby's pace. Allow plenty of time for feeding and to allow the baby to learn to swallow solids. Don't rush or 'force feed'. Most babies know when they've had enough to eat. Offer a wide variety of foods to avoid choosiness later on.

Food safety: Practice good hygiene. Wash hands before food preparation. Store foods safely. Serving immediately after preparation, using clean utensils and serving dishes. Avoid using feeding bottles, which are difficult to keep clean.

Food safety: Heat only what the baby will want. Don't reheat previously warmed food. Heat food thoroughly and allow it to cool. Don't refreeze food that's been warmed or previously frozen. Everything for feeding the baby needs to be really clean.

To be avoided: No specific guidelines

To be avoided: Added salt: Babies <6 months need <1g/day, and <1 year a maximum of 1g/day. Breastfed and formula-fed babies get enough salt. Don't add salt to cooked foods. Limit high-salt foods (cheese, bacon, sausages, processed foods, pasta sauces, breakfast cereal). Avoid sugar and honey: Sweeten stewed sour fruit like rhubarb with mashed banana, breast or formula milk. Don't use honey until after one year as it may contain harmful bacteria. Some foods can cause allergic reactions in some babies. Avoid the following before six months: Eggs, fish and shellfish. Wheat-based and gluten-containing foods (bread, wheat flour, breakfast cereals, rusks). If there is a family history of coeliac disease, consult a doctor before using wheat, rye or barley-based foods. Nuts and seeds – including peanuts, peanut butter and other nut spreads. Don't give whole peanuts to children under five years old because they can cause choking.

Vitamin-mineral supplements:
Use fortified complementary foods or vitamin-mineral supplements as needed.

Vitamin-mineral supplements:
No specific guidelines.

Starting ordinary cow's milk:
No specific guidelines.

Starting ordinary cow's milk:
Full-fat cow's milk not suitable as a drink until one year. Semi-skimmed milk not suitable as a drink until two years. Skimmed milk not suitable until five years.

Appendix 5:
Key nutritional concerns
and recommendations

	What has been done?	What needs to be done?
Providing personal support for breastfeeding	NICE Public Health Guidance 11(2008) 'Improving the nutrition of pregnant and breastfeeding mothers and children in low-income households'. Recommendation seven (as one of five key priorities) requires 'commissioners and managers of maternity and children's services to adopt a multifaceted approach or coordinated programme of interventions across different settings to increase breastfeeding rates'. All pregnant women now receive a DVD 'From bump to breastfeeding' which offers practical information and guidance through the medium of women's personal stories and experiences. This project is undertaken by the charity 'Best Beginnings' with Department of Health funding and endorsed by five Royal Colleges.	• Audit and strengthening of implementation through PCTs. • Midwifery care in the postnatal period needs strengthening. • Shortages in the workforce should be addressed through improving collaboration between professional and paid breastfeeding peer supporters. • Further evaluation of the effectiveness of the multifaceted approach. • This project has been extended* to support families of sick and premature babies. It aims to ensure that they are at the centre of their baby's care in ways that are known to improve health outcomes. * www.bestbeginnings.org.uk/small-wonders

	What has been done?	What needs to be done?
Targeted intervention to focus on the low socioeconomic groups	NICE PH Guidance 11 (2008) Recommendation 11 (as one of five key priorities) requires commissioners and managers of maternity and children's services to target 'Pregnant women and new mothers, particularly those who are less likely to breastfeed.'	• Audit and strengthening of implementation through PCTs. • Health visiting needs to be strengthened, particularly in disadvantaged areas.
Better understanding of the need for continuing support from significant health professionals and family members	NICE PH Guidance 11 (2008) Recommendation 10 requires health professionals (especially midwives, health visitors, and support workers) to 'provide continuing and proactive breastfeeding support at home, recording all advice in the mother's hand-held records'.	• Audit and strengthening of implementation through PCTs.
Local policy guidelines on support of breastfeeding should be published and monitored	NICE PH Guidance 11 (2008) Recommendation seven also requires maternity and children's services to implement a structured programme subject to external evaluation that encourages breast feeding; 'The UNICEF Baby Friendly Initiative should be considered a minimum standard'.	• Audit and strengthening of implementation through PCTs. • Continued funding for educational support and external audit provided through Unicef Baby Friendly Accreditation pathways.

	What has been done?	What needs to be done?
Help on return to work	NICE PH Guidance 11 (2008) Recommendation 20 requires those working in pre-school settings to support breastfeeding mothers by offering them the opportunity to breastfeed and by providing facilities for frozen storage of expressed milk. Recommendation 12 offers specific guidance on the safe storage of expressed breast milk. An NHS leaflet "Breastfeeding and Work: Information for employers and employers" clearly explains Health and Safety Executive guidance and relevant legislation in this area.	• Audit and strengthening of implementation through PCTs.
Greater emphasis should be placed on updating health professionals in order to increase their awareness of breastfeeding issues, promotion and management	NICE PH Guidance 11 (2008) Recommendation one requires professional bodies and skills councils to ensure that health professionals have appropriate knowledge and skills to advise on a range of early nutrition topics including breastfeeding. Growth charts used in UK since 2009 are based on the growth of breastfed infants and young children, reminding health	• Strengthen implementation of educational initiatives (for example, The University of York and Humberside NHS Region, have collaborated to develop a distance learning course providing modules at Master's level open to all health professionals.) • Endorsement of learning initiatives by Royal Colleges and review of Specialist Training

	What has been done?	What needs to be done?
	professionals that breastfeeding should represent a societal norm and reducing the risk that a healthy breastfed infant will be inappropriately perceived as showing faltering weight gain. Extensive multidisciplinary educational support on use of the new charts is provided through Royal College of Paediatrics and Child Health website (www.rcpch.ac.uk).	Curricula. This should be led by the Inter-Collegiate Group on Nutrition (www.icgnutrition.org.uk) through the Academy of Medical Royal Colleges. • Launch new four to growth chart. Realignment of obesity thresholds to overcome confusion about the difference between clinical and public health definitions (eighty-fifth to ninety-first vs ninety-first and ninety-fifth centiles)
Initiatives by lay groups eg National Childbirth Trust and La Leche League should be properly subsidised	NICE PH Guidance 11 (2008) requires commissioners and managers of maternity and children's services to: 'provide easily accessible breastfeeding peer support programmes [to include training] and ensure peer supporters are part of a multidisciplinary team.	• Audit and strengthening of implementation through PCTs.

	What has been done?	
Combine nutritional education with practical advice accompanied by quasi cash incentives to purchase healthier foods	'Healthy Start' was introduced in 2006 following a review of the WFS by COMA. NICE PH Guidance 11 (2008) Recommendation four promoted uptake of Healthy Start and use as an opportunity to offer eligible parents 'practical, tailored information, support and advice on a range of topics including increased purchase and consumption of fruit and vegetables, breastfeeding and introduction of complementary foods after six-months'.	• Audit of uptake and implementation is in progress (Department of Health Research & Development Directorate sponsored projects) • Audit and strengthening of implementation through PCTs.

Appendix 6: Child disability: useful websites

www.edcm.org.uk

www.councilfordisabledchildren.org.uk

www.education.gov.uk

www.dh.gov.uk

www.guardian.co.uk/society/disability

maxdavie.posterous.com (author's blog)

References

Chapter 1

1   Department of Health (2009) *Healthy lives, brighter futures – the strategy for children and young people's health*. London: Department of Health.
2   Marmot M, Allen J, Goldblatt P et al (2010) *Fair society, healthy lives: strategic review of health inequalities in England post 2010*. London: Marmot Review Team.
3   The United Nations Children's Fund (2007) *An overview of child well-being in rich countries. Innocenti report card 7*. Florence: United Nations Children's Fund Innocenti Research Centre.
4   United Nations Children's Fund (2013) *Child well-being in rich countries: a comparative overview. Innocenti Reprt Card 11*. Florence: United Nations Children's Fund Innocenti Research Centre.
5   www2.ohchr.org/english/bodies/crc/docs/AdvanceVersions/CRC.C.GBR.CO.4.pdf (accessed November 2012)
6   Organisation for Economic Co-operation and Development *(2000) Doing better for children*. Paris: Organisation for Economic Co-operation and Development.
7   Layard R & Dunn J (2009) *A good childhood: searching for values in a competitive age. The good childhood inquiry*. London: Children's Society.
8   The United Nations Children's Fund (2010) *Innocenti report card 9: the children left behind*. Florence: United Nations Children's Fund Innocenti Research Centre.
9   Children and Young People's Health Outcomes Forum (2012) *Report of the children and young people's health outcomes forum. Children and young people's health outcomes strategy*. London: Department of Health.
10 Law C, Parkin C & Lewis H (2012) Policies to tackle inequalities in child health: why haven't they worked (better)? *Archive of disease in childhood:* **97**: 301-3.
11 Wolfe I, Cass H, Thompson MJ et al (2011) Improving child health services in the UK: insights from Europe and their implications for the NHS reforms. *British Medical Journal* **342**: d1277.
12 Department of Health (2012) *Getting it right for children, young people and families*. London: Department of Health.
13 House of Commons Children, Schools and Families Committee *Sure start children's centres: fifth report of session 2009-2010*. HC 130, 2009-10.
14 Department of Health & Department for Education and Skills (2004) *National service framework for children, young people and maternity services: maternity services*. London: Department of Health.
15 Department for Education and Skills (2003) *Every child matters*. London: Department for Education and Skills.
16 Department for Education and skills (2004) *Every child matters: change for children*. London: Department for Education and skills.
17 www.legislation.gov.uk/ukpga/2004/31/pdfs/ukpga_20040031_en.pdf (accessed November 2012)
18 Department for Education (2007) *The children's plan: building brighter futures*. London: Department for Education.
19 webarchive.nationalarchives.gov.uk/+/http://www.hm-treasury.gov.uk/pbr_csr07_psaindex.htm (accessed November 2012)
20 webarchive.nationalarchives.gov.uk/+/www.dh.gov.uk/en/Publicationsandstatistics/Publications/DH_083645 (accessed November 2012)
21 Department of Health (2009) *Healthy child programme: pregnancy and the first five years of life*. London: Department of Health.
22 Department of Health (2009) *Healthy child programme: the two year review*. London: Department of Health.
23 Department of Health (2009) *Healthy child programme from 5 to 19 years old*. London: Department of Health.
24 Laming WH (2009) *The protection of children in England: a progress report*. London: The Stationery Office.
25 Department for Children, Schools and Families (2009) *The protection of children in England: action plan. The Government's response to Lord Laming*. London: HM Government.
26 www.legislation.gov.uk/ukpga/1989/41/contents (accessed November 2012)
27 www.workingtogetheronline.co.uk (accessed November 2012)
28 Department for Education (2011) *The Munro review of child protection: final report. A child-centred system*. London: HM Government.
29 Kennedy I (2010) *Getting it right for children and young people: overcoming cultural barriers in the NHS so as to meet their needs*. London: Department of Health.

30   Department of Health (2010) *Achieving equity and excellence for children*. London: Department of Health.
31   Scottish Executive (1999) *Towards a healthier Scotland*. Edinburgh: Scottish Executive.
32   Scottish Executive (2001) *For Scotland's children report: better integrated children's services*. Edinburgh: Scottish Executive.
33   Scottish Executive (2002) *It's everyone's job to make sure I'm alright - report of the child protection audit and review*. Edinburgh: Scottish Executive.
34   Scottish Executive (2004) *Consultation on the review of the children's hearings system: getting it right for every child*. Edinburgh: Scottish Executive.
35   Scottish Executive (2005) *Getting it right for every child: proposals for action*. Edinburgh: Scottish Executive.
36   Scottish Executive (2005) *Health for all children 4: guidance on implementation in Scotland 2005*. Edinburgh: Scottish Executive.
37   Scottish Executive (2008) *Early years framework*. Edinburgh: Scottish Executive.
38   Scottish Executive (2008) *Equally well: report of the ministerial task force on health inequalities*. Edinburgh: Scottish Executive.
39   Scottish Executive (2011) *Early years framework: progress so far*. Edinburgh: Scottish Executive.
40   www.maternal-and-early-years.org.uk (accessed November 2012)
41   Scottish Executive (2011) *Growing up in Scotland*. Edinburgh: Scottish Executive.
42   Scottish Executive (2012) *Getting it right for every child*. Edinburgh: Scottish Executive.
43   National Assembly for Wales (2000) *Children and young people: a framework for partnership*. Cardiff: National Assembly for Wales.
44   National Assembly for Wales (2001) *Child and adolescent mental health services: everybody's business*. Cardiff: National Assembly for Wales.
45   National Assembly for Wales (2002) *Seven core aims for children and young people*. Cardiff: National Assembly for Wales.
46   National Assembly for Wales (2004) *Children and young people: rights to action*. Cardiff: National Assembly for Wales.
47   National Assembly for Wales (2004) *All Wales youth offending strategy*. Cardiff: National Assembly for Wales.
48   National Assembly for Wales (2006) *Stronger partnerships for better outcomes: guidance on local co-operation under the Children Act 2004*. Cardiff: National Assembly for Wales.
49   National Assembly for Wales (2005) *The national service framework*. Cardiff: National Assembly for Wales.
50   www.ssiacymru.org.uk/index.cfm?articleid=3329 (accessed November 2012).
51   National Assembly for Wales (2006) *The child poverty strategy and implementation plan*. Cardiff: National Assembly for Wales.
52   National Assembly for Wales (2007) *Towards a stable life and a brighter future*. Cardiff: National Assembly for Wales.
53   National Assembly for Wales (2009) *Getting it right: a 5-year plan*. Cardiff: National Assembly for Wales.
54   National Assembly for Wales (2011) *Nurturing children, supporting families*. Cardiff: National Assembly for Wales.
55   National Assembly for Wales (2012) *The Children's rights scheme*. Cardiff: National Assembly for Wales.
56   Joint Working Party on Child Health Surveillance (1989) *Health for all children*. Oxford: Oxford University Press.
57   Hall MBD & Elliman D (2003) *Health for all children (4e)*. Oxford: Oxford Medical Publications.
58   Department of Health, Social Services and Public Safety (2006) *Health for all children: guidance and principles of practice for professional staff*. Belfast: Department of Health, Social Services and Public Safety.
59   Department of Health, Social Services and Public Safety (2010) *Healthy child, healthy future: a framework for the universal child health promotion programme in Northern Ireland*. Belfast: Department of Health, Social Services and Public Safety.
60   Office of the First Minister and Deputy First Minister (2006) *Our children and young people*. Belfast: Office of the First Minister and Deputy First Minister.
61   Office of the First Minister and Deputy First Minister (2008) *Our children and young people – our pledge: a ten year strategy for children and young people in Northern Ireland 2006 – 2016*. Belfast: Office of the First Minister and Deputy First Minister.
62   Department of Education Northern Ireland (2010) *Early years 0-6 strategy*. Bangor: Department of Education Northern Ireland.
63   Department of Health, Social Services and Public Safety (2010) *Health futures 2010-2015: the contribution of health visitors and school nurses in Northern Ireland*. Belfast: Department of Health, Social Services and Public Safety.
64   Department of Health, Social Services and Public Safety (2012) *A maternity strategy for Northern Ireland 2012-2018*. Belfast: Department of Health, Social Services and Public Safety.
65   The Guardian (15.2.12) *Cuts to children's services risk greater social inequality, says coalition adviser*.

Chapter 2

1   Dickens C (1859) *A tale of two cities*. Hertfordshire: Wordsworth Editions.
2   www.data.euro.who.int/hfadb/ (accessed December 2012)
3   The United Nations Children's Fund (2013) *Child well-being in rich countries: a comparative overview. Innocenti report Card 11*. Florence: United Nations Children's Fund Innocenti research Centre.
4   www.childrenssociety.org.uk (accessed December 2012)
5   The Children's Society (2012) *The good childhood report 2012: a review of our children's well-being*. London: The Children's Society.
6   The United Nations Children's Fund (2007) *An overview of child well-being in rich countries. Innocenti report card 7*. Florence: United Nations Children's Fund Innocenti Research Centre.
7   Department for Education and Skills (2003) *Every child matters*. London: Department for Education and Skills.
8   Children and Young People's Health Outcomes Forum (2012) *Report of the children and young people's health outcomes forum. Children and young people's health outcomes strategy*. London: Department of Health.
9   Modi N, Clark H, Wolfe I et al (2013) A healthy nation: strengthening children's health research in the UK. *The Lancet* **381**: 73-87.
10 Ghaffar A, Tran NT, Reddy KS et al (2013) Changing mindsets in health policy and systems research. *The Lancet* **381**: 436-7.
11 Department of Health (2011) *Mortality monitoring bulletin: infant mortality, inequalities*. London: Department of Health.
12 Nolte E & McKee M (2004) *Does healthcare save lives? Avoidable mortality revisited*. London: The Nuffield Trust.
13 Pearson G (Ed) (2008) *Why children die: a pilot study 2006, England (South West, North East and West midlands), Wales and Northern Ireland*. London: The Confidential Enquiry into Maternal and Child Health.
14 Wolfe I, Cass H, Thompson M et al (2011) How can we improve child health services? *British Medical Journal* **342**: d1277.
15 Wolfe I, Thompson M, Gill P et al (2013) Health services for children in Western Europe. *The Lancet*. Published online March 27, 2013 http://dx.doi.org/10.1016/S0140-6736(12)62085-6
16 www.chimat.org.uk (accessed December 2012)
17 Office for National Statistics (2010) *Child mortality statistics: childhood, infant and perinatal, 2008*. Newport: Office for National Statistics.
18 Sethi D (2008) *Europe report on childhood injury prevention*. Geneva: World Health Organization.
19 Viner R, Coffey C, Bloem P et al (2011) 50-year mortality trends in children and young people: a study of 50 low-income, middle-income, and high-income countries. *The Lancet* **377**: 1162-74.
20 Family Resources Survey 2011: www.research.dwp.gov (accessed December 2012)
21 Beasley R (1998) Worldwide variation in prevalence of symptoms of asthma, allergic rhinoconjunctivitis, and atopic eczema: ISAAC. *The Lancet* **351**: 1225-32.
22 Asher MI, Montefort S, Björkstén B et al (2006) Worldwide time trends in the prevalence of symptoms of asthma, allergic rhinoconjunctivitis, and eczema in childhood: ISAAC phases one and three repeat multicountry cross-sectional surveys. *The Lancet* **368**: 733-43.
23 Pearce N, Aït-Khaled N, Beasley R et al (2007) Worldwide trends in the prevalence of asthma symptoms: phase of the international study of asthma and allergies in childhood (ISAAC). *Thorax* **2**: 758-66.
24 www.asthma.org.uk (accessed December 2012)
25 Patterson CC, Dahlquist GG, Gyürüs E et al (2009) Incidence trends for childhood type 1 diabetes in Europe during 1989-2003 and predicted new cases 2005-20: a multicentre prospective registration study. *The Lancet* **373**: 2027-33.
26 Diabetes UK (2011) *National diabetes audit*. London: Diabetes UK.
27 Royal College of Paediatrics and Child Health (2012) *Epilepsy 12 national report: United Kingdom collaborative clinical audit of health care for children and young people with suspected epileptic seizures*. London: Royal College of Paediatrics and Child Health.
28 www.who.int (accessed November 2012)
29 Braddick F, Carral V, Jenkins R et al (2009) *Child and adolescent mental health in Europe: infrastructures, policy and programmes*. Luxembourg: European communities.
30 Green H, McGinnity A, Meltzer H et al (2005) *Mental health of children and young people in Britain, 2004*. London: Palgrave MacMillan.
31 Department of Health (2011) *No health without mental health: a cross-government mental health outcomes strategy for people of all ages*. London: Department of Health.

32   Taylor R & Rieger A (1985) Medicine as a social science: Rudolf Virchow on the typhus epidemic in Upper Silesia. *International Journal of Health Services:* **15**: 547-59.

33   Halfon N & Hochstein M (2002) Life course health development: an integrated framework for developing health, policy, and research. *Milbank Quarterly* **80**: 433-79.

34   Spencer NJ (2000) *Poverty and child health*. Oxford: Radcliffe Medical Press.

35   Marmot M, Allen J, Goldblatt P et al (2010) *Fair society, healthy lives: strategic review of health inequalities in England post 2010*. London: Marmot Review Team.

36   Waylen A, Stallard N & Stewart-Brown S (2008) Parenting and health in mid-childhood: a longitudinal study. *European Journal of Public Health* **18**: 300-5.

37   Stewart-Brown S, Fletcher L & Wadsworth M (2005) Parent-child relationships and health problems in adulthood in three UK national birth cohort studies. *European Journal of Public Health* **15**: 640-6.

38   Relationships Foundation (2011) *Relationships Foundation: family pressure gauge*. Cambridge: Relationships Foundation.

39   Department of Education (2010) *Children looked after in England (including adoption and care leavers) year ending 31 March 2010*. London: Department of Education.

40   Gilbert R, Fluke J, O'Donnell M et al (2012) Child maltreatment: variation in trends and policies in six developed countries. *The Lancet* **379**: 758-72.

41   Children and Family Court Advisory and Support Service press release (10.4.12) *CAFCASS care demand - latest figures for march 2012*.

42   Ofsted (2012) *Children's care monitor 2011*. Manchester: Ofsted.

43   Laylard R & Dunn J (2009) *A good childhood: searching for values in a competitive age*. London: Penguin.

44   The Guardian (15.2.12) *Cuts to children's services risk greater social inequality, says coalition adviser*.

45   Lake A (2011) Early childhood development – global action is due. *The Lancet* **378**: 1277-8.

46   Walker SP, Wachs TD, Grantham-McGregor S et al (2011) Inequality in early childhood: risk and protective factors for early child development. *The Lancet* **378**: 1325-38.

47   Engle PL, Fernald LCH, Alderman H et al (2011) Strategies for reducing inequalities and improving developmental outcomes for young children in low-income and middle-income countries. *The Lancet* **378**: 1339-53.

48   Bowlby J (1969) *Attachment and loss: vol. 1. Attachment*. New York, NY: Basic Books.

49   Cunha F, Heckman JJ, Lochner L et al (2005) *Interpreting the evidence on life cycle skill formation. Discussion Papers in Economics 05-02*. London: Department of Economics, University College London.

50   Clark C, Woodley J & Lewis F (2011) *The gift of reading in 2011: children and young people's access to books and attitudes towards reading*. London: National Literacy Trust.

51   The Organisation for Economic Co-operation and Development (2009) Doing better for children. Paris: The Organisation for Economic Co-operation and Development.

52   www.oecd-ilibrary.org/education/pisa_19963777 (accessed December 2012)

53   Currie C, Levin K & Todd J (2008) *Health behaviour in school-aged children: World Health Organization collaborative cross-national study (HBSC): findings from the 2006 survey in Scotland*. Edinburgh: Child and Adolescent Health Research Unit, University of Edinburgh.

54   Currie C, Roberts C, Morgan A et al (2004) *Young people's health in context: international report from the 2001/02 survey (Health Policy for Children and Adolescents, No.4)*. Copenhagen: World Health Organization Regional Office for Europe.

55   Riala K, Hakko H, Isohanni M et al (2004) Teenage smoking and substance use as predictors of severe alcohol problems in late adolescence and in young adulthood. *Journal of Adolescent Health* **35**: 245-54.

56   Vega WA, Chen KW & Williams J (2006) Smoking, drugs, and other behavioural health problems among multiethnic adolescents in the NHSDA. *Addictive Behaviors* **32**:1949-56

57   The Health and Social Care Information Centre (2011) *National child measurement programme: England, 2010/11 school year*. Leeds: The Information Centre.

58   Blair M, Stewart-Brown S & Waterston T (2010) *Child public health* (2e). Oxford: Oxford University Press.

59   Orton E, Kendrick D, West J et al (2012) Independent risk factors for injury in pre-school children: three population-based nested case-control studies using routine primary care data. *PLoS One* **7**: e35193.

60   The United Nations Children's Fund (2010) *Innocenti report card 9: the children left behind*. Florence: United Nations Children's Fund Innocenti Research Centre.

61   Mackenbach JP (2011) The English strategy to reduce health inequalities. *The Lancet* **377**: 1986-8

62   Department for Work and Pensions (2012) *Households below average income. An analysis of the income distribution 1994/95-2010/11*. London: Department for Work and Pensions.

63   Child Poverty Action Group (2012) *End child poverty: child poverty map of the UK*. London: Child Poverty Action Group.

64   Brewer M, Browne J & Joyce R (2011) *Child and working age poverty from 2010 to 2020*. London: Institute for Fiscal Studies.

65   The United Nations Childrens Fund (2012) *Measuring child poverty: new league tables of child poverty in the world's richest countries. Innocenti Report Card 10*. Florence: United Nations Children's Fund Innocenti Research Centre.

66   Royal College of Paediatrics and Child Health, Royal College of General Practitioners, College of Emergency Medicine et al (2010) *To understand and improve the experience of parents and carers who need assessment when a child has a fever (high temperature)*. London: Royal College of Paediatrics and Child Health.

67   Pollock A, Price D, Roderick P et al (2012) A flawed Bill with a hidden purpose. *The Lancet* **379**: 999.

68   Pollock AM, Price D, Roderick P et al (2012) How the Health and Social Care Bill 2011 would end entitlement to comprehensive health care in England. *The Lancet* **379**: 387-9.

69   Reynolds L & McKee M (2012) *Opening the oyster: the 2010-11 NHS reforms in England. Clinical Medicine* **12**:128-32.

70   www.rcpch.ac.uk/facingthefuture (accessed June 2012)

71   World Health Organization (2009) *Global health risks: mortality and burden of disease attributable to selected major risks*. Geneva: World Health Organization.

72   Sachs JD (2001) *Macroeconomics and health. Investing in health for economic development*. Geneva: World Health Organization.

73   The United Nations Children's Fund (1989) United Nations Convention on the Rights of the Child. New York, NY: The United Nations Children's Fund.

74   Court SDM (1976) *Fit for the future. The report of the Committee on child health services*. London: Her Majesty's Stationery Office.

75   Department of Health (2004) *National service framework for children young people and maternity services: core standards*. London: Department of Health.

76   Kennedy I (2010) *Getting it right for children and young people: overcoming cultural barriers in the NHS as to meet their needs*. London: Department of Health.

77   Kuh D , Ben-Shlomo Y, Lynch J et al (2003) Continuing professional education: life course epidemiology. *Journal of Epidemiology and Community Health* **57**: 778-83.

78   Royal College of Paediatrics and Child Health (2012) *Turning the tide: harnessing the power of child health research. A report by the Royal College of Paediatrics & Child Health commission on child health research*. London: Royal College of Paediatrics and Child Health.

79   Royal College of Paediatrics and Child Health (2007) *Services for children in emergency departments: report of the intercollegiate committee for services for children in the emergency department*. London: Royal College of Paediatrics and Child Health.

80   Van der Linden BA, Spreeuwenberg C & Schrijvers AJ (2001) Integration of care in The Netherlands: the development of transmural care since 1994. *Health Policy* **55**: 111-20.

81   Ahgren B & Axelsson R (2007) Determinants of integrated health care development: chains of care in Sweden. *The International Journal of Health Planning and Management* **22**: 145-57.

82   Glasgow R, Orleans C, Wagner E et al (2001) "Does the Chronic Care Model also Serve as a Template for Improving Prevention?" *The Milbank Quarterly* **79**: 579-612.

83   Ham C & Smith J (2010) *Removing policy barriers to integrated care in England*. London: Nuffield Trust.

84   Forrest CB, Simpson L & Clancy C (1997) Child health services research: challenges and opportunities. *Journal of the American Medical Association* **277**: 1787-93.

85   World Health Organization (2011) *Commission on information and accountability for women's and children's health. Keeping promises, measuring results*. Geneva: World Health Organization.

86   Council of Europe (2011) *Guidelines of the Committee of Ministers of the Council of Europe on child-friendly health care and their explanatory memorandum*. Strasbourg: Council of Europe.

87   Guhn M, Janus M & Hertzman C (2007) The early development instrument: translating school readiness assessment into community actions and policy planning. *Early Education and Development* **18**: 369-74.

88   Warwick I, Mooney A & Oliver C (2009) *National healthy schools programme: developing the evidence base. Project report*. London: Thomas Coram Research Unit, Institute of Education, University of London.

89   Melhuish E, Belsky J, Leyland AH et al (2008) Effects of fully-established sure start local programmes on 3 year-old children and their families living in England: a quasi-experimental observational study. *The Lancet* **372**: 1641-7.

90   Zubrick S, Ward K, Silburn S et al (2006) Prevention of child behavior problems through universal implementation of a group behavioural family intervention. *Prevention Science* **6**: 287-304.

91   Dretzke J, Frew E, Davenport C et al (2005) The effectiveness and cost-effectiveness of parent training/education programmes for the treatment of conduct disorder, including oppositional defiant disorder in children. *Health Technology Assessment* **9**: 1-250.

92   Simkiss D, Snooks H, Stallard N et al (2010) Measuring the impact and costs of a universal group based parenting programme: protocol and implementation of a trial. *BMC Public Health* **10**: 364.

93   Irwin L, Siddiqi A & Hertzman C (2007) *Early child development: a powerful equalizer. Final report for the World Health Organization's commission on the social determinants of health*. Geneva: World Health Organization.

94   Boyce T & Patel S (2009) *Health impacts of spatial planning decisions*. London: NHS Healthy Urban Development Unit (NUDU).

95   Planning Advisory Service (2008) *Prevention is still better than cure: planning for healthy communities*. London: Planning Advisory Service.

96   Waters E, de Silva-Sanigorski A, Hall BJ et al (2011) Interventions for preventing obesity in children. *Cochrane Database of Systematic Reviews* **20**: CD001871.

97   University of Sheffield (2012) *Model-based appraisal of alcohol minimum pricing and off-licensed trade discount bans in Scotland using the Sheffield alcohol policy model (v2): second update based on newly available data*. Sheffield: University of Sheffield.

98   Hammond D, Dockrell M, Arnott D et al (2009) Cigarette pack design and perceptions of risk among UK adults and youth. *European Journal of Public Health* **19**: 631-7.

99   Hammond D & Parkinson C (2009) The impact of cigarette package design on perceptions of risk. *Journal of Public Health* **31**: 345-53.

100 Germain D, Wakefield M & Durkin S (2010) Adolescents' perceptions of cigarette brand image: does plain packaging make a difference? *Journal of Adolescent Health* **46**: 385-92.

101 Rawls J (1971) *A theory of justice*. Cambridge, Massachusetts: Belknap Press, of Harvard University Press.

Chapter 3

1   Marmot M, Allen J, Goldblatt P et al (2010) *Fair society, healthy lives: strategic review of health inequalities in England post 2010*. London: Marmot Review Team.

2   Office for National Statistics (2011) *Statistical bulletin. Childhood, infant and perinatal mortality in England and Wales, 2009*. Newport: Office for National Statistics.

3   Office for National Statistics (2011) *Statistical bulletin. Trends in life expectancy by the National Statistics Socio-economic classification 1982-2006*. Newport: Office for National Statistics.

4   Smith MP, Olatunde O & White C (2010) Inequalities in disability-free life expectancy by area deprivation: England, 2001–04 and 2005–08. *Health Statistics Quarterly* **48**: 1-22.

5   Office for National Statistics (2011) *Statistical bulletin. Deaths registered in England and Wales in 2010, by cause*. Newport: Office for National Statistics.

6   Marmot M (2001) Sustainable development and the social gradient in coronary heart disease. *European Heart Journal* **22**: 740-50.

7   Bradbury B & Jäntti M (1999) *Child poverty across industrialized nations. Innocenti occasional papers economic and social policy series no.71*. Florence: United Nations Children's Fund Innocenti Research Centre.

8   Brewer M, Browne J & Joyce R (2011) *Child and working-age poverty from 2010 to 2020. IFC Commentary C121*. London: Institute of Fiscal Studies.

9   Platt L (2009) *Ethnicity and child poverty. Department for Work and Pensions research report No 576*. London: Department for Work and Pensions.

10   Pickett KE & Dorling D (2010) Against the organization of misery? The Marmot Review of health inequalities. *Social Sciences & Medicine* **71**: 1231-3.

11   Black D, Morris J, Smith C et al (1980) *Inequalities in health: report of a research working group*. London: Department of Health and Social Security.

12   Morgan O & Baker A (2006) Measuring deprivation in England and Wales using 2001 Carstairs scores. *Health Statistics Quarterly* **31**: 28-33.

13   British Medical Association (2011) *Social determinants of health – what doctors can do*. London: British Medical Association.

14   Bradshaw J (2011) Introduction. In: Bradshaw J (eds) *The well-being of children in the UK*. Bristol: Polity Press.

15   Department for Work and Pensions & Department for Education (2011) *A new approach to child poverty: tackling the cause of disadvantage and transforming families' lives*. London: The Stationery Office.

16   Lader D, Chadwick B, Chestnutt I et al (2005) *Children's Dental Health in the United Kingdom, 2003. Summary Report*. Newport: Office for National Statistics.

17   Botting B (1997) *Mortality in childhood*. In: Drever F & Whitehead M (eds) *Health Inequalities*. London: Office for National Statistics.

18   Messer J (2011) *An analysis of the socio-demographic characteristics of sole registered births and infant deaths. Health Statistics Quarterly 50*. Newport: Office for National Statistics.

19   Oakley L, Maconochie N, Doyle P et al (2009) Multivariate analysis of infant deaths in England and Wales in 2005-06, with focus on socio-economic status and deprivation. *Health Statistics Quarterly* **42**: 22-39.

20   Office for National Statistics (2010) *Child mortality statistics: childhood, infant and perinatal, 2008*. Newport: Office for National Statistics.

21   Mayhew E & Bradshaw J (2005) Mothers, babies and the risks of poverty. *Poverty* **121**: 13-6.

22   Office for National Statistics (2011) *Statistical bulletin. Gestation-specific infant mortality in England and Wales, 2009*. Newport: Office for National Statistics.

23   Pickett K & Wilkinson RG (2007) Child wellbeing and income inequality in rich societies: ecological cross sectional study. *British Medical Journal* **335**: 1080.

24   Siegler V, Al-Hamad A & Blane D (2010) Social inequalities in fatal childhood accidents and assaults: England and Wales, 2001–03. *Health Statistics Quarterly* **48**: 3-35.

25   Blane D, Bartley M & Smith GD (1997) Disease aetiology and materialist explanations of socioeconomic mortality differentials. *European Journal of Public Health* **7**: 385-91.

26   British Medical Association (2003) *Housing and health: building for the future*. London: British Medical Association.

27   Harker L (2006) *Chance of a lifetime. The impact of bad housing on children's lives*. London: Shelter.

28   Department of Health (2003) *Tackling health inequalities: a programme for action*. London: Department of Health.

29   Department of Health (2008) *Tackling health inequalities: 2007 status report on the programme for action*. London: Department of Health.

30   Marmot Review Team (2011) *The health impacts of cold homes and fuel poverty*. London: Friends of the Earth and the Marmot Review Team.

31   Barnes M, Butt S & Tomaszewski W (2008) *The dynamics of bad housing: the impact of bad housing on the living standards of children*. London: National Centre for Social Research.

32   Peat JK, Dickerson J & Li J (1998) Effects of damp and mould in the home on respiratory health: a review of the literature. *Allergy* **53**: 120-8.

33   Her Majesty's Stationery Office (2010) *Child Poverty Act, 2010*. London: The Stationery Office.

34   Department of Work and Pensions (2011) *Households below average income. An analysis of the income distribution 1994/95 – 2009/10*. London: Department of Work and Pensions.

35   Organisation for Economic Co-operation and Development (2011) *Doing better for families*. Paris: Organisation for Economic Co-operation and Development.

36   Bradshaw J, Middleton S, Davis A et al (2008) *A minimum income standard for Britain*. York: Joseph Rowntree Foundation and Loughborough University.

37   Kawachi I (2000) Income inequality and health. In: Berkman LF and Kawachi I (eds) *Social epidemiology*. Oxford: Oxford University Press.

38   Wilkinson RG (1996) *Unhealthy societies*. London: Routledge.

39   Morris JN, Wilkinson P, Dangour AD et al (2007) Defining a minimum income for healthy living (): older age, England. *International Journal of Epidemiology* **36**: 1300-7.

40   Department for Work and Pensions (2010) *Low-income dynamics. 1991-2008 (Great Britain)*. London: Department for Work and Pensions.

41   Beresford B, Sloper T & Bradshaw J (2005) Physical Health. In: Bradshaw J and Mayhew E (eds) *The well-being of children in the UK*. Plymouth: Save the Children UK and University of York.

42   Department for Children, Schools, and Families & Department of Health (2010) *Teenage pregnancy strategy: beyond 2010*. London: Department for Children, Schools, and Families.

43   Yeung WJ, Linver MR & Brookes-Gunn J (2002) How money matters for young children's development: parental investment and family processes. *Child Development* **73**: 1861-79.

44   Gregg P, Propper C & Washbrook E (2007) *Understanding the relationship between parental income and multiple child outcomes: a decomposition analysis*. London: Centre for Analysis of Social Exclusion (CASE) & London School of Economics.

45   LV= (2012) Cost of a child: from cradle to college (www.lv.com/upload/lv-rebrand-
      2009/pdfs/other/11665_LV_COAC.PDF accessed November 2012)
46   Dixon M & Margo J (2006) *Population politics.* London: Institute for Public Policy Research.
47   Hertzman C & Wiens M (1996) Child development and long-term outcomes: a population health
      perspective and summary of successful interventions. *Social Science and Medicine* **43**: 1083-95.
48   Carnegie Corporation of New York (1994) *Starting points. Meeting the needs of young children.* New-York,
      NY: Carnegie Corporation of New York.
49   Melhuish E & Hall D (2007) The policy background to sure start. In Belsky J, Barnes J & Melhuish E (eds) *The
      national evaluation of sure start. Does area-based early intervention work?* Bristol: Policy Press.
50   Waldfogel J & Washbrook E (2010) *Low income and early cognitive development in the U.K. A report for
      the Sutton Trust.* London: The Sutton Trust.
51   Belsky J, Melhuish E, Barnes J et al (2006) Effects of sure start local programmes on children and families:
      early findings from a quasi-experimental, cross sectional study. British Medical Journal **332**: 1476-578.
52   www.direct.gov.uk/en/Parents/Preschooldevelopmentandlearning/NurseriesPlaygroupsReceptionClasses/
      DG_173054 (accessed February 2012)
53   Melhuish E, Belsky J, Leyland AH et al (2008) Effects of fully-established sure start local programmes on 3-
      year-old children and their families living in England: a quasi-experimental observational study. *The Lancet*
      372: 1641-7.
54   Belsky J & Melhuish E (2007) Impact of sure start local programmes on children and families. In: Belsky J,
      Barnes J & Melhuish E (eds) *The national evaluation of sure start. Does area-based early intervention work?*
      Bristol: Policy Press.
55   Schweinhart LJ, Montie J, Xiang Z et al (2004) *The high/scope perry preschool study through age 40.
      Summary, conclusions, and frequently asked questions.* Ypsilanti, MI: High Scope Press.
56   Schweinhart L, Barnes H & Weikart D (1993) *Significant benefits: the high scope perry preschool study
      through age 27.* Ypsilanti, Michigan: High Scope Press.
57   Center on the Developing Child (2007) *A science-based framework for early childhood policy using
      evidence to improve outcomes in learning, behavior, and health for vulnerable children.* Boston,
      Massachusetts: Harvard University.
58   Department of Health & Department for Children, Schools and Families (2009) *Healthy child programme.
      Pregnancy and the first five years of life.* London: Department of Health.
59   Department of Health (2010) *The family nurse partnership (FNP) programme.* London: Department of Health.
60   Barnes J, Ball M, Meadows P et al (2011) *The family-nurse partnership programme in England: wave 1
      implementation in toddlerhood & a comparison between waves 1 and 2a of implementation in pregnancy
      and infancy.* London: Department of Health.
61   Lexmond J & Reeves R (2009) *Building character.* London: Demos.
62   MacMillan HC, Wathen CN, Barlow J et al (2009) Interventions to prevent child maltreatment and
      associated impairment. *The Lancet* **373**: 250–66.
63   Hughes JR & Gottlieb LN (2004) The effects of the Webster-Stratton parenting program on maltreating
      families: fostering strengths. *Child Abuse & Neglect* **28**: 1081-97.
64   Olds DL, Henderson CR, Chamberlin R et al (1986) Preventing child abuse and neglect: a randomized trial
      of nurse home visitation. *Pediatrics* **78**: 65-78.
65   Scott A (2010) National dissemination of effective parenting programmes to improve child outcomes.
      British Journal of Psychiatry **196**: 1-3
66   Butterfield R, Henderson J & Scott R (2009) *Public health and prevention expenditure in England. Health
      England Report No. 4.* London: Health England & Department of Health.
67   Organisation for Economic Co-operation and Development (2011) *Doing better for children.* Paris:
      Organisation for Economic Co-operation and Development.
68   Allen G (2011) *Early intervention: the next steps. an independent report to her majesty's government.
      Early intervention review team.* London: Cabinet Office.
69   Action for Children and New Economics Foundation (2009) *Backing the future: why investing in children
      is good for us all.* London: New Economics Foundation.
70   Committee for Economic Development (1987) *Children in need investment strategies for the educationally
      disadvantaged.* New York, NY: Committee for Economic Development.

Chapter 4

1   The Food Commission (2000) *Children's food examined*. London: The Food Commission.

2   Scientific Advisory Committee on Nutrition (2011) *The influence of maternal, fetal and child nutrition on the development of chronic disease in later life*. London: The Stationery Office.

3   Coulthard H & Harris G (2009) Delayed introduction of lumpy foods to children during the complementary feeding period affects child's food acceptance and feeding at 7 years of age. *Maternal and Child Nutrition* **5**: 75-85.

4   Savage SH, Reilly JJ, Edwards CA et al (1998) Weaning practice in the Glasgow longitudinal infant growth study. *Archives of Disease in Childhood* **79**: 153-6.

5   Hoet JJ & Hanson MA (1999) Intrauterine nutrition: its importance during critical periods for cardiovascular and endocrine development. *Journal of Physiology* **514**: 617-27.

6   Myatt L & Roberts V (2006) *Placental mechanisms and developmental origins of health and disease. Developmental origins of health and disease*. Cambridge: Cambridge University Press.

7   Prentice A (1996) *Constituents of human milk. Food and Nutrition Bulletin* **17**: 1-12.

8   Hamosh M (2001) Bioactive factors in human milk. *Pediatric Clinics of North America* **48**: 69-86.

9   British Medical Association (2009) *Early life nutrition and lifelong health*. London: British Medical Association.

10   Kramer MS & Kakuma R (2002) *The optimal duration of exclusive breastfeeding: a systematic review*. Geneva: World Health Organization.

11   Quigley MA, Kelly YJ & Sacker A (2007) Breastfeeding and hospitalization for diarrheal and respiratory infection in the United Kingdom millennium cohort study. *Pediatrics* **119**: 837-42.

12   Owen CG, Martin RM, Whincup PH et al (2005) Effect of infant feeding on the risk of obesity across the life course: a quantitative review of published evidence. *Pediatrics* **115**: 1367-77.

13   Arenz S, Ruckerl R & Koletzko B et al (2004) Breast-feeding and childhood obesity – a systematic review. *International Journal of Obesity and Related Metabolic Disorders* **28**: 1247-56.

14   World Cancer Research Fund (2007) *Food, nutrition physical activity and the prevention of cancer*. Washington, DC: World Cancer Research Fund.

15   World Cancer Research Fund (2009) *A closer look at breastfeeding*. London: World Cancer Research Fund.

16   McAndrew F, Thompson J, Fellows L et al (2012) *Infant feeding survey 2010*. London: The Information Centre.

17   Scientific Advisory Committee on Nutrition (2008) *Infant feeding survey 2005: a commentary on infant feeding practices in the UK*. London: The Stationery Office.

18   Dewey KG, Peerson JM, Brown KH et al (1995) World Health Organization working group on infant growth. Growth of breast-fed infants deviates from current reference data: a pooled analysis of US, Canadian and European data sets. *Pediatrics* **96**: 495-503.

19   Scientific Advisory Committee on Nutrition (2007) *Application of WHO growth standards in the UK*. London: The Stationery Office.

20   Wright CM, Parkinson K & Scott J (2006) Breastfeeding in a UK urban context: who breastfeeds, for how long and does it matter? *Public Health Nutrition* **9**: 686-91.

21   Lande B, Anderson LF, Baerug A et al (2003) Infant feeding practices and associated factors in the first six months of life: the Norwegian infant nutrition survey. *Acta Paediatrica* **92**: 152-61.

22   McFadden A & Toole G (2006) Exploring women's views of breastfeeding: a focus group study within an area with high levels of socio-economic deprivation. *Maternal & Child Nutrition* **2**: 156-68.

23   Dyson L, Renfrew M, McFadden A et al (2006) *Promotion of breastfeeding initiation and duration: Evidence into practice briefing*. London: National Institute for Health and Clinical Excellence.

24   Kramer MS, Chalmers B, Hodnett ED et al (2001) Promotion of breastfeeding intervention trial (PROBIT). *Journal of the American Medical Association* **285**: 413-20.

25   Broadfoot M, Britten J, Tappin DM et al (2005) The baby friendly hospital initiative and breast feeding rates in Scotland. *Archives of Disease in Childhood. Fetal and Neonatal Edition* **90**: 114-6.

26   Bartington S, Griffiths LJ, Tate AR et al (2006) Are breastfeeding rates higher among mothers delivering in baby friendly accredited maternity units in the UK? *International Journal of Epidemiology* **35**: 1178-86.

27   National Institute for Health and Clinical Excellence (2006) *Postnatal care: routine postnatal care of women and their babies*. London: National Institute for Health and Clinical Excellence.

28   Renfrew M, Dyson L, Wallace L et al (2005) *Breastfeeding for longer: what works?* London: National Institute for Health and Clinical Excellence.

29   National Institute for Health and Clinical Excellence (2008) *Public Health Guidance 11: improving the nutrition of pregnant and breastfeeding mothers and children in low-income households*. London: National Institute for Health and Clinical Excellence.

30   United Nations International Children's Emergency Fund (2012) *Preventing disease and saving resources: the potential contribution of increasing breastfeeding rates in the UK*. York: United Nations International Children's Emergency Fund.

31   UK Stationery Office (2007) *The infant formula and follow-on formula (England) regulations 2007*. London: UK Stationery Office.

32   World Health Organization (1981) *International code of marketing of breast-milk substitutes*. Geneva: World Health Organization.

33   Kandhai MC, Reij M, Gorris LGM et al (2004) Occurrence of *enterobacter sakazakii* in food production environments and households. *The Lancet* **363**: 39-40.

34   Renfrew MJ, Ansell P & Macleod KL (2003) Formula feed preparation: helping reduce the risks; a systematic review. *Archives of Disease in Childhood* **88**: 855-8.

35   Crawley H & Westland S (2011) *Infant milks in the UK*. Hertfordshire: Caroline Walker Trust.

36   www.firststepsnutrition.org (accessed November 2012)

37   European Union (2011) Commission Regulation (EU) No 440/2011 of 6 May 2011 on the authorisation and refusal of authorisation of certain health claims made on foods and referring to children's development and health. *Official Journal of the European Union* **L119**: 4-9.

38   www.sacn.gov.uk/pdfs/position_statement_2007_09_24.pdf (accessed November 2012)

39   Department of Health (2003) *Infant feeding recommendation*. London: Department of Health.

40   World Health Organization (2001) *54th World Health Assembly. Global strategy for infant and young child feeding. The optimal duration of exclusive breastfeeding*. Geneva: World Health Organization.

41   Scientific Advisory Committee on Nutrition (2003) *Subgroup on maternal and child nutrition: paper for discussion: introduction of solid foods*. London: Scientific Advisory Committee on Nutrition.

42   Robinson S, Marriott L, Poole J et al *(2007)* Dietary patterns in infancy: the importance of maternal and family influences on feeding practice. *British Journal of Nutrition* **98**: 1029-37.

43   Health and Safety Executive (2003) *A guide for new and expectant mothers who work*. London: Health and Safety Executive.

44   Department of Health (2011) *Breastfeeding and work: Information for employees and employers*. London: Department of Health.

45   National Institute for Health and Clinical Excellence (2008) *PH11 Maternal and child nutrition*. London: National Institute for Health and Clinical Excellence.

46   School Food Trust (2011) *Advisory panel on food and nutrition in early years. Laying the table. Recommendations for national food and nutrition guidance for early years settings in England*. London: School Food Trust.

47   Hills D, Child C, Jungle K et al (2006) *Healthy Start: rapid evaluation of early impact on beneficiaries, health professionals, retailers and contactors*. London: The Tavistock Institute.

48   Gregory JR, Collins DL, Davies PS et al (1995) *National diet and nutrition survey: children 1-1/2 to 4-1.2 years*. London: Her Majesty's Stationery Office.

49   British Medical Association (2005) *Preventing childhood obesity*. London: British Medical Association.

50   Bates B, Lennox A & Swan G (2010) *National diet and nutrition survey: headline results form year 1 of the rolling programme (2008/9)*. London: Food Standards Agency and the Department of Health.

51   Hypponen E, Virtanen S, Kenward MG et al (2000) Obesity, increased linear growth, and risk of type I diabetes in children. *Diabetes Care* **23**: 1755-60.

52   Must A, Spadano J, Coakley EH et al (1999) The disease burden associated with overweight and obesity. *Journal of the American Medical Association* **282**:1523-9.

53   Mokdad AH, Ford ES, Bowman BA et al (2003) Prevalence of obesity, diabetes, and obesity-related health risk factors, 2001. *Journal of the American Medical Association* **289**: 76-9.

54   Patterson RE, Frank LL, Kristal AR et al (2004) A comprehensive examination of health conditions associated with obesity in older adult. *American Journal of Preventive Medicine* **27**: 385-90.

55   Nuffield Council on Bioethics (2007) *Public health: ethical issues*. London: Nuffield Council on Bioethics.

56   British Medical Association (2012) *Behaviour change, public health and the role of the state – BMA position statement*. London: British Medical Association.

57   House of Commons Science and Technology Committee *Behaviour change: second report of session 2010-2012*. HC 179, 2010-12.

58   www.responsibilitydeal.dh.gov.uk (accessed October 2012)

59 National Heart Forum (2009) *Obesity: recent trends in children aged 2-11y and 12-19y*. London: National Heart Forum.
60 British Medical Association (2003) *Adolescent health*. London: British Medical Association.
61 The Office of Communications (2004) *Childhood obesity – food advertising in context*. London: The Office of Communications.
62 Which? (2008) *How TV food advertising restrictions work*. London: Which?
63 www.nhs.uk/Change4Life/Pages/change-for-life.aspx (accessed November 2012)
64 NHS Information Centre (2011) *National child measurement programme: England, 2010/11 school year*. London: NHS Information Centre.
65 Committee on Medical Aspects of Food Policy (1991) *Panel on dietary reference values. Dietary reference values for food energy and nutrients for the United Kingdom. Report on health and social subjects*. London: Her Majesty's Stationery Office.
66 Food and Agriculture Organization of the United Nations, World Health Organization & United Nations University (2004) *Expert consultation. Human energy requirements*. Rome: Food and Agriculture Organization of the United Nations.
67 Saunders KL (2007) Preventing obesity in pre-school children: a literature review. *Journal of Public Health* **29**: 368-75.
68 National Institute for Health and Clinical Excellence (2006) *Obesity: guidance on the prevention, identification, assessment and management of overweight and obesity in adults and children. Clinical Guideline 43*. London: National Institute for Health and Clinical Excellence.
69 Phillips R, Norden O, McGinigal S et al (2009) *Childcare and early years providers survey*. London: Department for Education.
70 Smith. R, Purdon S, Schneide V et al (2009) *Early education pilot for two year old children evaluation*. London: National Centre for Social Research.
71 Tickell C (2011) *The early years: foundations for life, health and learning*. London: Department for Education.
72 Local Authorities Coordinators of Regulatory Services (2011) *Councils working with nurseries to improve nutritional standards*. London: Local Authorities Coordinators of Regulatory Services.
73 Crawley H (2006) *Eating well for under 5s in child care. Practical and nutritional guidelines*. Hertfordshire: Caroline Walker Trust.
74 Crawley H (2006) *Eating well for under 5s in child care: Training materials for people working with under 5s in child care*. Hertfordshire: Caroline Walker Trust.
75 Caroline Walker Trust (2010) *Eating well for 1-4 year olds*. Hertfordshire: Caroline Walker Trust.
76 Caroline Walker Trust (2011) *Eating well: first year of life*. Hertfordshire: Caroline Walker Trust.
77 Marmot M, Allen J, Goldblatt P et al (2010) *Fair society, healthy lives: strategic review of health inequalities in England post 2010*. London: Marmot Review Team.
78 Lawson M, Thomas M & Hardiman A (1999) Dietary and lifestyle factors affecting plasma vitamin D levels in Asian children living in England. *European Journal of Clinical Nutrition* **53**: 268-72.
79 Scientific Advisory Committee on Nutrition (2007) *Update on vitamin D. Position statement by the Scientific Advisory Committee on Nutrition*. London: The Stationery Office.
80 Committee on Medical Aspects of Food and Nutrition Policy (2002) *Panel on child and maternal nutrition: scientific review of the welfare food scheme. Report on Health and Social Subjects*. London: The Stationery Office.
81 Scientific Advisory Committee on Nutrition (2010) *Iron and health*. London: The Stationery Office.
82 Thane CW, Walmsley CM, Bates CJ et al (2000) Risk factors for poor iron status in British toddlers: further analysis of data from the National Diet and Nutrition Survey of children aged 1.5-4.5 years. *Public Health Nutrition* **3**: 433-40.
83 Hetzel BS (2004) *Towards the global elimination of brain damage due to iodine deficiency*. New Delhi: Oxford University Press.
84 Bleichrodt N & Born MP (1994) *The damaged brain of iodine deficiency*. New York, NY: Cognizant Communication Corporation.
85 Hetzel BS (1983) Iodine deficiency disorders (IDD) and their eradication. *The Lancet* **2**: 1126-9.
86 Dunn JT (1996) *The conquest of iodine deficiency disorders*. New Delhi: Oxford University Press.
87 Vanderpump MPJ, Lazarus JH, Smyth PP et al (2011) Iodine status of UK schoolgirls: a cross-sectional survey. *The Lancet* **377**: 2007-12.
88 Scientific Advisory Committee on Nutrition (2012) *Paper for discussion: iodine and health*. London: Scientific Advisory Committee on Nutrition.

89   Vanderpump MP (2012) Commentary: iodine deficiency as a new challenge for industrialized countries: a
      UK perspective. *International Journal of Epidemiology* **41**: 601-4.
90   Petersen PE (2003) *The world oral health report 2003: continuous improvement of oral health in the 21st
      century.* Geneva: World Health Organization.
91   British Association for the Study of Community Dentistry (2007) *The caries experience of 5 year old children
      in Great Britain (2005/06).* London: British Association for the Study of Community Dentistry.
92   McDonagh M, Whiting P, Bradley M et al (2000) *A systematic review of public water fluoridation.* University
      of York: NHS Centre for Reviews and Dissemination.
93   Centers for Disease Control and Prevention (2001) *Morbidity and mortality weekly report:
      recommendations for using fluoride to prevent and control dental caries in the United States.* Atlanta:
      Centers for Disease Control and Prevention.
94   Medical Research Council (2002) *Water fluoridation and health.* London: Medical Research Council.
95   All Party Parliamentary Group on Primary Care and Public Health (2003) *Inquiry into water fluoridation.*
      London: All Party Parliamentary Group on Primary Care and Public Health.
96   World Health Organization (2002) *Environmental health criteria 227 – fluorides.* Geneva: World Health
      Organization.
97   Forum on Fluoridation (2002) *Forum on fluoridation.* Dublin: The Stationery Office.
98   National Health Medical Research Council (2007) *A systematic review of the efficacy and safety of
      fluoridation.* Canberra: National Health Medical Research Council.

Chapter 5

1   Barlow J & Calam R (2011) A public health approach to safeguarding in the 21st century. *Child Abuse
      Review* **20**: 238-55.
2   Reading R, Bissell S, Goldhagen J et al (2009) Promotion of children's rights and prevention of child
      maltreatment. *The Lancet* **373**: 332-43.
3   O'Donnell M, Scott D & Stanley F (2008) Child abuse and neglect – is it time for a public health approach?
      Australian and New Zealand Journal of Public Health **32**: 325-30.
4   World Health Organization (2004) *Violence prevention alliance. The public health approach.* Geneva: World
      Health Organization.
5   Sidebotham P (2001) An ecological approach to child abuse: creative use of scientific models in research
      and practice. *Child Abuse Review* **10**: 97-112.
6   Gilbert R, Widom CS, Browne K et al (2009) Burden and consequences of child maltreatment in high-
      income countries. *The Lancet* **373**: 68-81.
7   US Department of Health and Human Services, Administration on Children, Youth and Families (2008)
      Child maltreatment 2006. Washington DC: US Government Printing Office.
8   Fergusson DM & Mullen PE (1999) *Childhood sexual abuse – an evidence based perspective.* Thousand
      Oaks, California: Sage Publications.
9   Department for Education (2010) *Working together: an interagency guide to safegaurding and promoting
      the welfare of children.* London: Department for Education.
10   Leeb RT, Paulozzzi L, Melanson C et al (2008) *Child maltreatment surveillance. Uniform definitions for public
      health and recommended data elements.* Atlanta, Georgia: Centers for Disease Control and Prevention.
11   Runyan DK & Zolotor AJ (2011) International issues in child maltreatment. In: Jenny C (ed) *Child abuse and
      neglect: diagnosis, treatment, and evidence* (3e). Thousand Oaks, California: Sage Publications.
12   Runyan DK, Shankar V, Hassan F et al (2010) International variations in harsh child discipline. *Pediatrics* **126**:
      701-11.
13   Zolotor AJ, Runyan DK, Dunne MP et al (2009) ISPCAN child abuse screening tool children's version (ICAST-
      C): instrument development and multi-national pilot testing. *Child Abuse & Neglect* **33**: 833-41.
14   Sebre S, Sprugevica I, Novotni A et al (2004) Cross-cultural comparisons of child-reported emotional and
      physical abuse: rates, risk factors and psychosocial symptoms. *Child Abuse & Neglect* **28**: 113-27.
15   Gray J (2010) *World perspectives on child abuse* (9e). Aurora, CO: International Society for the Prevention
      of Child Abuse and Neglect.
16   Andrews G, Corry J, Slade T et al (2004) *Child sexual abuse. Comparative quantification of health risks.*
      Geneva: World Health Organization.
17   The United Nations Children's Fund (2010) *Child disciplinary practices at home: evidence from a range of
      low and middle income countries.* New York, NY: The United Nations Children's Fund.

18   Finkelhor D, Turner H, Ormrod R et al (2010) Trends in childhood violence and abuse exposure: evidence from 2 national surveys. *Archives of Pediatrics & Adolescent Medicine* **164**: 238-42.

19   Radford L, Corral S, Bradley C et al (2011) *Maltreatment and victimisation of children and young people in the UK* . London: National Society for the Prevention of Cruelty to Children.

20   Department for Education (2011) *Referrals, assessments and children who were the subject of a child protection plan (2010-11 children in need census, provisional)*. London: Department for Education.

21   Gilbert R, Kemp A, Thoburn J et al (2009) Recognising and responding to child maltreatment. *The Lancet* **373**: 167-80.

22   Rees G, Gorin S, Jobe A et al (2010) *Safeguarding young people: responding to young people aged 11-17 who are maltreated.* London: National Society for the Prevention of Cruelty to Children.

23   Finkelhor D, Turner H, Ormrod R et al (2009) Violence, abuse, and crime exposure in a national sample of children and youth. *Pediatrics* **124**: 1411-23.

24   Higgins DJ & Mccabe MP (2001) Multiple forms of child abuse and neglect: Adult retrospective reports. *Aggression and Violent behaviour* **6**: 547-78.

25   Dong M, Anda RF, Felitti VJ et al (2004) The interrelatedness of multiple forms of childhood abuse, neglect, and household dysfunction. *Child Abuse & Neglect* **28**: 771-84.

26   Turner HA, Finkelhor D & Ormrod R (2010) Poly-victimization in a national sample of children and youth. *American Journal of Preventative Medicine* **38**: 323-30.

27   Turner HA, Finkelhor D & Ormrod R (2010) The effects of adolescent victimization on self-concept and depressive symptoms. *Child Maltreatment* **15**: 76-90.

28   British Medical Association (2003) *Adolescent health*. London: British Medical Association.

29   Department for Education (2011) *Children looked after by local authorities in England (including adoption and care leavers) – year ending 31st march 2011: statistical first release*. London: Department for Education.

30   Campbell KA, Cook LJ, LaFleur BJ et al (2010) Household, family, and child risk factors after an investigation for suspected child maltreatment: a missed opportunity for prevention. *Archives of Pediatrics & Adolescent Medicine* **164**: 943-9.

31   MacMillan HL, Wathen CN & Barlow J (2009) Interventions to prevent child maltreatment and associated impairment. *The Lancet* **373**: 250-66.

32   Barth RP (2009) Preventing child abuse and neglect with parent training: evidence and opportunities. *Future Child* **19**: 95-118.

33   Munro E (2011) *The Munro review of child protection: final report – a child-centred system*. London: Department for Education.

34   Flaherty EG & Stirling J Jr (2010) Clinical report - the pediatrician's role in child maltreatment prevention. *Pediatrics* **126**: 833-41.

35   Stagner MW & Lansing J (2009) Progress toward a prevention perspective. *Future Child* **19**: 19-38.

36   www.legislation.gov.uk/ukpga/1989/41/contents (accessed November 2012)

37   Department of Health (1991) *Working together under the Children Act, 1989: a guide to arrangements for inter-agency co-operation for the protection of children from abuse*. London: Department of Health.

38   Department of Health, Home Office & Department for Education and Employment (1999) *Working together to safeguard children: a guide to inter-agency working to safeguard and promote the welfare of children*. London: Department of Health.

39   Department of Health (2000) *Framework for the assessment of children in need and their families*. London: Department of Health.

40   Department of Health (2002) *National service frameworks: a practical aid to implementation in primary care*. London: Department of Health.

41   Department for Education and Skills (2003) *Every child matters*. London: Department for Education and Skills.

42   www.legislation.gov.uk/ukpga/2004/31/contents (Accessed November 2012)

43   Department for Children, Schools and Families (2006) *Working together to safeguard children: a guide to inter-agency working to safeguard and promote the welfare of children*. London: Department for Children, Schools and Families.

44   National Institute for Health and Clinical Excellence (2009) *When to suspect child maltreatment*. London: National Institute for Health and Clinical Excellence.

45   Department for Children, Schools and Families (2010) *Working together to safeguard children: a guide to inter-agency working to safeguard and promote the welfare of children*. London: Department for Children, Schools and Families.

46 Department for Work and Pensions (2012) *Social Justice: transforming lives.* London: Department for Work and Pensions.

47 General Medical Council (2012) *Protecting children and young people: the responsibilities of all doctors.* London: General Medical Council.

48 www.legislation.gov.uk/ukpga/2012/7/contents/enacted (accessed November 2012)

49 Rose G, Khaw KT & Marmot M (2008) *Rose's strategy of preventive medicine.* Oxford: Oxford University Press.

50 Gilbert R, Fluke J, O'Donnell M et al (2012) Child maltreatment: variation in trends and policies in six developed countries. *The Lancet* **379**: 758-72.

51 Janson S, Längberg B & Svensson B (2010) Sweden: A 30 year ban on the physical punishment of children. In: Durrant JE & Smith A (eds) *Global pathways to abolishing physical punishment. Realizing children's rights.* London: Routledge.

52 Waldfogel J (2010) *Britain's war on poverty.* New York, NY: Russell Sage Foundation.

53 Brewer M, Browne J & Joyce R (2011) *Child and working-age poverty from 2010 to 2020.* London: Institute for Fiscal Studies.

54 Barnes M & Morris K (2008) Strategies for the prevention of social exclusion: an analysis of the Children's Fund. *Journal of Social Policy* **37**: 251-70.

55 Cawson P, Wattam C, Brooker S et al (2000) *Child maltreatment in the United Kingdom: a study of the prevalence of child abuse and neglect (executive summary).* London: National Society for the Prevention of Cruelty to Children.

56 Radford L, Corral S, Bradley C et al (2011) *Child cruelty in the UK: an NSPCC study into child abuse and neglect over the past 30 years.* London: National Society for the Prevention of Cruelty to Children.

57 Department of Health (2012) *Primary medical care.* London: Department of Health.

58 Office for National Statistics (2003) Figure 8.16 NHS general medical practitioner consultations: by age, 2000/01. In: Summerfield C & Babb P (eds) *Social trends no 33.* London: The Stationery Office.

59 Saxena S, Eliahoo J & Majeed A (2002) Socioeconomic and ethnic group differences in self reported health status and use of health services by children and young people in England: cross sectional study. *British Medical Journal:* **325**: 520.

60 Holge-Hazelton B & Tulinius C (2010) Beyond the specific child. What is 'a child's case' in general practice? *British Journal of General Practice* **60**: e4-9.

61 Sullivan PM & Knutson JF (2000) Maltreatment and disabilities: a population-based epidemiological study. *Child Abuse and Neglect* **24**: 1257-73.

62 Bastable R (2005) *Keep me Safe: the RCGP strategy for child protection.* London: Royal College of General Practitioners.

63 Royal College of General Practitioners & National Society for the Prevention of Cruelty to Children (2011) *Safeguarding children and young people in general practice: a toolkit.* London: Royal College of General Practitioners.

64 Royal College of General Practitioners (2004) *Grasping the nettle: information sharing and the child.* London: Royal College of General Practitioners.

65 Carter Y & Bannon M (2002) *The role of primary care in the protection of children from abuse and neglect: a position paper for the Royal College of General Practitioners.* London: Royal College of General Practitioners.

66 Care Quality Commission (2009) *Review of the involvement and action taken by health bodies in relation to the case of Baby P.* London: Care Quality Commission.

67 Fitzpatrick M (2011) How to protect general practice from child protection. *British Journal of General Practice* **61**: 299.

68 Allister J (2011) How to protect general practice from child protection. *British Journal of General Practice* **61**: 326.

69 Ford S (2011) Letter – response to letter 'How to protect general practice from child protection'. *British Journal of General Practice* Aug 19.

70 Tompsett H, Ashworth M, Atkins C et al (2010) *The child, the family and the GP: tensions and conflicts of interest for GPs in safeguarding children May 2006-October 2008: final report.* London: Kingston University.

71 Learner S (2011) After baby P: can GPs follow child protection guidance? *British Medical Journal:* **342**: d707.

72 Flaherty EG, Sege RD, Griffith J et al (2008) From suspicion of physical child abuse to reporting: primary care clinician decision-making. *Pediatrics* **122**: 611-9.

73 Dubowitz H, Lane WG, Semiatin JN et al (2011) The safe environment for every kid model: impact on pediatric primary care professionals. *Pediatrics* **127**: e962-970.

74 Feder GS, Hutson M, Ramsay J et al (2006) Women exposed to intimate partner violence: expectations and experiences when they encounter health care professionals: a meta-analysis of qualitative studies. *Archives of internal medicine* **166**: 22-37.

75 Feder G, Davies RA, Baird K et al (2011) Identification and referral to improve safety (IRIS) of women experiencing domestic violence with a primary care training and support programme: a cluster randomised controlled trial. *The Lancet* **378**: 1788-95.

76 Royal College of Psychiatrists (2011) *Parents as patients: supporting the needs of patients who are parents and their children*. London: Royal College of Psychiatrists.

77 Jenny C (2007) The intimidation of British pediatricians. *Pediatrics* **119**: 797-9.

78 Haines L & Turton J (2008) Complaints in child protection. *Archive of Disease in Childhood* 93: 4-6.

79 Kemp AM, Joshi AH, Mann M et al (2010) What are the clinical and radiological characteristics of spinal injuries from physical abuse: a systematic review. *Archives of Disease in Childhood* **95**: 355-60.

80 Kemp AM, Rajaram S, Mann M et al (2009) What neuroimaging should be performed in children in whom inflicted brain injury (iBI) is suspected? A systematic review. *Clinical Radiology* **64**: 473-83.

81 Maguire S, Pickerd N, Farewell D et al (2009) Which clinical features distinguish inflicted from non-inflicted brain injury? A systematic review. *Archives of Disease in Childhood* **94**: 860-7.

82 Kemp AM, Dunstan FD, Harrison S et al (2008) Patterns of skeletal fractures in child abuse: systematic review. *British Medical Journal:* **337**: a1518.

83 Royal College of Paediatrics and Child Health (2006) *Child protection companion*. London: Royal College of Paediatrics and Child Health.

84 Kirk CB, Lucas-Herald A & Mok J (2010) Child protection medical assessments: why do we do them? *Archives of Disease in Childhood* **95**: 336-40.

85 Trocme N, MacMillan H, Fallon B et al (2003) Nature and severity of physical harm caused by child abuse and neglect: results from the Canadian Incidence Study. *Canadian Medical Association Journal* **169**: 911-5.

86 Kugler B, Woodman J, Carroll J et al (2012) Child protection guidance needs to address parent behaviour. *Child: Care, Health and Development* (Article first published online: 2 November 2012; DOI: 10.1111/cch.12007)

87 Woodman J, Pitt M, Wentz R et al (2008) Performance of screening tests for child physical abuse in accident and emergency departments. *Health Technology Assessment* **12**: 1-95.

88 Woodman J, Brandon M, Bailey S et al (2011) Healthcare use by children fatally or seriously harmed by child maltreatment: analysis of a national case series 2005-2007. *Archives of Disease in Childhood* **96**: 270-5.

89 Jaudes PK & Mackey-Bilaver L (2008) Do chronic conditions increase young children's risk of being maltreated? *Child Abuse and Neglect* **32**: 671-81.

90 Children and Young People's Health Outcomes Forum (2012) *Report of the children and young people's health outcomes forum. Children and young people's health outcomes strategy*. London: Department of Health.

91 www.legislation.gov.uk/ukpga/1989/41 (accessed January 2012)

92 Department of Health & Department for Education and Skills (2001) *National service framework for children, young people and maternity services*. London: Department of Health.

93 www.legislation.gov.uk/ukpga/2004/31 (accessed January 2012)

94 Thoburn J (2010) Achieving safety, stability and belonging for children in out-of-home care. The search for 'what works' across national boundaries. *International Journal of Child and Family Welfare* **13**: 34-48.

95 Mansell J (2007) The underlying instability in statutory child protection: understanding the system dynamics driving risk assurance levels. *Social Policy Journal of New Zealand* **28**: 97-132.

96 Department for Education (2010) *Children in need in England, including their characteristics and further information on children who were the subject of a child protection plan (2009-10 children in need census, final)*. London: Department for Education.

97 Department of Health (2003) *Referrals, assessments and children and young people on child protection registers year ending 31 March 2002*. London: Department of Health.

98 Horwath J (2002) Maintaining a focus on the child? First impressions of the Framework for the Assessment of Children in Need and their Families in cases of child neglect. *Child Abuse Review* **11**: 195-213.

99 Parton N (2012) The Munro review of child protection: an appraisal. *Children & Society* **26**: 150-62.

100 Laming L (2003) *The Victoria climbie inquiry: report of an inquiry*. London: Her Majesty's Stationery Office.

101 Brandon M, Bailey S, Belderson P et al (2009) *Analysing child deaths and serious injury through abuse and neglect: what can we learn? A biennial analysis of serious case reviews 2005-2007*. London: Department for Children, Schools and Families.

102 Harper S (2009) Rose's strategy of preventive medicine. Geoffrey Rose with commentary by Kay-Tee Khaw and Michael Marmot. *International Journal of Epidemiology* **38**:1743-5.

103 Field F (2010) *The foundation years: preventing poor children becoming poor adults. The report of the independent review on poverty and life chances.* London: Cabinet Office.

104 Allen G (2011) *Early intervention: the next steps. An independent report to Her Majesty's Government.* London: Cabinet Office.

105 MacMillan HL, Wathen CN, Jamieson E et al (2009) Screening for intimate partner violence in health care settings: a randomized trial. *Journal of the American Medical Association* **302**: 493-501.

Chapter 6

1 www.councilfordisabledchildren.org.uk (accessed November 2012)

2 Her Majesty's Stationery Office (2010) *Disability and the Equality Act 2010.* London: The Stationery Office.

3 Blackburn CM, Spencer NJ & Read JM (2010) Prevalence of childhood disability and the characteristics and circumstances of disabled children in the UK: secondary analysis of the family resources survey. *BioMed Central Pediatrics* **10**: 21.

4 Department of Children, Families and Schools (2009) *Progression guidance 2009-2010.* London: Department of Children, Families and Schools.

5 The Children's Trust & Every Disabled Child Matters (2011) *Disabled children and health reform: questions, challenges and opportunities.* London. Every Disabled Child Matters.

6 Department of Health & Department for Education and Skills (2004) *National service framework for children, young people and maternity services.* London: The Stationery Office.

7 Bristol Royal Infirmary Inquiry (2001) *Learning from Bristol: the report of the public inquiry into children's heart surgery at the Bristol Royal Infirmary 1984 -1995.* Bristol Royal Infirmary Inquiry (www.bristol-inquiry.org.uk accessed November 2012)

8 Laming WH, Adjaye N & Fox J (2003) *The Victoria Climbié inquiry.* London: Department of Health.

9 Kennedy I (2010) *Getting it right for children and young people: overcoming cultural barriers in the NHS as to meet their needs.* London: Department of Health.

10 Waterman C (2010) *Take heed Mr Gove.* Buckinghamshire: Iris Press.

11 Graham J (2006) Impact of the national service framework for coronary heart disease on treatment and outcome of patients with acute coronary syndromes. *Heart* **92**: 301-6.

12 Children and Young People's Health Outcomes Forum (2012) *Report of the children and young people's health outcomes forum. Children and young people's health outcomes strategy.* London: Department of Health.

13 http://services.parliament.uk/bills/2012-13/childrenandfamilies.html (accessed February 2013)

14 Department for Education press release (9.5.12) *Children and Families Bill to give families support when they need it most.*

15 National Institute for Health and Clinical Excellence (2011) *Autism in children and young people.* London: National Institute for Health and Clinical Excellence.

16 Department of Health (2009) *Healthy child programme pregnancy and the first five years of life.* London: Department of Health.

17 Salmon G, Cleave H & Samuel C (2006) Development of multi-agency referral pathways for attention-deficit hyperactivity disorder, developmental coordination disorder and autistic spectrum disorders: reflections on the process and suggestions for new ways of working. *Clinical Child Psychology and Psychiatry* **11**: 63-81.

18 London Evening Standard (19.9.12) *NHS child care 'needs urgent change after years of neglect'.*

19 www.pencru.org/research_projects.php?op=view&projectid=115 (accessed November 2012)

20 www.bacch.org.uk (accessed November 2012)

21 Vize R (2012) Integrated care: a story of hard won success. *British Medical Journal* **344**: e3529.

22 www.dwp.gov.uk/policy/welfare-reform/legislation-and-key-documents/welfare-reform-act-2012/ (accessed November 2012)

23 Contact a Family (2012) *Counting the costs 2012: the financial reality for families with disabled children across the UK.* London: Contact a Family.

24 www.ofsted.gov.uk (accessed November 2012)

25 Department for Education (2011) *Support and aspiration: a new approach to special educational needs and disability. A consultation.* London Department for Education.

26 www2.ohchr.org/english/law/crc.htm (accessed November 2012)

Chapter 7

1   Taylor JA (1993) *Notes on an unhurried journey*. New York, NY: Four walls eight windows.

2   Collishaw S, Maughan B, Goodman R et al (2004) Time trend in adolescent mental health. *Journal of Child Psychology and Psychiatry*. **45**: 1350-62.

3   NHS Health Advisory Service (1995) *Together we stand: thematic review of the commissioning, role and management of child and adolescent mental health services*. London: The Stationery Office.

4   Zero to Three (2004) *Infant and early childhood mental health: promoting healthy social and emotional development*. Washington, DC: Zero to Three.

5   Barlow J, Parsons J & Stewart-Brown S (2005) Preventing emotional and behavioural problems: the effectiveness of parenting programmes with children less than 3 years of age. *Child Care, Health & Development*. **31**: 33-42.

6   Stallard P (1993) The behaviour of 3-year-old children: prevalence and parental perception of problem behaviour: a research note. *Journal of Child Psychology and Psychiatry and Allied Disciplines* **34**: 413-21.

7   Charlton T, Abrahams M & Jones K (1995) Prevalence rates of emotional and behavioural disorder among nursery class children in St Helen, South Atlantic: an epidemiological study. *Journal of Social Behaviour and Personality* **10**: 273-80.

8   Skuse D (1993) Identification and management of problem eaters. *Archives of Disease in Childhood*. **69**: 604-8.

9   Manikam R & Perman JA (2000) Pediatric feeding disorders. *Journal of Clinical Gastroenterology* **30**: 34-46.

10 Dinsdale H, Ridler C & Rutter H (2011) *National child measurement programme: changes in children's body mass index between 2006/07 and 2009/10*. Oxford: National Obesity Observatory.

11 Campbell SB (1995) Behaviour problems in preschool children: a review of recent research. *Journal of Child Psychology and Psychiatry* **36**: 113-49.

12 National Institute for Health and Clinical Excellence (2008) *Attention deficit hyperactivity disorder: diagnosis and management of ADHD in children, young people and adults*. London: National Institute for Health and Clinical Excellence.

13 Scheeringa MS (2009) Posttraumatic stress disorder. In: Zeanah Jr CH (ed) *Handbook of Infant Mental Health* (3e). New York, NY: Guilford Press.

14 Caspi A, Moffit TE, Newman DL et al (1996) Behavioral observations at three years predict adult psychiatric disorders: longitudinal evidence from a birth cohort. *Archives of General Psychiatry*. **53**: 1033-9.

15 Romeo R, Knapp M & Scott S (2006) Economic cost of severe antisocial behaviour and who pays it. *The British Journal of Psychiatry*. **188**: 547-53.

16 Scott S, Knapp M, Henderson J et al (2001) Financial cost of social exclusion: follow up study of antisocial children into adulthood. *British Medical Journal* **323**: 1-5.

17 Kim-Cohen J, Caspi A, Taylor A et al (2006) MAOA, maltreatment, and gene-environment interaction predicting children's mental health: new evidence and a meta-analysis. *Molecular Psychiatry* **11**: 903-13.

18 Bakermans-Kranenburg MJ, Van IJzendoorn MH, Pijlman FT et al (2008) Experimental evidence for differential susceptibility: Dopamine D4 receptor polymorphism (DRD4 VNTR) moderates intervention effects on toddlers' externalizing behaviour in a randomized controlled trial. *Developmental Psychology* **44**: 293-300.

19 Masten AS & Powell JL (2003) A resilience framework for research, policy and practice. In: Luthar SS (ed) *Resilience and vulnerability: adaptation in the context of childhood adversities*. Cambridge: Cambridge University Press.

20 Meltzer H, Gatward R, Goodman R et al (2000) *The mental health of children and adolescents in Great Britain*. London: Her Majesty's Stationery Office.

21 Hansen K & Joshi H (2010) *Children of the 21st century: the first five years*. Bristol: The Policy Press.

22 Manning C & Gregoire A (2009) Effects of parental mental illness on children. *Psychiatry*. **8**: 7-9.

23 Royal College of Psychiatrists (2012) *Parental mental illness: the problems for children. Information for parents, carers and anyone who works with young people*. London: Royal College of Psychiatrists.

24 British Medical Association (2007) *Fetal alcohol spectrum disorders: a guide for healthcare professionals*. London: British Medical Association.

25 Mayes LC (1995) Substance abuse and parenting. In: Bornstein MH (ed) *Handbook of parenting. Volume 4*. Hillsdale, NJ: Lawrence Erlbaum Associates.

26 Department of Health (2010) *Improving safety, reducing harm: children, young people and domestic violence. A practical toolkit for front-line practitioners*. Norwich: The Stationery Office.

27 British Medical Association (2007) *Domestic abuse*. London: British Medical Association.

28   Glover V (2001) The effects of prenatal stress on child behavioral and cognitive outcomes start at the beginning. In: Tremblay RE, Boivin M & Peters Rde V (eds) *Encyclopaedia on early childhood development* [online version]. Montreal, Quebec: Centre of Excellence for Early Childhood Development.

29   British Medical Association (2004) *Smoking and reproductive health.* London: British Medical Association.

30   Crittenden PM (2011) *Raising parents: attachment, parenting and child safety.* Abingdon: Taylor and Francis.

31   Prior V & Glaser D (2006) *Understanding attachment and attachment disorders: theory, evidence and practice.* London: Jessica Kingsley.

32   Bowlby J (1969) *Attachment and loss: Vol. 1. Attachment.* New York, NY: Basic Books.

33   Maccoby EE & Martin JA (1983) Socialization in the context of the family: parent–child interaction. In: Mussen PH & Hetherington EM (eds) *Handbook of child psychology: vol. 4. Socialization, personality, and social development.* New York, NY: Wiley.

34   Lamborn S, Mounts NS, Steinberg L et al (1991) Patterns of competence and adjustment among adolescents from authoritative, authoritarian, indulgent and neglectful families. *Child Development* **62**: 1049-65.

35   Masten AS (2001) Ordinary magic: resilience processes in development. *American Psychologist* **56**: 227-38.

36   Straus MA (2005) Children should never, ever be spanked no matter what the circumstances. In: Loseke DR, Gelles RL & Cavanaugh MM (eds) *Current controversies about family violence.* Thousand Oak CA: Sage Publications.

37   National Institute for Health and Clinical Excellence (2009) *When to suspect child maltreatment.* London: National Institute for Health and Clinical Excellence.

38   Springer KW, Sheridan J, Kuo D et al (2007) Long-term physical and mental health consequences of childhood physical abuse: results from a large population-based sample of men and women. *Child Abuse and Neglect* **31**: 517-30.

39   Vandell DL, Belsky J, Burchinal M et al (2010) Do effects of early childcare extend to age 15 years? Results from the NICHD study of early care and youth development. *Child Development.* **81**: 737-56.

40   EveryChild (2012) *Adopting better care: improving adoption services around the world.* London: EveryChild.

41   Greene R, Pugh R & Roberts D (2008) *Research briefing: black and minority ethnic parents with mental health problems and their children.* London: Social Care Institute for Excellence.

42   Sabates R & Dex S (2012) *Multiple risk factors in young children's development. CLS working paper 2012/1.* London: Centre for Longitudinal Studies.

43   Office of the Deputy Prime Minister (2004) *The impact of overcrowding on health and education: a review of evidence and literature.* London: Office of the Deputy Prime Minister.

44   Department of Health (2008) *Children and young people in mind.* London: Department of Health.

45   Department for Children Schools and Families (2009) *Think family toolkit: improving support for families at risk. Strategic overview.* London: Department for Children Schools and Families.

46   Department of Health (2011) *No health without mental health: a cross-government mental health outcomes strategy for people of all ages.* London: Department of Health.

47   Anning A & Ball M (2008) *Improving services for young children: from sure start to children's centres.* London: Sage Publications.

48   Poobalan AS, Aucott LS, Ross L et al (2007) Effects of treating postnatal depression on mother-infant interaction and child development: systematic review. *British Journal of Psychiatry* **191**: 378-86.

49   National Institute for Health and Clinical Excellence & Social Care Institute for Excellence (2006) *Parent training/education programmes in the management of children with conduct disorder.* London: National Institute for Health and Clinical Excellence.

50   National Institute for Health and Clinical Excellence (2008) *CG72 Attention deficit hyperactivity disorder (ADHD).* London: National Institute for Health and Clinical Excellence.

51   www.incredibleyears.com (accessed November 2012)

52   www.triplep.net (accessed November 2012)

53   Ence WA & Koegel RL (2012) *Effects of video feedback on parent implementation of pivotal response treatment.* West Hartford, CT: International Society for Autism Research.

Chapter 8

1   House of Commons Health Select Committee (1997) *The specific health needs of children and young people*. London: Her Majesty's Stationery Office.

2   Barker DJP (1995) Fetal origins of coronary heart disease. *British Medical Journal* **311**: 171-4.

3   Widdowson EM & McCance RA (1963) The effect of finite periods of undernutrition at different ages on the composition and subsequent development of the rat. *Proceedings of the Royal Society B: Biological Sciences* **158**: 329-42.

4   Barker DJP (1998) *Mothers, babies and health in later life*. Edinburgh: Churchill Livingstone.

5   Gluckman P & Hanson M (2006) (eds) *Developmental origins of health and disease*. Cambridge: Cambridge University Press.

6   Barker DJP & Osmond C (1986) Infant mortality, childhood nutrition and ischaemic heart disease in England and Wales. *The Lancet* **1**: 1077-81.

7   Gardner MJ, Winter PD & Barker DJP (1984) *Atlas of mortality from selected diseases in England and Wales 1968-1978*. Chichester: John Wiley and Sons.

8   Local Government Board (1910) *39th Annual report 1909-10. Supplement on infant and child mortality*. London: Her Majesty's Stationery Office.

9   Jansson T & Powell TL (2007) Role of the placenta in fetal programming: underlying mechanisms and potential interventional approaches. *Clinical Science* **113**: 1-13.

10 Burton GJ, Barker DJP, Moffett A et al (2010) *The placenta and human developmental programming*. Cambridge: Cambridge University Press.

11 Eriksson JG, Kajantie E, Barker DJP et al (2011) Mother's body size and placental size predict coronary heart disease in men. *European Heart Journal* **22**: 2297-303.

12 Barker DJP, Thornburg KL, Osmond C et al (2010) The surface area of the placenta and hypertension in the offspring in later life. *International Journal of Development Biology* **54**: 525-30.

13 Barker DJ, Gelow J, Thornburg K et al (2010) The early origins of chronic heart failure: impaired placental growth and initiation of insulin resistance in childhood. *European Journal of Heart Failure* **12**: 819-25.

14 Barker DJ, Thornburg KL, Osmond C et al (2010) The prenatal origins of lung cancer. II. The placenta. *American Journal of Human Biology* **22**: 512-6.

15 Fowden A (1995) Endocrine regulation of fetal growth. *Reproduction, Fertility and Development* **7**: 351-63.

16 Harding JE (2001) The nutritional basis of the fetal origins of adult disease. *International Journal of Epidemiology* **30**: 15-23.

17 Barker DJ, Bagby SP & Hanson MA (2006) Mechanisms of disease: in utero programming in the pathogenesis of hypertension. *Nature Clinical Practice Nephrology* **2**: 700-7.

18 British Medical Association (2009) *Early life nutrition and lifelong health*. London: British Medical Association.

19 Rudolph AM (1984) The fetal circulation and its response to stress. *Journal of Developmental Physiology* **6**: 11-9.

20 Phillips DIW (1996) Insulin resistance as a programmed response to fetal undernutrition. *Diabetologia* **39**:1119-22.

21 Oliver MH, Harding JE, Breier BH et al (1993) Glucose but not a mixed amino acid infusion regulates plasma insulin-like growth factor-1 concentrations in fetal sheep. *Pediatric Research* **34**: 62-5.

22 Barker DJP, Osmond C, Simmonds SJ et al (1993) The relation of small head circumference and thinness at birth to death from cardiovascular disease in adult life. *British Medical Journal* **306**: 422-6.

23 Leon DA, Lithell H, Vagero D et al (1997) Biological and social influences on mortality in a cohort of 15,000 Swedes followed from birth to old age. *Journal of Epidemiology and Community Health* **51**: 594.

24 Frankel S, Elwood P, Sweetnam P et al (1996) Birthweight, body-mass index in middle age, and incident coronary heart disease. *The Lancet* **348**: 1478-80.

25 Rich-Edwards JW, Stampfer MJ, Manson JE et al (1997) Birthweight and risk of cardiovascular disease in a cohort of women followed up since 1976. *British Medical Journal* **315**: 396-400.

26 Stein CE, Fall CHD, Kumaran K et al (1996) Fetal growth and coronary heart disease in South India. *The Lancet* **348**: 1269-73.

27 Martyn CN, Barker DJP & Osmond C (1996) Mothers' pelvic size, fetal growth, and death from stroke and coronary heart disease in men in the UK. *The Lancet* **348**: 1264-8.

28 Forsen T, Eriksson JG & Tuomilehto J (1997) Mother's weight in pregnancy and coronary heart disease in a cohort of Finnish men: follow-up study. *British Medical Journal* **315**: 837-40.

29. Osmond C, Kajantie E, Forsén T et al (2007) Infant growth and stroke in adult life: the Helsinki birth cohort study. *Stroke* **38**: 264-70.

30. Barker DJP, Osmond C, Forsén TJ et al (2005) Trajectories of growth among children who have coronary events as adults. *New England Journal of Medicine* **353**: 1802-9.

31. Paneth N & Susser M (1995) Early origin of coronary heart disease (the "Barker hypothesis"). *British Medical Journal* **310**: 411-2.

32. Barker DJP, Forsén T, Uutela A et al (2001) Size at birth and resilience to effects of poor living conditions in adult life: longitudinal study. *British Medical Journal* **323**: 1273-6.

33. Law CM & Shiell AW (1996) Is blood pressure inversely related to birthweight? The strength of evidence from a systematic review of the literature. *Journal of Hypertension* **14**: 935-41.

34. Hales CN, Barker DJP, Clark PMS et al (1991) Fetal and infant growth and impaired glucose tolerance at age 64. *British Medical Journal* **303**: 1019-22.

35. Koupilova I, Leon DA & Vagero D (1997) Can confounding by socio-demographic and behavioural factors explain the association between size at birth and blood pressure at age 50 in Sweden? *Journal of Epidemiology and Community Health* **51**: 14-8.

36. Rose G (1985) Sick individuals and sick populations. *International Journal of Epidemiology* **14**: 32-8.

37. British Medical Association (2007) *Fetal alcohol spectrum disorders – a guide for healthcare professionals.* London: British Medical Association.

38. Langley SC & Jackson AA (1994) Increased systolic blood pressure in adult rats induced by fetal exposure to maternal low protein diets. *Clinical Science* **86**: 217-22.

39. Petry CJ, Ozanne SE, Wang CL et al (1997) Early protein restriction and obesity independently induce hypertension in 1-year-old rats. *Clinical Science* **93**: 147-52.

40. Law CM, Barker DJP, Bull AR et al (1991) Maternal and fetal influences on blood pressure. *Archives of Disease in Childhood* **66**: 1291-5.

41. Whincup P, Cook D, Papacosta O et al (1994) Maternal factors and development of cardiovascular risk: evidence from a study of blood pressure in children. *Journal of Human Hypertension* **8**: 337-43.

42. Margetts BM, Rowland , Foord FA et al (1991) The relation of maternal weight to the blood pressures of Gambian children. *International Journal of Epidemiology* **20**: 938-43.

43. Campbell DM, Hall MH, Barker DJP et al (1996) Diet in pregnancy and the offspring's blood pressure 40 years later. *British Journal of Obstetrics and Gynaecology* **103**: 273-80.

44. Lever AF & Harrap SB (1992) Essential hypertension: a disorder of growth with origins in childhood? *Journal of Hypertension:***10**: 101-20.

45. Fall , Osmond C, Barker DJP et al (1995) Fetal and infant growth and cardiovascular risk factors in women. *British Medical Journal* **310**: 428-32.

46. Phipps K, Barker DJP, Hales CN et al (1993) Fetal growth and impaired glucose tolerance in men and women. *Diabetologia* **36**: 225-8.

47. Lithell HO, McKeigue PM, Berglund L et al (1996) Relation of size at birth to non-insulin dependent diabetes and insulin concentrations in men aged 50-60 years. *British Medical Journal* **312**: 406-10.

48. Olah KS (1996) Low maternal birthweight – an association with impaired glucose tolerance in pregnancy. *Journal of Obstetrics and Gynaecology* **16**: 5-8.

49. Curhan GC, Willett WC, Rimm EB et al (1996) Birthweight and adult hypertension and diabetes mellitus in US men. *American Journal of Hypertension* **94**: 3246-50.

50. McCance DR, Pettitt DJ, Hanson RL et al (1994) Birthweight and non-insulin dependent diabetes: thrifty genotype, thrifty phenotype, or surviving small baby genotype? *British Medical Journal* **308**: 942-5.

51. Law CM, Gordon GS, Shiell AW et al (1995) Thinness at birth and glucose tolerance in seven year old children. *Diabetic Medicine* **12**: 24-9.

52. Whincup PH, Cook DG, Adshead F et al (1997) Childhood size is more strongly related than size at birth to glucose and insulin levels in 10-11 year-old children. *Diabetologia* **40**: 319-26.

53. Taylor DJ, Thompson CH, Kemp GJ et al (1995) A relationship between impaired fetal growth and reduced muscle glycolysis revealed by 31P magnetic resonance spectroscopy. *Diabetologia* **38**: 1205-12.

54. Bjorntorp P (1995) Insulin resistance: the consequence of a neuroendocrine disturbance? *International Journal of Obesity* **19**: s6-10.

55. Barker DJP, Martyn CN, Osmond C et al (1993) Growth in utero and serum cholesterol concentrations in adult life. *British Medical Journal* **307**: 1524-7.

56. Martyn CN, Meade TW, Stirling Y et al (1995) Plasma concentrations of fibrinogen and factor in adult life and their relation to intra-uterine growth. *British Journal of Haematology* **89**: 142-6.

57 Reid DD & Fletcher CM (1971) International studies in chronic respiratory disease. *British Medical Bulletin* **27**: 59-64.

58 Osmond C, Barker DJP & Slattery JM (1990) Risk of death from cardiovascular disease and chronic bronchitis determined by place of birth in England and Wales. *Journal of Epidemiology and Community Health* **44**: 139-41.

59 Barker DJP, Godfrey KM, Fall C et al (1991) Relation of birthweight and childhood respiratory infection to adult lung function and death from chronic obstructive airways disease. *British Medical Journal* **303**: 671-5.

60 Holland WW, Halil T, Bennett AE et al (1969) Factors influencing the onset of chronic respiratory disease. *British Medical Journal* **2**: 205-8.

61 Reid DD (1969) The beginnings of bronchitis. *Proceedings of the Royal Society of Medicine* **62**: 311-6.

62 Samet JM, Tager IB & Speizer FE (1983) The relationship between respiratory illness in childhood and chronic air-flow obstruction in adulthood. *American Review of Respiratory Diseases* **127**: 508-23.

63 Phelan PD (1984) Does adult chronic obstructive lung disease really begin in childhood? *British Journal of Diseases of the Chest* **78**: 1-9.

64 Strachan DP (1990) Do chesty children become chesty adults? *Archives of Disease in Childhood* **65**: 161-2.

65 Barker DJP & Osmond C (1987) Childhood respiratory infection and adult chronic bronchitis in England and Wales. *British Medical Journal* **292**: 1271-5.

66 Mann SL, Wadsworth MEJ & Colley JRT (1992) Accumulation of factors influencing respiratory illness in members of a national birth cohort and their offspring. *Journal of Epidemiology and Community Health* **46**: 286-92.

67 Barker DJP, Godfrey KM, Fall C et al (1991) Relation of birthweight and childhood respiratory infection to adult lung function and death from chronic obstructive airways disease. *British Medical Journal* **303**: 671-5.

68 Shaheen SO, Barker DJP, Shiell AW et al (1994) The relationship between pneumonia in early childhood and impaired lung function in late adult life. *American Journal of Respiratory and Critical Care Medicine* **149**: 616-9.

69 Dexateux C & Stocks J (1997) Lung development and early origins of childhood respiratory illness *British Medical Bulletin* **53**: 40-57.

70 Fall C, Hindmarsh P, Dennison E et al (1998) Programming of growth hormone secretion and bone mineral density in elderly men: an hypothesis. *Journal of Clinical Endocrinology and Metabolism* **83**: 135-9.

71 Barker DJP, Winter PD, Osmond C et al (1996) Weight gain in infancy and cancer of the ovary. *The Lancet* **345**: 1087-8.

72 Michels KB, Trichopoulos D, Robins JM et al (1996) Birthweight as a risk factor for breast cancer. *The Lancet* **348**: 1542-6.

73 Barker DJ, Osmond C, Thornburg KL et al (2008) A possible link between the pubertal growth of girls and breast cancer in daughters. *American Journal of Human Biology* **20**: 127-31.

74 Eriksson JG, Thornburg KL, Osmond C et al (2010) The prenatal origins of lung cancer. I. The fetus. *American Journal of Human Biology* **22**: 508-11.

75 Susser E, Neugebauer R, Hoeak W et al (1996) Schizophrenia after prenatal exposure to famine. *Archives of General Psychiatry* **53**: 25-31.

76 Barker DJP, Osmond C & Pannett B (1992) Why Londoners have low death rates from ischaemic heart disease and stroke. *British Medical Journal* **305**: 1551-4.

77 Barker DJP & Osmond C (1987) Inequalities in health in Britain: specific explanations in three Lancashire towns. *British Medical Journal* **294**: 1351.

78 Turner SL, Hamilton H, Jacobs M et al (1997) The influence of fashion magazines on the body image satisfaction of college women: an exploratory analysis. *Adolescence* **32**: 603-14.

79 Grabe S, Ward LM & Hyde JS (2008) The role of the media in body image concerns among women: A meta-analysis of experimental and correlational studies. *Psychological Bulletin* **134**: 460-76.

80 Godfrey KM, Forrester T, Barker DJP et al (1994) The relation of maternal nutritional status during pregnancy to blood pressure in childhood. *British Journal of Obstetrics and Gynaecology* **101**: 398-403.

81 Clark PM, Atton C, Law CM et al (1998) Weight gain in pregnancy, triceps skinfold thickness and blood pressure in the offspring. *Obstetrics and Gynaecology* **91**: 103-7.

82 Leger J, Levy-Marchal C, Bloch J et al (1997) Reduced final height and indications for insulin resistance in 20 year olds born small for gestational age: regional cohort study. *British Medical Journal* **315**: 341-7.

83 Fall CHD, Stein CE, Kumaran K et al (1998) Size at birth, maternal weight, and type 2 diabetes in South India. *Diabetic Medicine* **15**: 220-7.

84   Ravelli ACJ, Van Der Meulen JHP, Michels RPJ et al (1998) Glucose tolerance in adults after prenatal exposure to famine. *The Lancet* **351**: 173-7.
85   BarkerDJP (2012) Sir Richard Doll Lecture. Developmental origins of chronic disease. *Public Health* **126**: 185-9.
86   Dubos R (1960) *Mirage of health*. London: Allen & Unwin.
87   Barker DJP (1989) The rise and fall of Western diseases *Nature* **338**: 371-2.
88   Floud R, Fogel RW, Harris B et al (2011) *The changing body*. Cambridge: Cambridge University Press.
89   Barker M, Baird J, Lawrence W et al (2011) The Southampton initiative for health: a complex intervention to improve the diets and increase the physical activity levels of women from disadvantaged communities. *Journal of Health Psychology* **16**: 178-91.
90   Lawrence W, Keyte J, Tinati T et al (2012) A mixed-methods investigation to explore how women living in disadvantaged areas might be supported to improve their diets. *Journal of Health Psychology* **17**: 785-98.
91   Black C, Cradock S, Ntani G et al (2012) Healthy conversation skills: increasing competence and confidence in front-line staff. *Public Health Nutrition* **19**: 1-8.

Chapter 9

1   Committee for Economic Development (1987) *Children in need investment strategies for the educationally disadvantaged*. New York, NY: Committee for Economic Development.
2   Kumar V (1996) *Poverty and inequality in the UK: the effects on children*. London: National Childrens Bureau.
3   Department for Education and Skills (2003) *Every child matters*. London: Department for Education and Skills.
4   Organisation for Economic Co-operation and Development (2000) *Doing better for children*. Paris: Organisation for Economic Co-operation and Development.
5   Marmot M, Allen J, Goldblatt P et al (2010) *Fair society, healthy lives: strategic review of health inequalities in England post 2010*. London: Marmot Review Team.
6   Office for National Statistics (2011) *Statistical bulletin. Trends in life expectancy by the national statistics socio-economic classification 1982-2006*. Newport: Office for National Statistics.
7   Office for National Statistics (2011) *Statistical bulletin. Childhood, infant and perinatal mortality in England and Wales, 2009*. Newport: Office for National Statistics.
8   Smith MP, Olatunde O & White C (2010) Inequalities in disability-free life expectancy by area deprivation: England, 2001–04 and 2005–08. *Health Statistics Quarterly* **48**: 1-22.
9   Relationships Foundation (2011) *Relationships Foundation: family pressure gauge*. Relationships Foundation. Cambridge.
10   R Laylard & J Dunn (2009) *A good childhood: searching for values in a competitive age*. London: Penguin.
11   Children and Family Court Advisory and Support Service press release (10.4.2012) *CAFCASS care demand - latest figures for March 2012*.
12   Department of Education (2010) *Children looked after in England (including adoption and care leavers) year ending 31 March 2010*. London: Department of Education.
13   Ofsted (2012) *Children's care monitor 2011*. Manchester: Ofsted.
14   Harker R (2012) *Children in care England: statistics*. London: House of Commons Library. Standard Note SN/SG/4470.
15   Family Resources Survey 2011(www.research.dwp.gov, accessed May 2012)
16   Department of Health (2011) *No health without mental health: a cross-government mental health outcomes strategy for people of all ages*. London: Department of Health.
17   The Health and Social Care Information Centre (2011) *National child measurement programme: England, 2010/11 school year*. Leeds: The Information Centre.
18   Pies C, Parthasarathy P & Posner SF (2012) Integrating the life course perspective into a local maternal and child health program. *Maternal and Child Health Journal* **16**: 649-55.
19   Court SDM (1976) *Fit for the future. The report of the Committee on Child Health Services*. London: Her Majesty's Stationery Office.
20   Department of Health (2004) *National service framework for children young people and maternity services: Core standards*. London: Department of Health.
21   Kennedy I (2010) *Getting it right for children and young people: overcoming cultural barriers in the NHS as to meet their needs*. London: Department of Health.
22   Neuspiel RN (1994) Starting points: meeting the needs of our youngest children. *The Journal of the American Medical Association* **272**: 1301.

23   Melhuish E & Hall D (2007) The policy background to sure start. In: Belsky J, Barnes J & Melhuish E (eds) *The national evaluation of sure start. Does area-based early intervention work?* Bristol: Policy Press.

24   Ball M & Niven L (2006) *National evaluation summary: outreach and home visiting services in sure start local programmes.* London: Her Majesty's Stationery Office.

25   HM Government (May 2010) *The coalition: our programme for government.* London: Cabinet Office.

26   Waldfogel J (2010) *Britain's war on poverty.* New York, NY: Russell Sage Foundation.

27   Brewer M, Browne J & Joyce R (2011) *Child and working-age poverty from 2010 to 2020.* London: Institute for Fiscal Studies.

28   Mackenbach JP (2011) The English strategy to reduce health inequalities. *The Lancet.* **377**: 1986-8

29   The United Nations Children's Fund (2007) *An overview of child well-being in rich countries. Innocenti Report Card 7.* Florence: United Nations Children's Fund Innocenti Research Centre.

30   Pollock A, Price D, Roderick P et al (2012) A flawed Bill with a hidden purpose. *The Lancet* **379**: 999.

31   Pollock AM, Price D, Roderick P et al (2012) How the Health and Social Care Bill 2011 would end entitlement to comprehensive health care in England. *The Lancet* **379**: 387-9.

32   Reynolds L & McKee M (2012) Opening the oyster: the 2010-11 NHS reforms in England. *Clinical medicine* **12**: 128-32.

33   The United Nations Children's Fund (2013) *Child well-being in rich countries: a comprehensive overview. Innocenti Report Card 11.* Florence: United Nations Children's Fund Innocenti Research Centre.

34   www.kpmg.com/UK/en/IssuesAndInsights/ArticlesPublications/NewsReleases/Pages/One-in-five-UK-workers-paid-less-than-the-Living-Wage.aspx (accessed December 2012)

35   Reed H (2012) *In the eye of the storm: Britain's forgotten children and families. A research report for Action for Children, The Children's Society and NSPCC.* London: Action for Children, The Children's Society and the National Society for the Prevention of Cruelty to Children.

36   www.nhs.uk/Change4Life/Pages/change-for-life.aspx (accessed December 2012)

37   www.livingstreets.org.uk/walk-with-us/walk-to-school (accessed December 2012)

38   Wolfe I (2012) Three 'Ps' for progress. *Public Service Review: European Union* **24**.

39   Frenk J, Chen L, Bhutta ZA et al (2010) Health professions for a new century. Transforming education to strengthen health systems in an interdependent world. *The Lancet* **376**: 1923-58.

40   Parton N (2012) The Munro review of child protection: an appraisal. *Children & Society* **26**: 150-62.

41   Allen G (2011) *Early intervention: the next steps – an independent report to Her Majesty's Government.* London: Department for work and pensions.

42   Butterfield R, Henderson J & Scott R (2009) *Public health and prevention expenditure in England. Health England report no. 4.* London: Health England & Department of Health.

43   Organisation for Economic Co-operation and Development (2011) *Doing better for children.* Paris: Organisation for Economic Co-operation and Development.

44   ICF GHK in partnership with Barnardo's (2012) *The value of early intervention. Identifying the social return of Barnardo's Children's Centre services.* Birmingham: ICF GHK.

45   www.chimat.org.uk (accessed May 2012)

46   Scott A (2010) National dissemination of effective parenting programmes to improve child outcomes. *The British Journal of Psychiatry* **196**: 1-3.

47   Brandon M, Bailey S, Belderson P et al (2009) *Analysing child deaths and serious injury through abuse and neglect: what can we learn? A biennial analysis of serious case reviews 2005-2007.* London: Department for Children, Schools and Families.

48   Center on the Developing Child (2007) *A science-based framework for early childhood policy using evidence to improve outcomes in learning, behavior, and health for vulnerable children.* Boston, MA: Harvard University.

49   Department of Health & Department for Children, Schools and Families (2009) *Healthy child programme. Pregnancy and the first five years of life.* London: Department of Health.

50   Barnes J, Ball M, Meadows P et al (2011) *The family-nurse partnership programme in England: wave 1 implementation in toddlerhood & a comparison between waves 1 and 2a of implementation in pregnancy and infancy.* London: Department of Health.

51   Melhuish E, Belsky J, Leyland AH et al (2008) Effects of fully-established sure start local programmes on 3-year-old children and their families living in England: a quasi-experimental observational study. *The Lancet* **372**: 1641-7.

52   Belsky J & Melhuish E (2007) Impact of sure start local programmes on children and families. In: Belsky J, Barnes J & Melhuish E (eds) *The national evaluation of sure start. Does area-based early intervention work?* Bristol: Policy Press.

53   Schweinhart LJ (2004) *High/Scope perry preschool study through age 40. Summary, conclusions, and frequently asked questions.* Ypsilanti, MI: High Scope Press.

54   Willis TA, Protrata B, Hunt C et al (2012) Training community practitioners to work more effectively with parents to prevent childhood obesity. The impact of HENRY upon Children's Centres and their staff. *Journal of Human Nutrition and Dietetics* **25**: 460-8.

Chapter 10

1   World Health Organization (2011) *Health at key stages of life – the life-course approach to public health.* Geneva: World Health Organization.

2   Pies C, Parthasarathy P & Posner SF (2012) Integrating the life course perspective into a local maternal and child health program. *Maternal and Child Health Journal* **16**: 649-55.